D0580309

NorthStar 4

LISTENING AND SPEAKING

THIRD EDITION

AUTHORS
Tess Ferree
Kim Sanabria

SERIES EDITORS
Frances Boyd
Carol Numrich

PEARSON
Longman

NorthStar: Listening and Speaking Level 4, Third Edition

Copyright © 2009, 2004, 1998 by Pearson Education, Inc.
All rights reserved.

No part of this publication may be reproduced, stored in a retrieval system, or transmitted in any form or by any means, electronic, mechanical, photocopying, recording, or otherwise, without the prior permission of the publisher.

Pearson Education, 10 Bank Street, White Plains, NY 10606

Contributor credit: Linda Lane, American Language Program at Columbia University, authored and edited PRONUNCIATION material for *NorthStar: Listening and Speaking Levels 1–5, Third Edition.*

Staff credits: The people who made up the *NorthStar: Listening and Speaking Level 4, Third Edition* team, representing editorial, production, design, and manufacturing, are Aerin Csigay, Dave Dickey, Ann France, Melissa Leyva, Sherry Preiss, Debbie Sistino, Kelly Tavares, Paula Van Ells, Mykan White, and Dorothy Zemach

Cover art: Silvia Rojas/Getty Images
Text composition: ElectraGraphics, Inc.
Text font: 11.5/13 Minion
Credits: See page 247.

Library of Congress Cataloging-in-Publication Data

Northstar. Listening and speaking. — 3rd ed.
        4 v. ; cm.
    Rev. ed. of: Northstar / Robin Mills and Helen Solórzano, 2nd. ed. 2004.
    The third edition of the Northstar series has been expanded to 4 separate volumes. Each level is in a separate volume with different contributing authors.
        Includes bibliographical references.
        Contents: Level 2: Basic Low Intermediate /Laurie Frazier, Robin Mills — Level 3: Intermediate / Helen Solórzano, Jennifer P.L. Schmidt — Level 4: High Intermediate / Tess Ferree, Kim Sanabria — Level 5: Advanced / Sherry Preiss.
        ISBN-13: 978-0-13-240988-9 (pbk. : student text bk. level 2 : alk. paper)
        ISBN-10: 0-13-240988-7 (pbk. : student text bk. level 2 : alk. paper)
        ISBN-13: 978-0-13-613313-1 (pbk. : student text bk. level 3 : alk. paper)
        ISBN-10: 0-13-613313-4 (pbk. : student text bk. level 3 : alk. paper)
        [etc.]
    1. English language—Textbooks for foreign speakers. 2. English language—Spoken English—Problems, exercises, etc. 3. Listening—Problems, exercises, etc. I. Mills, Robin, 1964– Northstar. II. Title: Listening and speaking.
    PE1128.N674 2008
    428.2'4—dc22

                                                    2008024491

ISBN 10: 0-13-205677-1
ISBN 13: 978-0-13-205677-9

Printed in the United States of America
11 12 13 14 15—V011—17 16 15 14 13

CONTENTS

WELCOME TO NORTHSTAR
THIRD EDITION

NorthStar, now in its third edition, motivates students to succeed in their **academic** as well as **personal** language goals.

For each of the five levels, the two strands—*Reading and Writing* and *Listening and Speaking*—provide a fully integrated approach for students and teachers.

WHAT IS SPECIAL ABOUT THE THIRD EDITION?

NEW THEMES

New themes and **updated content**—presented in a **variety of genres**, including literature and lectures, and in **authentic reading and listening selections**—challenge students intellectually.

ACADEMIC SKILLS

More purposeful **integration of critical thinking** and an enhanced focus on **academic skills** such as inferencing, synthesizing, note taking, and test taking help students develop strategies for **success** in the **classroom** and on **standardized tests.** A **culminating productive task** galvanizes content, language, and **critical thinking skills**.

➤ In the *Listening and Speaking* strand, a **structured approach** gives students opportunities for **more extended and creative oral practice**, for example, presentations, simulations, debates, case studies, and public service announcements.

➤ In the *Reading and Writing* strand, a new, **fully integrated writing section** leads students through the **writing process** with engaging writing assignments focusing on various rhetorical modes.

NEW DESIGN

Full **color pages** with more **photos**, **illustrations**, **and graphic organizers** foster student engagement and make the content and activities come alive.

MyNorthStarLab

MyNorthStarLab, an easy-to-use **online learning and assessment program**, offers:

➤ Unlimited access to reading and listening selections and DVD segments.

➤ Focused test preparation to help students succeed on international exams such as TOEFL® and IELTS®. Pre- and post-unit assessments improve results by providing individualized instruction, instant feedback, and personalized study plans.

➤ Original activities that support and extend the *NorthStar* program. These include pronunciation practice using voice recording tools, and activities to build note taking skills and academic vocabulary.

➤ Tools that save time. These include a flexible gradebook and authoring features that give teachers control of content and help them track student progress.

THE NORTHSTAR APPROACH

The *NorthStar* series is based on **current research in language acquisition** and on the **experiences of teachers and curriculum designers**. Five principles guide the *NorthStar* approach.

PRINCIPLES

1 **The more profoundly students are stimulated intellectually and emotionally, the more language they will use and retain.**

The thematic organization of *NorthStar* promotes intellectual and emotional stimulation. The 50 sophisticated themes in *NorthStar* present intriguing topics such as recycled fashion, restorative justice, personal carbon footprints, and microfinance. The authentic content engages students, links them to language use outside of the classroom, and encourages personal expression and critical thinking.

2 **Students can learn both the form and content of the language.**

Grammar, vocabulary, and culture are inextricably woven into the units, providing students with systematic and multiple exposures to language forms in a variety of contexts. As the theme is developed, students can express complex thoughts using a higher level of language.

3 **Successful students are active learners.**

Tasks are designed to be creative, active, and varied. Topics are interesting and up-to-date. Together these tasks and topics (1) allow teachers to bring the outside world into the classroom and (2) motivate students to apply their classroom learning in the outside world.

4 **Students need feedback.**

This feedback comes naturally when students work together practicing language and participating in open-ended opinion and inference tasks. Whole class activities invite teachers' feedback on the spot or via audio/video recordings or notes. The innovative new MyNorthStarLab gives students immediate feedback as they complete computer-graded language activities online; it also gives students the opportunity to submit writing or speaking assignments electronically to their instructor for feedback later.

5 **The quality of relationships in the language classroom is important because students are asked to express themselves on issues and ideas.**

The information and activities in *NorthStar* promote genuine interaction, acceptance of differences, and authentic communication. By building skills and exploring ideas, the exercises help students participate in discussions and write essays of an increasingly complex and sophisticated nature.

THE NorthStar UNIT

① FOCUS ON THE TOPIC

This section introduces students to the unifying theme of the listening selections.

PREDICT and **SHARE INFORMATION** foster interest in the unit topic and help students develop a personal connection to it.

BACKGROUND AND VOCABULARY activities provide students with tools for understanding the first listening selection. Later in the unit, students review this vocabulary and learn related idioms, collocations, and word forms. This helps them explore content and expand their written and spoken language.

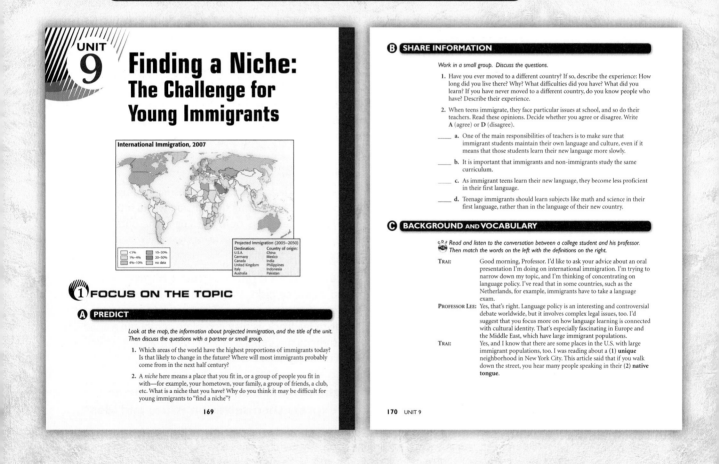

UNIT
9

Finding a Niche:
The Challenge for Young Immigrants

International Immigration, 2007

Projected Immigration (2005–2050)	
Destination:	Country of origin:
U.S.A.	China
Germany	Mexico
Canada	India
United Kingdom	Philippines
Italy	Indonesia
Australia	Pakistan

<1%   1%–4%   4%–10%   10–20%   20–50%   no data

① FOCUS ON THE TOPIC

Ⓐ PREDICT

Look at the map, the information about projected immigration, and the title of the unit. Then discuss the questions with a partner or small group.

1. Which areas of the world have the highest proportions of immigrants today? Is that likely to change in the future? Where will most immigrants probably come from in the next half century?

2. A *niche* here means a place that you fit in, or a group of people you fit in with—for example, your hometown, your family, a group of friends, a club, etc. What is a niche that you have? Why do you think it may be difficult for young immigrants to "find a niche"?

169

Ⓑ SHARE INFORMATION

Work in a small group. Discuss the questions.

1. Have you ever moved to a different country? If so, describe the experience: How long did you live there? Why? What difficulties did you have? What did you learn? If you have never moved to a different country, do you know people who have? Describe their experience.

2. When teens immigrate, they face particular issues at school, and so do their teachers. Read these opinions. Decide whether you agree or disagree. Write **A** (agree) or **D** (disagree).

_____ **a.** One of the main responsibilities of teachers is to make sure that immigrant students maintain their own language and culture, even if it means that those students learn their new language more slowly.

_____ **b.** It is important that immigrants and non-immigrants study the same curriculum.

_____ **c.** As immigrant teens learn their new language, they become less proficient in their first language.

_____ **d.** Teenage immigrants should learn subjects like math and science in their first language, rather than in the language of their new country.

Ⓒ BACKGROUND AND VOCABULARY

Read and listen to the conversation between a college student and his professor. Then match the words on the left with the definitions on the right.

TRAI: Good morning, Professor. I'd like to ask your advice about an oral presentation I'm doing on international immigration. I'm trying to narrow down my topic, and I'm thinking of concentrating on language policy. I've read that in some countries, such as the Netherlands, for example, immigrants have to take a language exam.

PROFESSOR LEE: Yes, that's right. Language policy is an interesting and controversial debate worldwide, but it involves complex legal issues, too. I'd suggest that you focus more on how language learning is connected with cultural identity. That's especially fascinating in Europe and the Middle East, which have large immigrant populations.

TRAI: Yes, and I know that there are some places in the U.S. with large immigrant populations, too. I was reading about a (1) **unique** neighborhood in New York City. This article said that if you walk down the street, you hear many people speaking in their (2) **native tongue**.

170 UNIT 9

② FOCUS ON LISTENING

This section focuses on understanding two contrasting listening selections.

> **LISTENING ONE** is a radio report, interview, lecture, or other genre that addresses the unit topic. In levels 1 to 3, listenings are based on authentic materials. In levels 4 and 5, all the listenings are authentic.
>
> **LISTEN FOR MAIN IDEAS** and **LISTEN FOR DETAILS** are comprehension activities that lead students to an understanding and appreciation of the first selection.
>
> The **MAKE INFERENCES** activity prompts students to "listen between the lines," move beyond the literal meaning, exercise critical thinking skills, and understand the listening on a more academic level. Students follow up with pair or group work to discuss topics in the **EXPRESS OPINIONS** section.

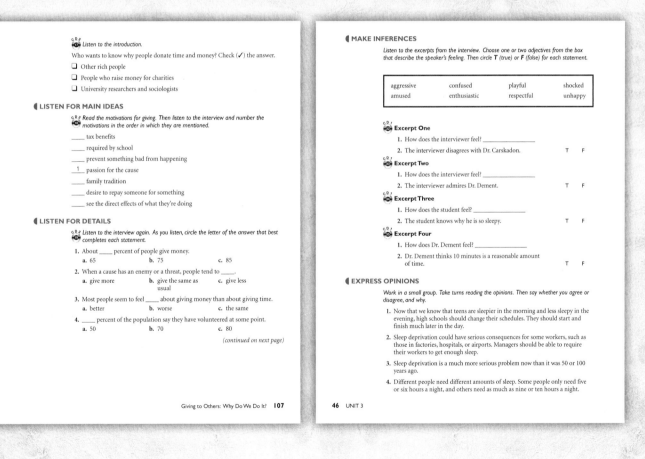

Listen to the introduction.

Who wants to know why people donate time and money? Check (✔) the answer.

❑ Other rich people

❑ People who raise money for charities

❑ University researchers and sociologists

◖ LISTEN FOR MAIN IDEAS

Read the motivations for giving. Then listen to the interview and number the motivations in the order in which they are mentioned.

_____ tax benefits

_____ required by school

_____ prevent something bad from happening

__1__ passion for the cause

_____ family tradition

_____ desire to repay someone for something

_____ see the direct effects of what they're doing

◖ LISTEN FOR DETAILS

Listen to the interview again. As you listen, circle the letter of the answer that best completes each statement.

1. About _____ percent of people give money.
   a. 65   **b.** 75   **c.** 85

2. When a cause has an enemy or a threat, people tend to _____.
   a. give more   **b.** give the same as   **c.** give less
                        usual

3. Most people seem to feel _____ about giving money than about giving time.
   a. better   **b.** worse   **c.** the same

4. _____ percent of the population say they have volunteered at some point.
   a. 50   **b.** 70   **c.** 80

(continued on next page)

Giving to Others: Why Do We Do It?   **107**

◖ MAKE INFERENCES

*Listen to the excerpts from the interview. Choose one or two adjectives from the box that describe the speaker's feeling. Then circle **T** (true) or **F** (false) for each statement.*

aggressive	confused	playful	shocked
amused	enthusiastic	respectful	unhappy

Excerpt One

1. How does the interviewer feel? _____

2. The interviewer disagrees with Dr. Carskadon.   T   F

Excerpt Two

1. How does the interviewer feel? _____

2. The interviewer admires Dr. Dement.   T   F

Excerpt Three

1. How does the student feel? _____

2. The student knows why he is so sleepy.   T   F

Excerpt Four

1. How does Dr. Dement feel? _____

2. Dr. Dement thinks 10 minutes is a reasonable amount of time.   T   F

◖ EXPRESS OPINIONS

Work in a small group. Take turns reading the opinions. Then say whether you agree or disagree, and why.

1. Now that we know that teens are sleepier in the morning and less sleepy in the evening, high schools should change their schedules. They should start and finish much later in the day.

2. Sleep deprivation could have serious consequences for some workers, such as those in factories, hospitals, or airports. Managers should be able to require their workers to get enough sleep.

3. Sleep deprivation is a much more serious problem now than it was 50 or 100 years ago.

4. Different people need different amounts of sleep. Some people only need five or six hours a night, and others need as much as nine or ten hours a night.

46   UNIT 3

LISTENING TWO offers another perspective on the topic and is usually another genre. Again, in levels 1 to 3, the listenings are based on authentic materials and in levels 4 and 5, they are authentic. This second listening is followed by an activity that challenges students to question ideas they formed about the first listening, and to use appropriate language skills to analyze and explain their ideas.

INTEGRATE LISTENINGS ONE AND TWO presents culminating activities. Students are challenged to take what they have learned, organize the information, and synthesize it in a meaningful way. Students practice skills that are essential for success in authentic academic settings and on standardized tests.

B LISTENING TWO: *Food in a Bowl*

What are the food trends in California? You will hear some comments from *Satellite Sisters*, a radio show featuring five sisters who live in different parts of the world and share their thoughts—via satellite—on everyday life. In this segment, Lian talks about life in California.

1 Listen to the report and answer the questions.

1. Why was Lian surprised in the supermarket?
   a. She found unusual food items in bowls.
   b. She thought the bowls were too expensive.

2. Why does Lian think this food-in-bowls trend is happening?
   a. People are too hurried to be careful about eating.
   b. Bowls keep food warmer than plates.

3. Lian jokes that maybe the next new eating style will be _____.
   a. eating while keeping one hand on the phone
   b. eating without using our hands

4. Lian exaggerates by using humor when she says, "just get yourself a nice *trough*, and put the lasagna in there." Why does she mention an animal food container?
   a. Many Californians are vegetarians and don't eat animal products.
   b. She thinks that people do not have good manners.

trough

5. Lian thinks that teaching children to eat with a knife and fork _____.
   a. is a parent's responsibility
   b. won't be necessary in the future

6. Lian's sister, Julie, in Bangkok, also makes a comment. What is her attitude toward the subject?
   a. She shares Lian's feelings about food in bowls.
   b. She seems to have no problem accepting food in bowls.

7. What does Lian's sister Liz, in New York, struggle with?
   a. eating food on *skewers*
   b. finding lamb in a bowl

skewers

2 Work in a small group. Discuss the questions.
   • Do you think it's important for families to eat meals together? Why or why not? What are some reasons that families might not eat together?
   • What factors are most important for you when choosing a meal: taste, price, convenience, or something else?

Goodbye to the Sit-Down Meal **155**

C INTEGRATE LISTENINGS ONE AND TWO

STEP 1: Organize

Work in groups of three. *Fill in the chart with ideas from Listenings One and Two about food trends.*

CATEGORIES	GOODBYE, SIT-DOWN MEAL	FOOD IN A BOWL
1. Examples of changes in eating habits (diet and style of eating)	• French bakeries are serving sandwiches now	
2. Reasons our eating habits are changing		
3. Speakers' attitudes toward these changes		
4. Speakers' tone		

STEP 2: Synthesize

Continue working with the same group and perform a role play. Student A is a reporter asking Student B (Fishlere) and Student C (Satellite Sister) questions from the categories on the left of the chart. The reporter also asks for examples and explanations. Use a tone similar to that of the speakers you heard.

Example

A: Most people seem to agree that our eating habits are changing in many ways. Can you give me some examples?
B: Yes, that's true. In France, for example . . .
C: Well, where I live . . .

156 UNIT 8

---

③ FOCUS ON SPEAKING

This section emphasizes development of productive skills for speaking. It includes sections on vocabulary, grammar, pronunciation, functional language, and an extended speaking task.

> The **VOCABULARY** section leads students from reviewing the unit vocabulary, to practicing and expanding their use of it, and then working with it—using it creatively in both this section and in the final speaking task.
>
> Students learn useful structures for speaking in the **GRAMMAR** section, which offers a concise presentation and targeted practice. Vocabulary items are recycled here, providing multiple exposures leading to mastery. For additional practice with the grammar presented, students and teachers can consult the GRAMMAR BOOK REFERENCES at the end of the book for corresponding material in the *Focus on Grammar* and Azar series.

---

③ FOCUS ON SPEAKING

Ⓐ VOCABULARY

◀ REVIEW

Work with a partner. Look at a student's PowerPoint presentation about the experience of one young immigrant to France and read his comments. Fill in the blanks with words from the box. Then compare your answers with a partner's.

assimilate	interpret	mainstream	set her apart	tight-knit
boned up on	intimidated	niche	support	unique

One Immigrant's Adjustment	Hi, uh, my presentation today is called "One Immigrant's Adjustment." I'm going to focus on Mai Lam, who is 16 years old. She moved to France with her family three years ago from Vietnam. Here's a picture of Mai with her classmates before she left home. She loved school because she had a _____ group of friends.
	1.

[graph]	I'm going to show you a graph about immigration to France. Uh . . . it isn't really clear, but you can see that there are a lot of immigrants in France—actually about 8% of the population—including about 100,000 from Vietnam. It's the fourth line down. So Mai wasn't _____. There are immigrants from many other countries too, like Algeria, Portugal, Spain, and Tunisia. **2.**

Ⓑ GRAMMAR: Reported Speech

1 *Work with a partner. Read the conversation and answer the questions.*

> **A:** I just did the assignment about animal communication. The article reported that some parrots could recognize themselves in a mirror.
>
> **B:** Yeah, and it said they **were able to** string three or four words together, too. Actually, my professor told us that he **had just written** a paper on how parrots learn language. He said he **was going to** publish it next month.
>
> **A:** What did the paper say?
>
> **B:** Well, apparently it warned that researchers **had to** study animal intelligence more carefully before drawing conclusions.

  1. Do we know the exact words of the article and the professor?

  2. Why do you think speaker B chose not to quote the article and the professor directly?

REPORTED SPEECH

Reported speech (also called indirect speech) reports what a speaker said without using his or her exact words.

Use words like *said (that), told, indicated, mentioned, reported,* etc., to show that you are reporting information that someone else said.

When you are reporting what a speaker or article said, "backshift" the verb in the indirect speech statement.

Original: "We **are conducting** some interesting research with chimps."
Reported: The scientist explained that she **was conducting** some interesting research with chimps.

The verb in the reported speech has shifted back in time, in this case from the present continuous to the past continuous. See more examples in the chart below.

NOTE: If you are reporting a person's unchanging beliefs or a general truth, rather than an event, it is not necessary to change the tense of the original verb.

Original: "Many animals **are** remarkably intelligent."
Reported: The zoologist **told her students** that many animals **are / were** remarkably intelligent.

The **PRONUNCIATION** section presents both controlled and freer, communicative practice of the sounds and patterns of English. Models from the listening selections reinforce content and vocabulary. This is followed by the **FUNCTION** section where students are exposed to functional language that prepares them to express ideas on a higher level. Examples have been chosen based on frequency, variety, and usefulness for the final speaking task.

The **PRODUCTION** section gives students an opportunity to integrate the ideas, vocabulary, grammar, pronunciation, and function presented in the unit. This final speaking task is the culminating activity of the unit and gets students to exchange ideas and express opinions in sustained speaking contexts. Activities are presented in a sequence that builds confidence and fluency, and allows for more than one "try" at expression. When appropriate, students practice some presentation skills: audience analysis, organization, eye contact, or use of visuals.

C SPEAKING

PRONUNCIATION: Reducing and Contracting Auxiliary Verbs

- When they talk, native speakers often use contractions of the verbs *be* and *have* after a pronoun. These contractions sound friendlier and less formal, and native speakers find them easier to say than the full forms.
  I've been watching the news more and more recently. My husband says I watch too much. He's started reading more instead.
- After nouns, auxiliary verbs *are*, *have*, and *has* have reduced pronunciations. *Are* sounds like an *-er* ending. It is joined with the preceding word.
  Doctors are worried about our health.
  (Say "Doctorser worried.")
  Have is pronounced /əv/ (like the preposition *of*). It is joined closely with the preceding word.
  Some have chosen to turn off the news.
  (Say "Somev chosen . . .")
  Has is pronounced /əz/ (like the "long plural") after some words.
  My boss has become addicted to the news.
  (Say "bosses.")

1 *Listen to the sentences. As you listen, underline the auxiliary verbs that are reduced. Then read the sentences aloud to a partner, using contractions and reductions.*

1. The United States has become a nation of people addicted to the news.
2. Americans are offered news in many forms.
3. Critics have been concerned about the amount of news we watch.
4. Academics are worried about the amount of news we consume.

2 *Listen to the paragraph about our addiction to the news media. As you listen, fill in the auxiliary verb or contraction that you hear. Then read the paragraph aloud to a partner.*

People _____ offered many sources of news, some of which
                          1.
_____ available 24/7. The country _____ become a
            2.   3.
nation of "news junkies," or people who _____ addicted to the news.
                                                      4.
Some academics _____ started to ask serious questions about the
                          5.
role of the news media in society. Some people believe that the media _____
                                                                                    6.
focusing on negative stories. Therefore, it focuses less on the important issues

---

PRODUCTION: A Class Presentation

In this activity, you will work with a group to *identify arguments for and against a position related to animals and their relationship to people.* You will then present the issue to the class. Try to use the vocabulary, grammar, pronunciation, and language for giving and asking for examples that you learned in the unit.*

Step 1: Divide the class into enough groups so that each one can choose a different topic. Then each group selects its topic from the list or proposes a new one. Consider the question in terms of whether animals are intelligent or not.

1. Should animals be kept in zoos?
2. Should people eat animals?
3. Should people conduct experiments on animals?
4. Should people be allowed to hunt animals?
5. Should people pass stricter laws to protect endangered species?

Step 2: Study the example outline. Then organize your ideas in the outline on page 81. Be sure to think of reasons and examples for both sides of the argument.

Topic: Should people wear fur or leather?	
I. People should not wear fur or leather.	II. People should be allowed to wear fur or leather.
A: Killing animals for fur is cruel.	A: Animals are raised specifically for fur.
1. Animals raised for fur are kept in inhumane conditions.	1. Many rabbits wouldn't be alive unless people bred them for their fur. They weren't wild animals that were shot.
2. They are killed before they reach old age.	
B: Fur is not necessary for people.	2. Example:
1. They can wear other materials.	B: Reason:
2. Example:	1. Example:
	2. Example:

*For Alternative Speaking Topics, see page 81.

ALTERNATIVE SPEAKING TOPICS are provided at the end of the unit. They can be used as *alternatives* to the final speaking task, or as *additional* assignments. RESEARCH TOPICS tied to the theme of the unit are organized in a special section at the back of the book.

COMPONENTS

TEACHER'S MANUAL WITH ACHIEVEMENT TESTS

Each level and strand of *NorthStar* has an accompanying Teacher's Manual with step-by-step **teaching suggestions**, including unique guidance for using *NorthStar* in secondary classes. The manuals include time guidelines, expansion activities, and techniques and instructions for using MyNorthStarLab. Also included are reproducible unit-by-unit achievement **tests** of **receptive** and **productive** skills, **answer keys** to both the student book and tests, and a unit-by-unit **vocabulary** list.

DVD

The *NorthStar* DVD has **engaging**, **authentic video clips**, including animation, documentaries, interviews, and biographies, that correspond to the themes in *NorthStar*. Each theme contains a three- to five-minute segment that can be used with either the *Reading and Writing* strand or the *Listening and Speaking* strand. The video clips can also be viewed in MyNorthStarLab.

COMPANION WEBSITE

The companion website, www.longman.com/northstar, includes resources for teachers, such as the **scope and sequence**, **correlations** to other Longman products and to state standards, and **podcasts** from the *NorthStar* authors and series editors.

MyNorthStarLab

PEARSON LONGMAN
mynorthstarlab

AVAILABLE WITH the new edition of
NORTHSTAR

NorthStar is now available with **MyNorthStarLab**—an easy-to-use **online** program **for students and teachers** that saves time and improves results.

➢ **STUDENTS** receive **personalized instruction** and **practice** in all four skills. Audio, video, and test preparation are all in **one** place—available **anywhere, anytime**.

➢ **TEACHERS** can take advantage of many resources including online **assessments**, a flexible **gradebook**, and **tools for monitoring student progress**.

CHECK IT OUT! GO TO www.mynorthstarlab.com FOR A PREVIEW!

TURN THE PAGE TO SEE KEY FEATURES OF **MyNorthStarLab**.

MYNORTHSTARLAB

MyNorthStarLab supports students with **individualized instruction, feedback,** and **extra help**. A wide array of resources, including a flexible **gradebook**, helps teachers manage student progress.

The MyNorthStarLab **WELCOME** page **organizes assignments and grades,** and **facilitates communication** between students and teachers.

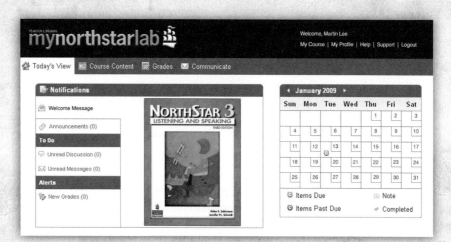

For each unit, MyNorthStarLab provides a **READINESS CHECK**.

➤ Activities **assess** student knowledge **before** beginning the unit and **follow up** with individualized instruction.

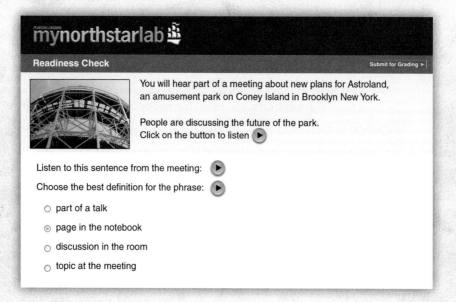

Student book material and **new** practice activities are available to students online.

➤ Students benefit from virtually unlimited **practice anywhere, anytime**.

Interaction with **Internet** and **video** materials will:

➤ Expand students' knowledge of the topic.

➤ Help students practice new vocabulary and grammar.

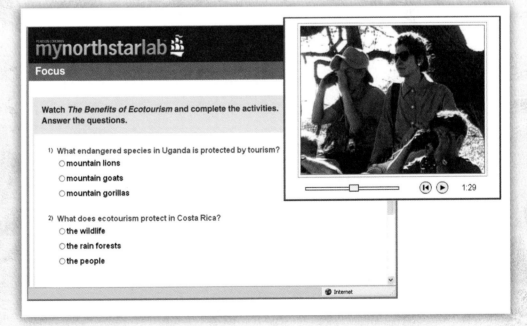

INTEGRATED SKILL ACTIVITIES in MyNorthStarLab challenge students to bring together the **language skills** and **critical thinking skills** that they have practiced throughout the unit.

PEARSON LONGMAN
mynorthstarlab

Integrated Task - Read, Listen, Write

Submit for Grading ▶

THE ADVENTURE OF A LIFETIME

We at the Antarctic Travel Society <u>encourage</u> you to consider an excited guided tour of Antarctica for your next vacation.

The Antarctic Travel society carefully plans and operates tours of the Antarctic by ship. There are three trips per day leaving from <u>ports</u> in South America and Australia. Each ship carries only about 100 passengers at a time. Tours run from November through March to the ice-free areas along the coast of Antarctica.

In addition to touring the coast, our ships stop for on-land visits, which generally last for about three hours. Activities include guided sightseeing, mountain climbing, camping, <u>kayaking</u>, and <u>scuba diving</u>. For a longer stay, camping trips can also be arranged.

Our tours will give you an opportunity to experience the richness of Antarctica, including its wildlife, history, active research stations, and, most of all, its natural beauty.

Tours are <u>supervised</u> by the ship's staff. The staff generally includes <u>experts</u> in animal and sea life and other Antarctica specialists. There is generally one staff member for every 10 to 20 passengers. Theses trained and responsible individuals will help to make your visit to Antarctica safe, educational, and <u>unforgettable</u>.

READ, LISTEN AND WRITE ABOUT TOURISM IN ANTARCTICA
Read.
Read the text. Then answer the question.

According to the text, how can tourism benefit the Antartic?

▶ **Listen.**
Click on the Play button and listen to the passage.
Use the outline to take notes as you listen.

Main idea:

Seven things that scientists study:

The effects of tourism:

Write.
Write about the potential and risks in Antarctica.
Follow the steps to prepare.

Step 1
• Review the text and your outline from the listening task.
• Write notes about the benefits and risks of tourism.

Step 2
Write for 20 minutes. Leave 5 minutes to edit your work.

The MyNorthStarLab **ASSESSMENT** tools allow instructors to customize and deliver achievement tests online.

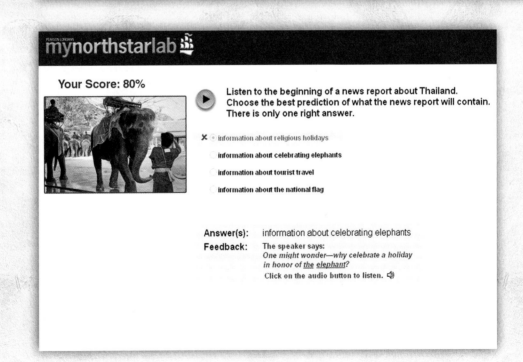

SCOPE AND SEQUENCE

UNIT	CRITICAL THINKING	LISTENING

1 **Information Overload**
 	
Theme: Media
Listening One: *News Resisters*
  A radio report
Listening Two: *Does the Media Overwhelm Our Lives?*
  A radio interview
	Compare sources of news
	Recognize assumptions about media
	Interpret graphs
	Infer information not explicit in the interview
	Hypothesize another's point of view
	Analyze goals of news reporting
	Analyze effects of news reporting styles
	Reflect on the role news has in individual's lives
		Make predictions
		Listen for main ideas
		Listen for details
		Provide evidence to support answers
		Relate listenings to personal values
		Organize and synthesize information from the listenings
		Listen to student broadcasts and analyze them

2 **The Achilles Heel**
 	
Theme: Overcoming obstacles
Listening One: *Dreams of Flying and Overcoming Obstacles*
  A radio broadcast
Listening Two: *The Achilles Track Club Climbs Mount Kilimanjaro*
  A television news broadcast
	Identify personal obstacles
	Rank the value of personal qualities
	Analyze narrative techniques in an essay
	Hypothesize another's point of view
	Analyze sensitive language referring to disabilities
	Infer meaning not explicit in the listening
	Compare and contrast two life histories
	Frame contrasting points of view
		Make predictions
		Summarize main ideas
		Listen for details
		Relate listenings to knowledge of the world
		Identify connecting themes between two listenings
		Identify thought groups in speech
		Listen to classmates' reports and pose questions

3 **Early to Bed, Early to Rise . . .**
 	
Theme: Medicine
Listening One: *Teen Sleep Needs*
  A radio news report
Listening Two: *Get Back In Bed*
  A radio interview
	Interpret a cartoon
	Interpret a proverb
	Compare and contrast sleep habits
	Hypothesize scenarios
	Draw conclusions about sleep deprivation
	Propose solutions to problems
	Analyze a case of sleep deprivation and its consequences
		Make predictions
		Take notes
		Summarize main ideas
		Listen for details
		Interpret speakers' tone and emotions
		Relate listenings to personal experiences
		Compare information from two listenings
		Identify emphasis in speech and its meaning

SPEAKING	VOCABULARY	GRAMMAR	PRONUNCIATION
Summarize points Act out a scripted conversation Give a newscast Express and defend opinions	Use context clues to find meaning Find and use synonyms Use idiomatic expressions Use descriptive adjectives	Passive voice	Reducing and contracting auxiliary verbs
Share experiences Construct and tell a story from provided notes Conduct an interview Practice storytelling Plan and give a three-minute speech	Use context clues to find meaning Define words Differentiate between literal versus figurative language	Gerunds and infinitives	Thought groups
Use new vocabulary in a guided conversation Make contrastive statements Act out scripted dialogues Form and express opinions Interrupt politely to clarify or confirm information Role play asking for and giving advice Role play a meeting situation	Use context clues to find meaning Define words Use idiomatic expressions	Present unreal conditionals	Contrastive stress

SCOPE AND SEQUENCE

UNIT	CRITICAL THINKING	LISTENING
4 Animal Intelligence **Theme:** Animal intelligence **Listening One:** *The Infinite Mind: Animal Intelligence* 　A radio interview **Listening Two:** *What Motivates Animals?* 　A radio interview	Recognize speakers' attitudes Support opinions with information from the reports Make judgments Support generalizations with examples Infer information not explicit in the interview	Make predictions Relate previous knowledge to the listenings Identify main ideas Listen for details Infer word meaning from context Listen for specific information Infer speakers' attitudes
5 Longevity: Refusing to Be Invisible **Theme:** Longevity **Listening One:** *The Red Hat Society* 　A radio interview **Listening Two:** *On Vinegar and Living to the Ripe Old Age of 115* 　A radio interview	Recognize feeling from tone of voice Draw conclusions from graphs Support opinions with information from the reports Create graphs from opinions	Make predictions Relate previous knowledge to the listenings Identify main ideas Listen for specific information Infer information not explicit in the interview Identify speakers' feelings
6 Giving to Others: Why Do We Do It? **Theme:** Philanthropy **Listening One:** *Why We Give* 　A radio interview **Listening Two:** *The Mystery Donor* 　A radio report	Read and interpret graphs Make judgments about motivations for philanthropy Identify personal assumptions Hypothesize rationales for philanthropic actions Compare and contrast information Rank desirable employee qualities	Make predictions Identify main ideas Listen for details Listen and take notes using a graphic organizer Organize and synthesize information from the listenings Listen to and evaluate students' presentations
7 What's the Use of Homework? **Theme:** Education **Listening One:** *Effects of Homework on Family Life* 　A radio interview **Listening Two:** *A Duty to Family, Heritage, and Country: Another Perspective on Homework* 　A radio commentary	Interpret a cartoon Identify and evaluate assumptions Hypothesize another's point of view Connect opinions to specific people Evaluate own opinions concerning others' thoughts	Predict content Listen for main ideas Listen for details Support answers with details Relate listenings to personal experiences Organize and synthesize information from the listenings

SPEAKING	VOCABULARY	GRAMMAR	PRONUNCIATION
Give and ask for examples Form and express opinions Report on research Construct and perform a presentation Evaluate the opinions of others	Use context clues to find meaning Define words Find and use synonyms	Reported speech	Questions with *or*
Make suggestions Form and express opinions Call in to a radio talk show Ask and answer questions Role-play a family meeting	Use context clues to find meaning Define words Find and use synonyms	Tag questions	Recognizing word blends with *you*
Express opinions about philanthropy Discuss examples of charitable efforts Prioritize and rank ideas Practice correct intonation Develop and perform a public service announcement	Use context clues to find meaning Find and use synonyms Identify correct word forms	Adjective clauses	Intonation in lists
Express opinions Restate information for clarification Restate statements Perform a role play Conduct a town meeting	Use context clues to find meaning Find and use synonyms Use idiomatic expressions	*Make, let, help,* and *get*	Stressed and unstressed vowels

SCOPE AND SEQUENCE

UNIT	CRITICAL THINKING	LISTENING
8 **Goodbye to the Sit-Down Meal** **Theme:** Food **Listening One:** *French Sandwiches* A radio report **Listening Two:** *Food in a Bowl* A radio report	Identify and analyze food trends Relate general factors to specific behaviors Compare food practices Interpret meaning from context Infer situational context Infer word meaning from context	Make predictions Summarize main ideas Listen for details Interpret speakers' tone and attitude Relate the listening to local food trends Compare and contrast two restaurants Classify vowel sounds Listen to and evaluate student food shows using a rubric
9 **Finding a Niche: The Challenge for Young Immigrants** **Theme:** Immigration **Listening One:** *A World within a School* A radio news report **Listening Two:** *The Words Escape Me* A song	Compare personal experiences Recognize personal assumptions Hypothesize scenarios Infer word meaning from context Compare and contrast two experiences Infer meaning not explicit in the listening Propose solutions Interpret graphs	Make predictions Identify main ideas Listen for details Interpret speakers' tone and pitch Relate the listenings to personal values Understand and interpret song lyrics
10 **No Technology? No Way!** **Theme:** Technology **Listening One:** *Noise in the City* A radio news report **Listening Two:** *Technology Talk* A radio interview	Interpret cartoons Draw conclusions from a graph Compare opinions about technology Infer situational context Make judgments Hypothesize scenarios Draw conclusions Define a problem and propose a solution	Make predictions Listen for main ideas Listen for supporting details Interpret speakers' tone and word usage Take notes while listening Listen for specific information Listen for emphasis in speech Identify and name sounds

SPEAKING	VOCABULARY	GRAMMAR	PRONUNCIATION
Share ideas on food trends Use tone of voice to indicate attitude Use new vocabulary in free conversation Compose and perform a dialogue Practice gambits that call attention to a particular item Explain how to use a tool Develop and perform a food show	Use context clues to find meaning Find and use synonyms Analyze figurative meanings of words Use idiomatic expressions	Phrasal verbs	Spelling and sounds: *oo* and *o*
Express opinions Practice gambits to hesitate in response to a question Ask and answer questions about a chart Simulate a town meeting Conduct an interview	Use context clues to find meaning Find and use synonyms Define words Use idiomatic expressions	Present and past—contrasting verb tenses	*ship* /ʃ/, *measure* /ʒ/, *cheap* /tʃ/, and *jazz* /dʒ/
Discuss opinions Act out scripted dialogues Discuss possible future outcomes Practice gambits to express frustration Role-play a conflict between neighbors Develop and present a new technological gadget	Find and use synonyms Define words Use context clues to find meaning Use descriptive adjectives	Future perfect and future progressive	Adverbial particles

ACKNOWLEDGMENTS

To friends, family, and colleagues who have supported us throughout this third edition of *NorthStar*, our heartfelt thanks. Each of you has left an imprint on these pages.

The project has been guided and enriched by the contributions of many people. We would like to thank Frances Boyd and Carol Numrich, our watchful *NorthStar* series editors. We thank the wonderful editorial staff at Pearson Education, particularly Debbie Sistino for her deft control of this huge endeavor, and Dorothy Zemach, whose professionalism and demeanor are outstanding. In addition, the many interviewees and commentators heard in the listenings are part of *NorthStar*. We also extend gratitude and warm wishes to students and friends at Randolph Township Schools and Eugenio María de Hostos Community College.

And of course, we thank Jay and Miranda, Carlos, Kelly and Victor.

Tess Ferree
Kim Sanabria

Reviewers

For the comments and insights they graciously offered to help shape the direction of the Third Edition of *Northstar,* the publisher would like to thank the following reviewers and institutions.

Gail August, Hostos Community College; **Anne Bachmann**, Clackamas Community College; **Aegina Barnes**, York College, CUNY; **Dr. Sabri Bebawi**, San Jose Community College; **Kristina Beckman**, John Jay College; **Jeff Bellucci**, Kaplan Boston; **Nathan Blesse**, Human International Academy; **Alan Brandman**, Queens College; **Laila Cadavona-Dellapasqua**, Kaplan; **Amy Cain**, Kaplan; **Nigel Caplan**, Michigan State University; **Alzira Carvalho**, Human International Academy, San Diego; **Chao-Hsun (Richard) Cheng**, Wenzao Ursuline College of Languages; **Mu-hua (Yolanda) Chi**, Wenzao Ursuline College of Languages; **Liane Cismowski**, Olympic High School; **Shauna Croft**, MESLS; **Misty Crooks**, Kaplan; **Amanda De Loera**, Kaplan English Programs; **Jennifer Dobbins**, New England School of English; **Luis Dominguez**, Angloamericano; **Luydmila Drgaushanskaya**, ASA College; **Dilip Dutt**, Roxbury Community College; **Christie Evenson**, Chung Dahm Institute; **Patricia Frenz-Belkin**, Hostos Community College, CUNY; **Christiane Galvani**, Texas Southern University; **Joanna Ghosh**, University of Pennsylvania; **Cristina Gomes**, Kaplan Test Prep; **Kristen Grinager**, Lincoln High School; **Janet Harclerode**, Santa Monica College; **Carrell Harden**, HCCS, Gulfton Campus; **Connie Harney**, Antelope Valley College; **Ann Hilborn**, ESL Consultant in Houston; **Barbara Hockman**, City College of San Francisco; **Margaret Hodgson**, NorQuest College; **Paul Hong**, Chung Dahm Institute; **Wonki Hong**, Chung Dahm Institute; **John House**, Iowa State University; **Polly Howlett**, Saint Michael's College; **Arthur Hui**, Fullerton College; **Nina Ito**, CSU, Long Beach; **Scott Jenison**, Antelope Valley College; **Hyunsook Jeong**, Keimyung University; **Mandy Kama**, Georgetown University; **Dale Kim**, Chung Dahm Institute; **Taeyoung Kim**, Keimyung University; **Woo-hyung Kim**, Keimyung University; **Young Kim**, Chung Dahm Language Institute; **Yu-kyung Kim**, Sunchon National University; **John Kostovich**, Miami Dade College; **Albert Kowun**, Fairfax, VA; **David Krise**, Michigan State University; **Cheri (Young Hee) Lee**, ReadingTownUSA English Language Institute; **Eun-Kyung Lee**, Chung Dahm Institute; **Sang Hyock Lee**, Keimyung University; **Debra Levitt**, SMC; **Karen Lewis**, Somerville, MA; **Chia-Hui Liu**, Wenzao Ursuline College of Languages; **Gennell Lockwood**, Seattle, WA; **Javier Lopez Anguiano**, Colegio Anglo Mexicano de Coyoacan; **Mary March**, Shoreline Community College; **Susan Matson**, ELS Language Centers; **Ralph McClain**, Embassy CES Boston; **Veronica McCormack**, Roxbury Community College; **Jennifer McCoy**, Kaplan; **Joseph McHugh**, Kaplan; **Cynthia McKeag Tsukamoto**, Oakton Community College; **Paola Medina**, Texas Southern University; **Christine Kyung-ah Moon**, Seoul, Korea; **Margaret Moore**, North Seattle Community College; **Michelle Moore**, Madison English as a Second Language School; **David Motta**, Miami University; **Suzanne Munro**, Clackamas Community College; **Elena Nehrbecki**, Hudson County CC; **Kim Newcomer**, University of Washington; **Melody Nightingale**, Santa Monica College; **Patrick Northover**, Kaplan Test and Prep; **Sarah Oettle**, Kaplan, Sacramento; **Shirley Ono**, Oakton Community College; **Maria Estela Ortiz Torres**, C. Anglo Mexicano de Coyoac'an; **Suzanne Overstreet**, West Valley College; **Linda Ozarow**, West Orange High School; **Ileana Porges-West**, Miami Dade College, Hialeah Campus; **Megan Power**, ILCSA; **Alison Robertson**, Cypress College; **Ma. Del Carmen Romero**, Universidad del Valle de Mexico; **Nina Rosen**, Santa Rosa Junior College; **Daniellah Salario**, Kaplan; **Joel Samuels**, Kaplan New York City; **Babi Sarapata**, Columbia University ALP; **Donna Schaeffer**, University of Washington; **Lynn Schneider**, City College of San Francisco; **Errol Selkirk**, New School University; **Amity Shook**, Chung Dahm Institute; **Lynn Stafford-Yilmaz**, Bellevue Community College; **Lynne Ruelaine Stokes**, Michigan State University; **Henna Suh**, Chung Dahm Institute; **Sheri Summers**, Kaplan Test Prep; **Martha Sutter**, Kent State University; **Becky Tarver Chase**, MESLS; **Lisa Waite-Trago**, Michigan State University; **Carol Troy**, Da-Yeh University; **Luci Tyrell**, Embassy CES Fort Lauderdale; **Yong-Hee Uhm**, Myongii University; **Debra Un**, New York University; **José Vazquez**, The University of Texas Pan American; **Hollyahna Vettori**, Santa Rosa Junior College; **Susan Vik**, Boston University; **Sandy Wagner**, Fort Lauderdale High School; **Joanne Wan**, ASC English; **Pat Wiggins**, Clackamas Community College; **Heather Williams**, University of Pennsylvania; **Carol Wilson-Duffy**, Michigan State University; **Kailin Yang**, Kaohsing Medical University; **Ellen Yaniv**, Boston University; **Samantha Young**, Kaplan Boston; **Yu-san Yu**, National Sun Yat-sen University; **Ann Zaaijer**, West Orange High School

Information Overload

1 FOCUS ON THE TOPIC

A PREDICT

Look at the cartoon and the title of the unit. Then discuss the questions with a partner or small group.

1. In what ways is this person affected by modern means of communication?

2. What is the message of the cartoon? Do you agree or disagree with it?

B SHARE INFORMATION

Where do you look for news and information? On the chart, check (✓) the news media you use most frequently. Then compare your answers with a small group. Discuss the reasons for your choices.

TYPES OF INFORMATION	NEWS MEDIA					
	Newspapers	TV	Radio	Internet	Magazines	Other people
Local news						
National news						
International news						
Weather						
Traffic reports						
Sports						
Business news						
Technology news						
Entertainment (art, movies, music)						

1 CD 7 *Read and listen to the survey and check (✓) the response that is most similar to your own. Then analyze your results on page 4.*

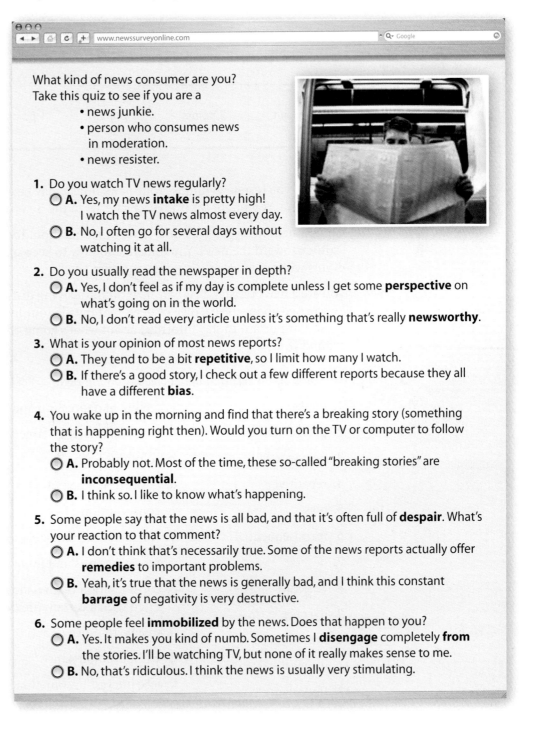

000   www.newssurveyonline.com   Q- Google

What kind of news consumer are you?
Take this quiz to see if you are a
- news junkie.
- person who consumes news in moderation.
- news resister.

1. Do you watch TV news regularly?
○ **A.** Yes, my news **intake** is pretty high! I watch the TV news almost every day.
○ **B.** No, I often go for several days without watching it at all.

2. Do you usually read the newspaper in depth?
○ **A.** Yes, I don't feel as if my day is complete unless I get some **perspective** on what's going on in the world.
○ **B.** No, I don't read every article unless it's something that's really **newsworthy**.

3. What is your opinion of most news reports?
○ **A.** They tend to be a bit **repetitive**, so I limit how many I watch.
○ **B.** If there's a good story, I check out a few different reports because they all have a different **bias**.

4. You wake up in the morning and find that there's a breaking story (something that is happening right then). Would you turn on the TV or computer to follow the story?
○ **A.** Probably not. Most of the time, these so-called "breaking stories" are **inconsequential**.
○ **B.** I think so. I like to know what's happening.

5. Some people say that the news is all bad, and that it's often full of **despair**. What's your reaction to that comment?
○ **A.** I don't think that's necessarily true. Some of the news reports actually offer **remedies** to important problems.
○ **B.** Yeah, it's true that the news is generally bad, and I think this constant **barrage** of negativity is very destructive.

6. Some people feel **immobilized** by the news. Does that happen to you?
○ **A.** Yes. It makes you kind of numb. Sometimes I **disengage** completely **from** the stories. I'll be watching TV, but none of it really makes sense to me.
○ **B.** No, that's ridiculous. I think the news is usually very stimulating.

2 Work with a partner. Use the key to score your partner's news habits. Then discuss the results. Do you each agree with the evaluation? Why or why not?

	QUESTION 1	QUESTION 2	QUESTION 3	QUESTION 4	QUESTION 5	QUESTION 6
Answer A	2 points	2 points	1 point	1 point	2 points	1 point
Answer B	1 point	1 point	2 points	2 points	1 point	2 points

11–12 Uh-oh—you're a news junkie! Your news intake may be excessive and could be stressful. You might want to disengage from the news occasionally.

8–10 Congratulations—you consume news in moderation. You have a healthy attitude toward the news. You understand how to keep up with current events without letting the news overwhelm you.

6–7 You are a news resister. You may have an **underlying** distrust of the media or be worried about the barrage of news that invades our lives 24/7.* However, it's still important to stay informed about what's going on in the world around you.

3 Match the words on the left with the definitions on the right.

_____ 1. intake   **a.** feeling of depression and sadness

_____ 2. perspective   **b.** constant attack, in large amounts

_____ 3. newsworthy   **c.** solutions

_____ 4. repetitive   **d.** basic; fundamental

_____ 5. bias   **e.** consumption

_____ 6. inconsequential   **f.** worthy of the media's attention

_____ 7. despair   **g.** repeating the same thing over and over

_____ 8. remedies   **h.** consideration of an issue from only one side, often with a certain prejudice

_____ 9. barrage   **i.** unable to move or act

_____ 10. immobilized   **j.** without importance

_____ 11. disengage from   **k.** lose interest in something

_____ 12. underlying   **l.** sensible point of view

*24/7: 24 hours a day, 7 days a week. Said of something that is constant or is available all the time.

2 FOCUS ON LISTENING

A LISTENING ONE: News Resisters

How does news affect our lives? You will listen to a radio reporter who talks to a medical doctor and other professionals, all with strong opinions on the topic.

 Listen to the introduction and answer the questions. Compare your answers with a partner's.

1. What does Dr. Weil hope people can do at the end of eight weeks of his program?

   _____

2. The reporter interviews some news resisters, people who avoid taking in too much news. In what professions do you think she will find them? Check (✓) your guesses.

   _____ artist   _____ doctor

   _____ business executive   _____ lawyer

   _____ clergy member   _____ novelist

   _____ college professor   _____ restaurant worker

◖ LISTEN FOR MAIN IDEAS

Listen to National Public Radio's Margot Adler interview people about how much news we need. Draw a line from each person to his or her opinion.

1. Andrew Weil
   (doctor, author)

2. Mark Harris
   (author)

3. Gabrielle Spiegel
   (Johns Hopkins University)

4. John Sommerville
   (author, history professor)

5. Tupton Shudrun
   (Buddhist nun, teacher)

a. Novels are more interesting than the news.

b. It's better not to read the news every day.

c. People should gradually reduce their news intake.

d. The news focuses too much on problems and doesn't offer solutions.

e. Fantasy and humor are more important than the news.

CD 7

5 *Listen to the interviews again. Circle the best answer to complete each statement.*

1. Mark Harris wrote an essay in the *New York Times* in the early 1970s about newspapers. Since then, he has _____.
   a. changed his opinion completely
   b. adjusted his opinion a little
   c. maintained the same opinion

2. In Harris's opinion, novels get readers to focus on interesting people, such as _____.
   a. sports figures who don't win
   b. teachers at small universities
   c. historical figures who are little known

3. The period in history that Gabrielle Spiegel studies is the _____ centuries.
   a. thirteenth and fourteenth
   b. fifteenth and sixteenth
   c. nineteenth and twentieth

4. Spiegel doesn't read newspapers because _____.
   a. they are repetitive
   b. she doesn't have enough time
   c. she wants to spend time with her children

5. In Sommerville's opinion, daily news _____.
   a. gives too much information
   b. keeps people from seeing connections
   c. should focus more on religion

6. Sommerville reads the news _____.
   a. every week
   b. every three or four months
   c. almost never

7. Tupton Shudrun is critical of the media because it _____.
   a. doesn't explain problems well
   b. creates a sense of despair
   c. is difficult to understand

8. Gabrielle Spiegel thinks that children _____.
   a. can't understand much of the news they hear
   b. need to spend more time alone
   c. should listen to the news with their parents

◖ MAKE INFERENCES

Listen to the excerpts and circle the correct answer. Then discuss with a partner how you chose the answer: For example, was it tone of voice, special vocabulary, or something else?

CD 1
6 **Excerpt One**

1. Mark Harris believes that reading a newspaper _____.
   - a. should be done in the evening instead of the morning
   - b. is a habit or a routine

CD 1
7 **Excerpt Two**

2. Professor Spiegel thinks that _____.
   - a. there are more important things to do than pay attention to the news
   - b. the news should cover longer, more historical events

CD 1
8 **Excerpt Three**

3. John Sommerville believes that _____.
   - a. daily newspapers don't choose the best stories to cover
   - b. some news stories are more important than others

CD 1
9 **Excerpt Four**

4. The news people working at NPR _____.
   - a. didn't think a story against the news was a good idea
   - b. believed they had a problem taking in too much news

◖ EXPRESS OPINIONS

Work in a small group. Discuss the questions.

1. What is a news resister? What are some advantages and disadvantages to being a news resister?

2. The reporter interviewed a doctor, a novelist, two professors, and a nun. They are all news resisters. Which of their ideas do you agree with? Which do you disagree with?

3. Do you think that responsible citizens have to keep up with the news? How much time do you think you should spend keeping up with the news? What news sources do you prefer, and why?

You will hear a radio interview with Todd Gitlin, author of *Media Unlimited*. He claims that when the news media jumps around from story to story, we get distracted and overwhelmed.

1 🔟 *Listen to the interview and circle the best answer to complete each statement.*

1. Todd Gitlin is a _____.
   a. college professor
   b. TV news reporter

2. Mr. Gitlin believes that media _____.
   a. will completely surround us in the future
   b. has already overtaken our lives

3. Mr. Gitlin lists _____ main problems associated with media consumption.
   a. two
   b. three

4. When claiming that we have developed a kind of "national attention deficit disorder," Gitlin gives the example of our _____.
   a. addiction to blogs (Web logs)
   b. fascination with sensational TV

5. Gitlin says we must _____.
   a. develop a sense of community
   b. be more concerned about people like ourselves

6. According to Gitlin, the average child interacts with some form of media _____ hours a day.
   a. 4 ½
   b. 6 ½

7. A negative consequence of children's use of TV and video games is that children _____.
   a. are exposed to too much violence
   b. expect teachers to be as entertaining as these media

2 *Work in a small group. Discuss the questions.*

1. Do you agree with Todd Gitlin that the media has a mostly negative influence on our lives? If so, what should we be doing to limit this influence? If not, why not?

2. Even though many people have pointed out the dangers of media overload, the media is still popular. What are some possible reasons for this?

C INTEGRATE LISTENINGS ONE AND TWO

◀ STEP 1: Organize

In Listening One, you heard why some people dislike daily news. Listening Two discussed more general consequences of media overload. Complete the chart with the information you heard.

	NEWS RESISTERS	IS MEDIA OVERWHELMING?
Problems with the way news is presented now	• Can't focus on all of the interesting stories	• There is a media overload
Effects on individuals' behavior	• People become addicted to the news	
Effects on individuals' feelings		
Effects on children		
Effects on society as a whole		

◀ STEP 2: Synthesize

Work with a partner. Role play a discussion between a news reporter and a commentator. The reporter asks the commentator about problems with how news is presented these days. Use the information in the chart in your questions and answers. Take turns being the reporter and the commentator.

Example

REPORTER: Good afternoon. I'd like to ask you about how news is presented today. Do you think there are any problems?
COMMENTATOR: Well, yes, I do. For one thing, I think there's a media overload. There's just too much news every day! And because the news is presented daily, it's hard to focus on a lot of the interesting stories out there. For example, . . .

③ FOCUS ON SPEAKING

Ⓐ VOCABULARY

◖REVIEW

1 *Two roommates are talking about the TV news. Complete their conversation with words from the box. Then practice the conversation with a partner.*

barrage	evading	makes a connection	regardless of
bias	inconsequential	newsworthy	remedy
comes in second	lethal	perspective	repetitive

A: What's on TV?

B: I'm watching the news. But you know, I just heard the same story that they reported last night! The news is so _____.
                                                                  1.

A: I know. And I also don't like the _____ in most of the TV news. I
                                                        2.
mean, it just doesn't present an objective viewpoint.

B: I know what you mean. And many times the stories are so _____;
                                                                              3.
they really don't affect our lives in any way.

A: Well, that's why I prefer the Internet. The news stories there are more interesting
and _____. For example, this morning I read about how some
              4.
dangerous chemicals were found in a popular brand of dog food. Apparently,
they could be _____.
                        5.

B: Well, there's an example of news that really _____ with people's
                                                                      6.
lives.

A: Exactly. I read that the Internet is people's first choice for news these days. TV
news _____, and radio and print media come last.
              7.

B: That's not surprising, is it? These days most people have access to online news
sources, _____ where they live.
                  8.

A: Right. But there are plenty of news sources to choose from—and they all have a
different _____.
                    9.

10 UNIT I

B: You know, I'm sick of this constant _____ of boring news

10.

stories on TV. And I waste a lot of time watching TV. I'm afraid I'm

_____ my other responsibilities.

11.

A: I have the perfect _____. Why don't we go out for a walk?

12.

2 *Decide if the words and phrases in the box have a positive or negative connotation, and write them into the appropriate category below.*

barrage	inconsequential	newsworthy
bias	lethal	remedy
evade	make a connection	repetitive

POSITIVE CONNOTATION	NEGATIVE CONNOTATION

◖ **EXPAND**

Read the descriptions of some TV news programs. Circle the correct words and phrases.

1. Regional Recap	Are you (**1. addicted to / plugged into**) the news? This Friday morning program features all of your favorite stories from the previous week, so you can enjoy them all again. Especially useful for busy people who didn't (**2. raise / catch**) all of the details of their favorite stories during the week.
2. All News is Good News!	If you need to (**3. take a break from / have an focus on**) negative news stories, you'll appreciate our (**4. coverage / addiction**) of only positive stories. We (**5. get the scoop on / make a connection to**) stories about success, lucky breaks, and ordinary people who have become heroes in their communities. Join us for our (**6. daily / fantasy**) messages of hope and happiness.
3. What's Happening?	The perfect (**7. remedy / perspective**) for people who find the regular news too serious. Our reporters have a sense of (**8. reason / humor**) and find the stories that will make you laugh! We cover only true stories, but our (**9. underlying / inconsequential**) purpose is to amuse and entertain you.
4. Sunday Night Special: Unplugged	Tonight we interview Dr. John Martin, the well-known educator who (**10. raises / recommends**) not allowing teenagers to use computers, even to (**11. track down / take on**) information on the Internet or e-mail, because these activities (**12. addict / distract**) them from school work and family time. In fact, Dr. Martin claims that overexposure to the Internet is one of the causes of (**13. bias / attention deficit disorder**).

Work with a partner or group. Discuss the four news programs in Expand using the words in the box. Check (✓) every word you use. Can you use them all?

Example

A: I think *Regional Recap* sounds **repetitive**.

B: You're right. And if the week's stories are **inconsequential**, there's no need to hear them again. I wouldn't **recommend** that program.

addiction, be addicted to	evade	put an emphasis on
attention deficit disorder (ADD)	fantasy	raise (children)
barrage	focus	recommend
bias	get the scoop on	regardless of
catch the news	inconsequential	remedy
come in second	lethal	repetitive
coverage	make a connection	sense of humor
daily	newsworthy	take a break (from)
distract	perspective	track down
distraction, distract from	plugged in	underlying

B GRAMMAR: Passive Voice

1 *Work with a partner. Read the conversation and answer the questions.*

A: You know, we**'re surrounded by** the news 24/7. Do you think that's a bad thing?

B: Well, I have mixed feelings. On the one hand, I know that we**'re being overloaded** with information. On the other hand, I am sometimes grateful for all the news.

1. Who is surrounded?

2. What surrounds them?

3. Who is being overloaded?

4. What is overloading them?

Forming the Passive Voice

To form the **passive**, use the correct form of *be* + the **past participle**. If the agent of the action is known and important, use *by* + the agent.

Active	**Passive**
Too much news **distracts** you from the things you really need to do.	You **are distracted** from the things you really need to do.
The reporter **discussed** the upcoming election.	The upcoming election **was discussed by** the reporter.

Using the Passive Voice

News reports often use the passive voice; for example, when the agent of the action is unknown or not important, or when the speaker or writer wants to avoid saying who the agent is.

- Use the passive voice to shift focus from the agent of the action to the person or thing being described.

  Tabloid newspapers **are read** by people all over the world.

  In this case, *tabloid newspapers* is more important than *people all over the world*.

- Use the passive voice when you do not know the agent of the action, or when the agent is not important.

  The news about the robbery **is being reported** in great detail.

- Use the passive voice when you don't want to mention the agent, particularly to avoid blaming the agent.

  Some factual mistakes **were made** in the article about the murder trial.

2 Complete the TV news reports with the passive voice, using the verbs in parentheses and the verb tenses indicated. Then take turns with a partner reading the reports aloud.

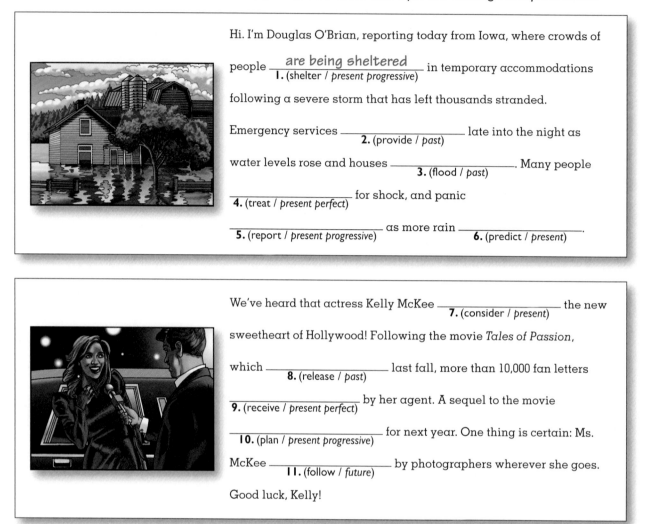

Hi. I'm Douglas O'Brian, reporting today from Iowa, where crowds of

people ___are being sheltered___ in temporary accommodations
　　　　　 1. (shelter / *present progressive*)

following a severe storm that has left thousands stranded.

Emergency services _____ late into the night as
　　　　　　　　　　 2. (provide / *past*)

water levels rose and houses _____. Many people
　　　　　　　　　　　　　　　 3. (flood / *past*)

_____ for shock, and panic
4. (treat / *present perfect*)

_____ as more rain _____.
5. (report / *present progressive*)　　　　　　 **6.** (predict / *present*)

We've heard that actress Kelly McKee _____ the new
　　　　　　　　　　　　　　　　　　　 7. (consider / *present*)

sweetheart of Hollywood! Following the movie *Tales of Passion*,

which _____ last fall, more than 10,000 fan letters
　　　 8. (release / *past*)

_____ by her agent. A sequel to the movie
9. (receive / *present perfect*)

_____ for next year. One thing is certain: Ms.
10. (plan / *present progressive*)

McKee _____ by photographers wherever she goes.
　　　 11. (follow / *future*)

Good luck, Kelly!

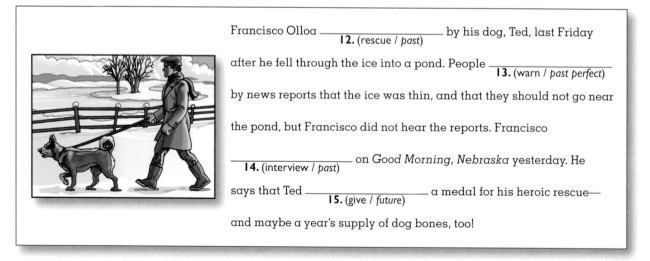

Francisco Olloa _____ by his dog, Ted, last Friday
　　　　　　　　　 12. (rescue / *past*)

after he fell through the ice into a pond. People _____
　　　　　　　　　　　　　　　　　　　　　　　 13. (warn / *past perfect*)

by news reports that the ice was thin, and that they should not go near

the pond, but Francisco did not hear the reports. Francisco

_____ on *Good Morning, Nebraska* yesterday. He
14. (interview / *past*)

says that Ted _____ a medal for his heroic rescue—
　　　　　　　 15. (give / *future*)

and maybe a year's supply of dog bones, too!

3 *Work with a partner.*

Student A: Read the statements.

Student B: Respond to the statements by completing the sentence using a passive form of the verb and the verb tense indicated.

Student A	Student B
1. Mark Harris found a remedy for his problem: He left his job with the newspaper.	1. Yes, it seems that he _____ to teaching. (attract / *past*)
2. There seem to be a lot of news resisters in universities.	2. That's right. Universities _____ with people (fill / *present*) who reject the daily news.
3. Professor Spiegel said that reading helps you develop your imagination.	3. Yes, I agree. Your imagination _____ when you read. (stimulate / *present*)
4. Tupton Shudrun seems to think that most news can be immobilizing and depressing.	4. That's definitely true. I remember many times when I _____ by (depress / *present perfect*) bad news on TV.

Now switch roles.

5. Apparently we spend countless hours with TV, the Internet, and the radio.	5. True. We _____ by (overload / *present progressive*) the media.
6. Todd Gitlin says that media overload has a terrible effect on us.	6. Yes, he thinks that our civic life _____ by our addiction (weaken / *present*) to news.
7. Kids these days watch a lot of TV after school and on weekends.	7. Yes, and when they come to school, they _____ down in front (plunk / *present perfect*) of a TV for a couple of hours already!
8. It's scary to think we spend so much time listening to news, right?	8. Yeah. When I heard these reports, I _____ to control the (inspire / *past*) amount of TV I watch.

◖ PRONUNCIATION: Reducing and Contracting Auxiliary Verbs

- When they talk, native speakers often use contractions of the verbs *be* and *have* after a pronoun. These contractions sound friendlier and less formal, and native speakers find them easier to say than the full forms.

  I've been watching the news more and more recently. My husband says I watch too much. He's started reading more instead.

- After nouns, auxiliary verbs *are*, *have*, and *has* have reduced pronunciations. *Are* sounds like an *-er* ending. It is joined with the preceding word.

  Doctors are worried about our health.
  (Say "Doctorser worried.")

  Have is pronounced /əv/ (like the preposition *of*). It is joined closely with the preceding word.

  Some have chosen to turn off the news.
  (Say "Someəv chosen . . .")

  Has is pronounced /əz/ (like the "long plural") after some words.

  My boss has become addicted to the news.
  (Say "bosses.")

1 ᶜᴰ ⁊ ⑪ *Listen to the sentences. As you listen, underline the auxiliary verbs that are reduced. Then read the sentences aloud to a partner, using contractions and reductions.*

  1. The United States has become a nation of people addicted to the news.

  2. Americans are offered news in many forms.

  3. Critics have been concerned about the amount of news we watch.

  4. Academics are worried about the amount of news we consume.

2 ᶜᴰ ⁊ ⑫ *Listen to the paragraph about our addiction to the news media. As you listen, fill in the auxiliary verb or contraction that you hear. Then read the paragraph aloud to a partner.*

  People _____ offered many sources of news, some of which
  _____ 1.

  _____ available 24/7. The country _____ become a
  _____ 2.   3.

  nation of "news junkies," or people who _____ addicted to the news.
                                            4.

  Some academics _____ started to ask serious questions about the
                    5.

  role of the news media in society. Some people believe that the media _____
                                                                          6.

  focusing on negative stories. Therefore, it focuses less on the important issues

that we face. We _____ being entertained by gossip about celebrities
7.

and politicians, but we _____ stopped worrying about serious
8.

problems that affect our society.

FUNCTION: Stating an Opinion

In any conversation or discussion, it is important to state your own opinion or viewpoints clearly. Read these excerpts from Listenings One and Two. Notice the phrases that the speakers use to introduce their opinions.

- **A:** People keep themselves plugged in because they don't know how to be alone with themselves. Historian Gabrielle Spiegel agrees.

  B: **I think that** there are two things you really need to get through life.

- **A:** Spending time with the media is the main way we use our time. Is that a problem?

  B: **Maybe, but** it's important to know what's happening in the world.

Here are some expressions that can be used to state an opinion, agree with someone else's opinion, politely disagree, and avoid giving an opinion.

STATING AN OPINION			
Offer an Opinion	**Agree**	**Disagree**	**Not Give an Opinion**
If you ask me, . . . In my opinion, . . . Well, as far as I know, . . . As I see it, . . .	I couldn't agree more. That's just what I was going to say! Yes, exactly.	Maybe / Perhaps, but . . . You have a good point, but . . . Yes, but on the other hand . . . That's not exactly the way I see it. I think . . .	I'm not really sure. I don't know what to think. I haven't made up my mind. Beats me. (informal)

Work with a partner. Take turns presenting and responding to these ideas. Use an expression from the box on page 17 when you state your opinion.

1. **A:** Most reporters are just looking for sensational stories. All they want is to sell more newspapers.

   B: I couldn't agree more. As I see it, that's why we're faced with a barrage of bad news.

2. **A:** News resisters are crazy!

   B: _____

3. **A:** I could easily give up reading newspapers every day, couldn't you?

   B: _____

4. **A:** Do you think that news is always depressing?

   B: _____

5. **A:** Fantasy and a sense of humor are enough for me.

   B: _____

6. **A:** Sometimes people on the street are interviewed on TV news. How do you like hearing their opinions on important topics?

   B: _____

7. **A:** Perhaps it's true that children expect their teachers to act like cartoon characters.

   B: _____

8. **A:** Newspapers will soon disappear. Everyone will be reading news on the Internet.

   B: _____

9. **A:** Do you agree that people don't know how to be alone these days?

   B: _____

10. **A:** Do you think it's better to get your news monthly, not daily?

    B: _____

In this activity, you will work in pairs to **present news stories for a TV or radio broadcast**. One person will be the reporter, who gives the stories. The other person will be a commentator, who will explain the significance of the stories and why people should care about them, and agree or disagree with opinions from the stories. Try to use the vocabulary, grammar, pronunciation, and language for stating an opinion that you learned in the unit.*

Step 1: Choose two or three current news stories from categories such as:

- International news
- National news
- Local news
- Sports
- Features (health, lifestyle, fashion)

Step 2: Work together to write your news stories and the commentator's opinions, or make notes that you could speak from. Practice giving and commenting on the news stories. Then present your broadcast to the class.

Example

REPORTER: This week in sports, a team of women mountain climbers set a new record on Mt. Everest in Nepal. However, two of the team members were severely injured. The Nepali government flew both women off the mountain in a helicopter.

COMMENTATOR: This story raises an interesting question: Who should be responsible for the safety of international climbers in Nepal? As I see it, the team itself should be responsible.

Step 3: Listen to your classmates present their news reports and grade them according to the categories below.

	Superior	Good	OK	Needs Help
Presentation:	❏	❏	❏	❏
Interest:	❏	❏	❏	❏
Creativity:	❏	❏	❏	❏
Suggestions for improvement: _____

Step 4: As a class, decide which news reports were the most interesting, the most creative, and the most newsworthy.

_____
*For Alternative Speaking Topics, see page 20.

Work in a small group. Take turns reading the quotations about the news. Discuss what they mean. Do you agree or disagree with the quotations?

Use phrases such as these to explain the quotes:

> *In other words, . . .*
> *What she's saying is . . .*
> *I think he means that . . .*

Example

A: "No news is good news." **In other words,** if you don't hear any news, then there isn't any bad news.

B: **I think so too,** because . . .

1. No news is good news. *(Proverb)*

2. For most folks, no news is good news; for the press, good news is not news. *(Gloria Borger, journalist)*

3. When a dog bites a man, that is not news, because it happens so often. But if a man bites a dog, that is news. *(John B. Bogart, newspaper editor)*

4. It's amazing that the amount of news that happens in the world every day always just exactly fits the newspaper. *(Jerry Seinfeld, comedian)*

5. I fear three newspapers more than a hundred thousand bayonets. *(Napoleon Bonaparte, French general)*

6. Newspapers should have no friends. *(Joseph Pulitzer, publisher)*

7. I believe in equality for everyone, except reporters and photographers. *(Mohandas Gandhi, Indian leader)*

8. On an average day seven minutes of news happens. Yet there are currently three full-time, 24-hour news networks. *(Jon Stewart, commentator and comedian)*

RESEARCH TOPICS, see page **218.**

The Achilles Heel

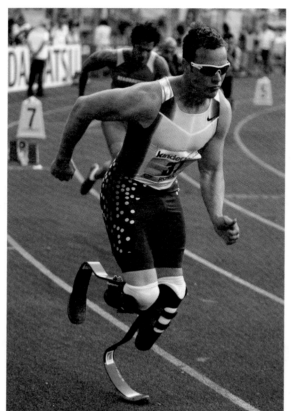

①FOCUS ON THE TOPIC

Ⓐ PREDICT

Look at the photograph and the title of the unit. Then discuss the questions with a partner or small group.

1. The photograph shows Oscar Pistorius, a disabled athlete from South Africa who holds a world record for running in his category in the 100, 200, and 400 meter events. In addition to his physical challenges, what mental or emotional obstacles do you think he has had to overcome?

2. The title of this unit, *The Achilles Heel**, is an expression that is used to refer to problems and obstacles that people face in their lives. What kinds of challenges do you predict this unit will be about?

---

*Achilles is a figure in Greek mythology whose one weakness was a weak or vulnerable spot in his heel.

Many people believe that each of us has an "Achilles heel" to overcome. Look at the list of common obstacles.

illness	discrimination	learning disability
injury	lack of money	lack of self-confidence
shyness	physical or mental disability	family problems

Work in a small group. Discuss the questions.

- Which of the obstacles do you think would be the most difficult to overcome? Which would be the least difficult?
- Do you know anyone who has faced any of these obstacles? Did the person overcome the obstacle or not?
- What other kinds of obstacles do you think people commonly face?

C BACKGROUND AND VOCABULARY

Personal essays are used in combination with grades, test scores, and recommendations to determine who will gain admission to particular colleges. These essays tell the admissions committee about the students' background and experiences. The topics of these essays often include overcoming obstacles or meeting personal challenges.

1 *Look at excerpts from two essays and the admissions committee's comments. Fill in the blanks with a word or phrase from the list.*

1. **collapsed:** fell down suddenly

2. **crushed:** pressed something so hard it broke

3. **crutches:** special sticks used under the arms to help a person walk

4. **in store for:** planned for

5. **landscape:** a view across an area of land

6. **limitations:** things that keep you from going beyond certain boundaries

7. **overcome:** succeed in controlling a problem

8. **proof:** facts or evidence that prove that something is true

9. **revelation:** insight; sudden realization

10. **scars:** marks left on skin from a cut or wound

11. **soared:** flew very high or fast

APPLICANT 1

A Person I Admire

My mother walks with (a.) _____ and has (b.) _____ all over her legs. When she was a young girl, she was walking past a building site when a piece of machinery fell on her and mangled her legs. The doctors thought she would never walk again. However, she believed that life still had a lot of opportunities (c.) _____ her, and she was right. Now she has four children, volunteers at the library, and has become a teacher.

APPLICANT 2

An Experience that Changed My Life

I spent last summer volunteering in a village in the Andes. The (d.) _____ was so beautiful. Birds (e.) _____ above us. However, I discovered that I was afraid of heights. I was so scared that I actually (f.) _____ once. I worked hard to face my fears, though, and while I'm still nervous, I know how to control myself. In short, I learned a lot about my mental (g.) _____ and how to meet those challenges.

COMMENTS:

1. This applicant admires people who are able to (h.) _____ serious obstacles.

2. This experience was a (i.) _____ to the candidate.

3. This is (j.) _____ that we need to make this kind of experience available to all our students.

4. The story about how the machinery (k.) _____ the applicant's mother's legs was really moving.

2 CD 1 ●13 Now listen to and read the essays and comments. Then work with a partner and decide which essay each comment refers to.

2 FOCUS ON LISTENING

A LISTENING ONE: Dreams of Flying and Overcoming Obstacles

Bob Edwards, of National Public Radio, talked about the college application process on the *Morning Edition* show. As part of the program, one college student, Richard Van Ornum, was invited to read his application essay aloud.

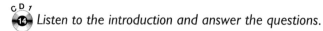

CD 1 ⑭ *Listen to the introduction and answer the questions.*

1. More than 150 essays were sent to the radio station. Thinking about the theme of the unit, how do you think the radio station chose which essays to broadcast?

   _____

2. What do you imagine the essay will include? Check (✓) your predictions.

   ○ a description of a challenge

   ○ the writer's personal history

   ○ the writer's hopes for the future

   ○ advice to the listeners

   ○ information about the college the writer wants to attend

   ○ a request for help

◖ LISTEN FOR MAIN IDEAS

CD 1 ⑮ *You will hear Richard Van Ornum describe his dreams and his reality. Listen to the essay and answer the questions.*

1. What did Richard dream about when he was young?

   _____

2. What happened to Richard when he was a young boy?

   _____

3. What was the revelation that Richard had?

   _____

4. What lessons has Richard learned from his experiences?

   _____

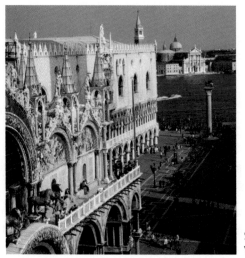

**San Marco Square
Venice, Italy**

LISTEN FOR DETAILS

 Listen to the essay again. As you listen, write **T** (true) or **F** (false) for each statement. If the statement is false, correct it.

_____ 1. As a child, Richard used to dream he was in an airplane.

_____ 2. Richard always dreamed about the same landscape.

_____ 3. Richard had an accident when he was six.

_____ 4. He was forced to get around in a wheelchair.

_____ 5. Richard was standing on the ground when he had a revelation.

_____ 6. He heard a song called "Drive Away with Me."

_____ 7. Richard can now walk.

_____ 8. He dreamed he was a boy again.

MAKE INFERENCES

Listen to the excerpts and answer the questions. Then compare your answers with a partner's.

CD 1 17 Excerpt One

1. What do you think "flying" symbolized to Richard?
   a. becoming injured or killed
   b. having freedom and possibilities
   c. being able to travel easily

CD 1 18 Excerpt Two

2. What would Richard say if someone asked him why he stopped dreaming?
   a. "It was boring to repeat the same dream every night."
   b. "I realized I couldn't actually fly."
   c. "It's natural for older children to stop dreaming."

CD 1 19 Excerpt Three

3. Why does Richard talk about the rooftop of the cathedral, winged horses, and pigeons?
   a. To help the listener picture what Venice, Italy looks like.
   b. To remind the listener of how important flying is to him.
   c. To show his frustration at not being able to move around freely.

CD 1 20 Excerpt Four

4. What was the meaning of Richard's dream?
   a. He knew he would do a lot of traveling in the future.
   b. He felt hopeful about the future.
   c. He realized that his accident was not important.

EXPRESS OPINIONS

Work in a small group. Discuss the questions.

1. Richard says "I . . . knew what my first obstacle had been: a runaway truck . . . with no compassion for preschoolers on a field trip." Why do you think Richard says "truck" instead of "truck driver"? What does this tell you about Richard's personality or about his attitude towards the accident?

2. Richard's essay was selected for broadcast throughout the United States. What qualities might make this essay appeal to many people? What parts of the essay appeal to you? Why?

3. What do you think led to Richard's revelation—his personality, being able to travel abroad, or encouragement from other people?

4. How important are the following factors in helping people overcome physical challenges in their life?
   - personality and attitude
   - help from friends and family
   - medical care
   - health and physical condition

B | LISTENING TWO: The Achilles Track Club Climbs Mount Kilimanjaro

Mount Kilimanjaro is a mountain in Tanzania, East Africa. Its peak is the highest point in Africa at 19,340 feet (5,895 meters). Approximately 200 miles south of the equator, Kilimanjaro's climate is extreme, with tropical weather at the base and arctic-like temperatures and strong winds closer to the peak.

You will hear a television news report about a group of athletes who climbed Mount Kilimanjaro. The athletes belong to the Achilles Track Club, an organization of athletes with physical disabilities such as blindness, deafness, or the loss of an arm. Before you listen, think about what would be difficult about climbing this mountain. Then think about what might make it even more difficult for a person with these disabilities to do so. Discuss your ideas with the class.

1 ⚫ *Listen to the report and answer the questions. Share your answers with the class.*

   1. How many climbers were there?

   _____

   2. What disabilities did the climbers have?

   _____

   3. What feelings did the climbers experience on their expedition?

   _____

   4. What record did the group set?

   _____

   5. Who inspired the climbers?

   _____

2 *Work in a small group. Discuss the questions.*

   1. What is your reaction to the story of the Achilles Track Club project? What makes it special and inspirational to other people?

   2. What could an able-bodied volunteer learn by joining the Achilles Track Club climb as a helper? Would you like to volunteer on a climb such as this? Why or why not?

   3. Many people dislike the term *disabled*. They would rather use terms such as *differently abled* or *physically challenged*. What do you think is the difference among these terms? What term do you think the Achilles Track Club athletes would choose to describe themselves? Why?

◀ STEP 1: Organize

Complete the Venn diagram with information about Richard Van Ornum and members of the Achilles Track Club. Inside the circles, list:

- challenges
- goals and hopes
- personal qualities

In the green intersection of the circles, list:

- ways the stories overlap

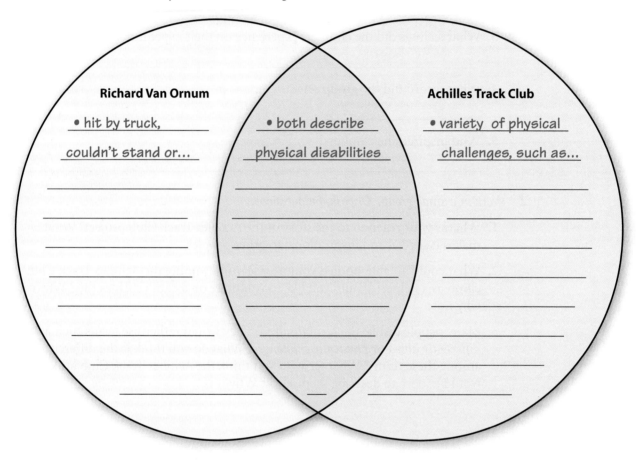

Richard Van Ornum

- hit by truck, couldn't stand or...

- both describe physical disabilities

Achilles Track Club

- variety of physical challenges, such as...

◀ STEP 2: Synthesize

Work in groups of three. Role play a reporter interviewing Richard Van Ornum and a member of the Achilles Track Club. The interviewer asks about each person's challenges, goals, and hopes. The interviewer comments on similarities and differences between the two people's experiences. Use information from the diagram in your questions and answers.

3 FOCUS ON SPEAKING

A VOCABULARY

◖ REVIEW

During their ascent of Mount Kilimanjaro, one of the members of the Achilles Track Club kept an online journal similar to the one below. Fill in the blanks with the words that are listed above each paragraph.

challenging	eagles	landscape
determined	inspiration	scattered

Ascent of Mt. Kilimanjaro

To: All my friends   **Subject:** Day One

Dear friends in New York,

   Hi, everyone! We're at the foot of this amazing mountain. It's over 5,895 meters high. That's 19,340 feet. This will be the most _____ thing I've ever done, but I'm really _____ to
           1.   **2.**
succeed. I think we're carrying a message of _____ and hope. I think I've set a high goal
                                        3.
for myself. If I push myself to do my best, maybe others will do the same.

   From up here, the _____ is spectacular. There are some houses _____
                    4.   **5.**
around the base of the hill. I saw some large birds that looked like _____ . They were
                                         6.
absolutely beautiful!

(continued on next page)

collapsed	inspirational	recognition	recognize

Ascent of Mt. Kilimanjaro

To: All my friends   **Subject:** Day Three

Dear all,

   We have spent the last two days getting used to the altitude. The air is kind of thin up here! After a day

of climbing, I _____ into bed last night. When I opened the tent this morning, I saw a small
       7.

figure in the distance. At first I didn't _____ her, but when I called out, "Hello," she responded
              8.

by waving. It was one of the other athletes. She was admiring the beauty of the sunrise. It was a very

_____ moment. Now I can't wait to get going!
    9.

   I am getting a lot of _____ from the others. They're always commenting on the things I
           10.

do well and telling me how strong I am, both physically and emotionally. The guides are very strong

climbers, and they give us the physical support we need, and of course I appreciate that.

courageous	judging	perseverance
empowerment	limitations	

Ascent of Mt. Kilimanjaro

To: All my friends   **Subject:** Day Five

Hi, everyone,

   I can't believe I am writing this, but the summit is very close. This is such a spectacular and imposing

place. I am so glad I decided to take part in this project. And now our _____ is finally
           11.

paying off. I will be able to say that as a cancer survivor, I have scaled one of the highest mountains in

the world! Sometimes people seem to look at disabled people with sympathy. It's as if they are

_____ us negatively, which can be very hard.
    12.

   But now, I think that despite all our _____, we have done something really special—
           13.

something that hardly anybody manages to do. I feel so proud that my teammates have been so

_____. I think that we are bringing a message of _____ to everyone
    14.   **15.**

who wants to overcome a difficult challenge.

altitude	peak	soaring
in store for	proof	tough

Ascent of Mt. Kilimanjaro

To: All my friends   **Subject:** Day Seven

Hello, everyone,

Get ready to hear the good news . . . We're here! We're at the _____ ! When we got to the
16.
top, we took a photo of the group as _____ that we made it! Then we released a bag of feathers
17.
into the air, to symbolize our story going out to other people. This has been an amazing experience, but
you can't believe how _____ it was. I can't believe we made it. Last week we were standing at
18.
the bottom of the mountain, and we didn't know what was _____ us. The _____ was
19.   20.
really hard to deal with, but we didn't give up!

There are birds _____ below us, and the air is clear. I want to remember this day forever.
21.

◀ **EXPAND**

Read the information and do the exercise that follows.

In Listening One, Richard Van Ornum uses certain words and phrases to mean
something different from what they most commonly mean. For example, look at
the way the word *weight* is used in the first sentence. Compare it to the way Van
Ornum uses it in the second sentence:

- The **weight** of most cars is over 1,000 pounds.
- "I would realize that no real person could fly, and I'd collapse on the floor under
  the **weight** of my own limitations."

In the first sentence, *weight* means the heaviness of something in pounds or
kilograms. It is concrete and physical. This meaning is called the *literal meaning*. In
the second sentence, *weight* means mental burden or pressure. This meaning is
called the *figurative meaning*. It creates a picture or image in the mind.

(continued on next page)

*Work with a partner. Read the sentences and focus on the bold phrases. Write **L** (literal) or **F** (figurative) for each sentence. Discuss your choices with each other. Then explain them to the class.*

1. _____ **a.** The Achilles athletes **reached a high point** in their climb and stopped to admire the view.

   _____ **b.** I **reached a high point** in my career when I finally got the recognition I felt I deserved.

2. _____ **a.** At first, Amar needed a **crutch** in order to walk.

   _____ **b.** Her disability never became her **crutch** in life; she was independent and proud.

3. _____ **a.** After several film failures at the box office, the movie director knew he had to **turn** his career **around** by doing something very different.

   _____ **b.** When the runner realized he was going in the wrong direction, he **turned around** and headed the other way.

4. _____ **a.** Jackie dropped his keys in the lake and had to **reach deep down** into the mud to find them.

   _____ **b.** When the mountain climber thought she was too weak to take another step, she **reached deep down** inside herself and found the determination to make it back to the camp.

5. _____ **a.** After dropping off the supplies, the helicopter **soared** into the clouds.

   _____ **b.** The runner accepted every challenge and **soared** to great heights in his athletic career.

6. _____ **a.** I was **crushed** by the news of my neighbor's accident.

   _____ **b.** Peter's legs were **crushed** in a motorcycle accident.

◖ CREATE

Work with a partner. Take turns asking each other questions. Use the bold words in your answers. Before you begin, look at the questions and jot down a few notes to help you when it's your turn to speak.

1. Tell about a time when you or someone you know **got to the top of** your class in a particular subject. Were you or they a **determined** student? When the material you were studying was **challenging**, how did you react? Who or what was your **inspiration**?

2. The Achilles athletes really wanted to **make it** to the top. They were very **courageous** and showed great **perseverance**. Which qualities do you think help people succeed in **tough** situations?

3. After Richard had an experience of personal **revelation** in Italy, he was able to really **turn** his life **around**. How could his family or friends help him to **recognize** his potential? How do you think his story could help others accept their physical **limitations**?

GRAMMAR: Gerunds and Infinitives

1 *Work with a partner. Read the conversation and answer the questions.*

A: My son wants to volunteer with the Achilles Track Club. He's planning **to train** with a blind athlete in the park every Sunday.

B: Isn't **running** with a blind person a bit dangerous?

A: Well, the Achilles Track Club teaches the volunteers how **to run** safely. The blind runners hold on to a short rope that the sighted people use **to guide** them.

B: **Volunteering** for this organization sounds like a very special experience.

1. In A's lines, what do the bold words have in common?

2. In B's lines, what do the bold words have in common?

GERUNDS AND INFINITIVES

Gerunds	Examples
To form the gerund, add **-ing** to the base form of the verb.	It's a story of **reaching** new heights and **overcoming** great odds.
Some Uses of the Gerund	
Use the gerund as the subject of a sentence.	**Getting** to the top of the mountain was a great achievement for the athletes.
Use the gerund after a preposition, such as *for*, *in*, *of*, and *about*.	Throughout his childhood, Richard thought **about walking** again.

Infinitives	Examples
To form the infinitive, use **to** and the base form of the verb.	I'd leap off my bed expecting **to soar** out of the window.
Some Uses of the Infinitive	
Use the infinitive after a **be** + **adjective** combination such as *easy*, *difficult*, *hard*, *happy*, *possible*, *willing*, and *prepared*.	It was very **hard** for the Achilles Track Club **to climb** Mount Kilimanjaro.
Use the infinitive after certain verbs, including *agree*, *decide*, *expect*, *hope*, *learn*, *manage*, *need*, *try*, and *want*.	One of the Achilles athletes did not **expect to reach** the summit and almost turned back several times.

2 *Look at the flyer. It contains a list of devices that can help the disabled. Work with a partner. Discuss how these devices could improve the everyday lives of disabled people. Use the expressions below the flyer with gerunds and infinitives.*

Example

Ramps at the entrances to buildings would **make it easier** for people in wheelchairs **to use** those buildings.

Tips to Make Your Home or Community Accessible for the Disabled

ramp   grip bar   mechanical lift

- Ramps at the entrances to buildings
- Braille signs in public elevators
- Wide doorways and hallways
- Baths / showers with grip bars
- Mechanical lifts

- Contrasting colors on ledges, counter edges, and steps
- Strobe lights on smoke and burglar alarms
- Raised buttons on appliances
- New ideas? _____

. . . make it easier . . .	. . . give people freedom . . .
. . . allow people . . .	. . . good for . . .
. . . stop people from . . .	. . . make people aware of . . .
. . . make it possible	. . . help people avoid . . .

3 *Read the information and do the exercise that follows.*

Since the Americans with Disabilities Act was passed in the United States in 1990, more people have become aware of the changes that must be made in public places to allow disabled individuals to deal with their challenges. Government and city officials have more responsibility to provide access to services for people with disabilities.

Work with a partner. Think about the difficulties that a person with a physical disability has doing everyday tasks. Complete the chart so that each statement indicates the view of an advocate for the disabled or the view of a government or city official. Use infinitives and gerunds. Add as much information as you can.

Discuss other innovations that might help the disabled. Then discuss whether your town or city has implemented such ideas.

ADVOCATE FOR DISABLED INDIVIDUALS	GOVERNMENT OR CITY OFFICIAL
_____ is very hard.	The city has agreed _____
_____ presents a real challenge.	We need _____
_____ must be extremely difficult.	We are willing _____
Disabled people are forced _____	We are prepared _____
They often can't manage _____	We are ready _____
I'm sure they would be happy _____	We should avoid _____

C SPEAKING

◖ PRONUNCIATION: Thought Groups

- When we speak, we group words together and join the groups into sentences. The groups are called thought groups. They help the listener organize the meaning of the sentence.

 CD 1
22 *Listen to the thought groups in the following sentences.*

My Achilles heel was shyness.

I hated going to parties by myself.

And I was terrified when I had to speak in class.

- Thought groups are often grammatical phrases or structures, such as prepositional phrases or short clauses.

CD 1
23 *Listen to the thought groups in this sentence.*

When I was little, I dreamed I was flying.

- Words can be combined into thought groups in different ways. Speakers sometimes choose groups of similar length to create a more pleasing rhythm. In other cases, the speaker may include two phrases in one group to show that the two phrases are part of the same idea. If the speaker wants to show that the two phrases are different ideas, they will be in different thought groups.

CD 1

24 *Listen to the two ways the words in the sentence are grouped.*

1. I realized that everyone is born with gifts.

2. I realized that everyone is born with gifts.

In the first sentence, the speaker expresses three separate thoughts. The fact that the speaker realized something ("I realized") is important. The choice to use three groups also slows the sentence down and gives each group more emphasis.

In the second sentence, the rhythm sounds faster because there are more words in each group. In this sentence, what the speaker realized about everyone ("is born with gifts") is most important.

- Pronounce the words in a thought group together smoothly. Join thought groups together by holding the end of a thought group briefly before you start the next group.

CD 1

25 *Listen to the sentences.*

My Achilles heel was shyness.
hold briefly

I dreamed I was flying.
hold briefly

I just didn't imagine it would be so tough.
hold briefly

1 **CD 1** **26** *Listen to the sentences. As you listen, mark the thought groups. Compare answers with a partner's. Then take turns reading the sentences to each other. Remember to hold the end of a thought group briefly before you start a new one.*

1. When Richard was little, he dreamed he was flying.

2. He looked at his scar and imagined it was an eagle.

3. When he visited Venice, he realized that he had great gifts.

4. He suddenly realized that he could overcome his obstacles.

5. The essay he wrote about his experience was chosen for broadcast.

2 *Look at the two charts. They contain three sentences each. Take turns creating sentences by choosing one thought group from each column. If the sentence you create is true, your partner will say, "That's right." If the sentence you create is not true, your partner will say, "I don't think that's right." Continue until you and your partner have created three true sentences for each chart.*

1	2	3	4
Richard's scar	struck the boy	in the accident	in preschool.
A runaway truck	looked like an eagle	on a field trip	as the sun set.
The young boy's leg	was mangled	soaring through the air	on a May morning.

1	2	3	4
Organizers from the Achilles Track Club	helped each other	on the trail	in late August.
Newspaper reporters	looked like an eagle	to the mountain summit	when the going got tough.
The inspiring athletes	accompanied the climbers	up the mountain	for a year.

◀ **FUNCTION: Sharing a Personal Story**

Stories of personal achievement often include details about background information, challenges or obstacles, and success or accomplishment. They also sometimes refer to a life lesson.

SHARING A PERSONAL STORY

Background	• Richard Van Ornum is a student who is preparing to send in an application to college. • The Achilles Track Club is a club for physically disabled athletes.
Challenge	• Richard's biggest physical challenge was that he was hit by a truck when he was young, and he could hardly walk. • It was challenging for the Achilles athletes when they tried to climb one of the world's tallest mountains.
Accomplishment	• As a result of great effort, Richard learned to walk again and overcame his mental obstacles. • After a tremendous physical and mental effort, the Achilles athletes climbed Mount Kilimanjaro.
Life Lesson	• Richard says, "If we recognize our talents and make the best of them, we've got a fighting chance to overcome our obstacles and succeed in life." In the end, his story shows us . . . • The Achilles team calls their expedition a testament to the human spirit and a chance to empower themselves and others. From their experiences, we can learn . . .

1 *Divide the class into three groups. Each group studies the background information, challenges, and successes of one of the people below, and also decides if the person's story has a greater meaning for other people.*

1. **Stephen Hawking**
   • world renowned British astrophysicist born in 1942
   • as a child he was very active: for example, he enjoyed horseback riding
   • symptoms of Lou Gehrig's disease began to appear when he was in college
   • at age 21, was given only three years to live; now, is almost completely paralyzed and mute
   • author of bestseller *A Brief History of Time* (1988)
   • made a flight to space, achieving zero gravity, in 2007
   • despite his disease, he describes himself as "lucky"

2. **Sabriye Tanberken**
- German, blind by age of 13 from retinal disease
- studied Tibet and the Tibetan language at Bonn University and created Tibetan Braille
- learned about large number of neglected blind children in Tibet and wanted to do something
- applied to do research with various non-government organizations but was refused
- with some partners, went to Tibet and opened her own school
- raised money for the project by selling her autobiography
- rides a horse to get around in Tibet
- says, "There should be no limits for the blind"

3. **Hirotada Ototake**
- Japanese, born without arms or legs
- parents wanted him to have no special treatment at school
- participated in schooling and sports (basketball)
- had his friends take him up a mountain
- wrote *No One's Perfect*, second-best-selling book in Japan in 50 years
- famous for his smile and his charming attitude
- appointed full-time teacher at an elementary school in Tokyo
- his mission is to make Japan "barrier free" for wheelchairs

2 *Divide into new groups, with at least one person to talk about each individual above. Take turns telling the people's stories. Include details about their background, challenges, and successes. Explain what lesson ordinary people can learn from them.*

◖ **PRODUCTION: A Personal Speech**

In this activity, you will **create and present to the class a 2–3 minute speech** about an obstacle you have overcome or a challenge you have faced. You can look back at Share Information on page 22 for ideas. Try to use the vocabulary, grammar, pronunciation, and typical parts of a personal story that you learned in the unit.*

―――――――――――――
*For Alternative Speaking Topics, see page 40.

Step 1: Use the information in the left column of the chart below to plan your speech. Take notes in the right column. Practice your presentation a few times aloud or in your mind.

Background Information about yourself and the setting of your story **Challenge** A description of the obstacle or challenge you faced; the personal qualities you needed to face this challenge **Outcome** What happened; what you achieved or accomplished **Life Lesson** What you learned from facing the challenge	

Step 2: Present your speech to the class or record it to play for the class.

Step 3: Listen to your classmates' speeches and write at least one question to ask them about their stories. Then ask your question clearly and listen to the presenters' responses.

ALTERNATIVE SPEAKING TOPICS

Work in a small group. Discuss the questions.

1. If you had to write a college application essay that showed something about your character, what topic would you choose? Discuss your ideas with your group, and prepare an oral version of your essay. Present it to your classmates.

2. In some cities and towns, buses, trains, and subways are not accessible to disabled people. Should all cities and towns change to accommodate people with disabilities? If so, who should pay for these changes: employers? taxpayers?

3. Which of the following do you think should be considered disabilities and provided for and protected by law?

   - obesity
   - phobias (great fear of something, like crowds, heights, or closed places)
   - very poor eyesight
   - extreme shortness or tallness
   - other

RESEARCH TOPICS, see page **219.**

Early to Bed,
Early to Rise . . .

"I couldn't sleep."

①FOCUS ON THE TOPIC

Ⓐ PREDICT

Look at the cartoon and the title of the unit. Then discuss the questions with a partner or small group.

1. Describe the cartoon. What is the man doing? Why?

2. The title of this unit comes from a fifteenth-century proverb about the importance of sleep: "Early to bed, early to rise, makes you healthy, wealthy, and wise." What does it mean? Do you agree with this proverb?

3. Do you think most people get enough sleep, too much sleep, or not enough sleep?

B SHARE INFORMATION

What are your sleep habits? Exchange information with a partner. Take notes and report your findings to the class. Mention anything interesting or unusual that you find out.

	YOU	YOUR PARTNER
Just before going to bed: • Do you usually eat or drink anything? If so, what? • Do you watch TV or read? What do you read or watch, and for how long? • Do you spend time thinking or planning the next day? • Do you worry a lot? • Do you do anything special to help you fall asleep?		
During the night: • Do you often wake up during the night? If so, how many times? Do you have trouble getting back to sleep? • Do you ever have nightmares? • Do you snore, talk, or move in your sleep? • Do you remember your dreams?		
In the morning: • Are you in a good mood? • Do you need an alarm clock to wake up? • Do you drink tea or coffee to feel alert?		

C BACKGROUND AND VOCABULARY

CD 1
27
Many students complain that they can't get enough sleep. Read and listen to the questions that a student and her mother wrote to a school counselor. Then match the words in bold with the correct definitions. Write the correct numbers in the blanks on page 43.

Please state your problem as specifically as possible:

Dear Dr. Jennings,
    I'm writing to you about my daughter Eden, who's a sophomore in high school. She's **(1) chronically** tired. I've noticed that on the weekend, her eyelids begin to **(2) droop** by mid-morning, and she wants to take a nap. If the lights are **(3) dim**, she gets **(4) waves of sleepiness**, and she's constantly **(5) blinking** and rubbing her eyes. At night, on the other hand, she gets a **(6) surge** of energy. The rest of my family goes to bed around 11:00, but she's wide awake then, so she's completely **(7) out of sync** with the rest of us. If this is what's happening at home, I'm sure it's the same when she's at school! What should I do?

Sincerely,

Sylvia Peterson

QUICK-RESPONSE ONLINE

Please state your problem as specifically as possible:

Dear Dr. Jennings,
    My mom said I should contact you because she's worried about my school work. I get really tired in the morning, even though I'm pretty **(8) alert** late at night, especially if there's something particularly **(9) captivating** on TV. Well anyway, my mom's worried about me. I think it's because I tend to get a bit **(10) irritable** when she wakes me up for school. Do you think it could be **(11) hormones** or something?

Thanks,

Eden Peterson

_____ **a.** chemical substances
        in the body

_____ **b.** very interesting

_____ **c.** closing and opening
        the eyes quickly

_____ **d.** able to think clearly

_____ **e.** permanently, constantly

_____ **f.** a boost, increase

_____ **g.** on a completely different
        schedule

_____ **h.** easily and quickly
        annoyed

_____ **i.** hang or bend down

_____ **j.** low, not bright

_____ **k.** strong feelings of
        fatigue, tiredness

②FOCUS ON LISTENING

Why are teenagers tired? Listen to this radio report by Michelle Trudeau from National Public Radio. It includes interviews with some experts in the field.*

CD 7 • 29 *Listen to the introduction and answer the questions.*

1. About how long do teenagers and young children want to sleep?

_____

2. Why do you think teenagers are out of sync with everyone else?

_____

3. What do you think you might learn from this report? Make some predictions.

_____

◀ LISTEN FOR MAIN IDEAS

CD 7 • 30 *You will hear comments by several authorities on sleep, including Dr. William Dement, Dr. Mary Carskadon, and researcher Ronald Dahl. Listen to the report and answer the questions.*

1. What is melatonin?

   It's a hormone that . . . _____

2. Why do teenagers feel less sleepy at night and sleepier in the morning?

   _____

3. How does Dr. Carskadon say that sleep deprivation affects teenagers' school experience?

   _____

4. According to the listening, what dangers can adolescents face as a result of their sleep deprivation?

   _____

5. According to the listening, how does sleepiness affect teenagers' emotional state?

   _____

---

*Tracks 28–31 include the complete radio report. Listen to Track 29 to answer the introduction questions. Listen to Track 30 for Listen to Main Ideas (above) and Listen for Details (page 45).

CD 7
30 *Listen to the interview again. As you listen, circle the letter of the correct answer.*

1. When is melatonin secreted in adolescents?
   a. before 10:00 P.M.
   b. around 11:00 P.M.
   c. after midnight

2. What time do most U.S. high schools begin?
   a. 7:30 A.M.
   b. 8:00 A.M.
   c. 9:00 A.M.

3. How many minutes does it take for high school students to fall asleep in a morning or afternoon auditorium class?
   a. about two
   b. about five
   c. about ten

4. In Dr. Dement's lab experiments conducted during the morning in a quiet environment, how long did it take for the teenagers to fall asleep?
   a. less than two and a half minutes
   b. less than three and a half minutes
   c. less than eight and a half minutes

5. About how many *more* hours per night do teenagers need on average?
   a. one
   b. two
   c. three

6. How many high school students in the U.S. are chronically sleep-deprived?
   a. 35 percent
   b. 85 percent
   c. 97 percent

7. About how far does a car travel during the time it takes for a person to blink?
   a. 6 feet
   b. 16 feet
   c. 60 feet

8. About how many traffic accidents are caused by teenagers?
   a. fewer than half
   b. more than half
   c. 89 percent

9. Which of the following effects of sleep deprivation is *not* mentioned?
   a. reaction time
   b. sadness and frustration
   c. poor family relationships

◖ MAKE INFERENCES

*Listen to the excerpts from the interview. Choose one or two adjectives from the box that describe the speaker's feeling. Then circle **T** (true) or **F** (false) for each statement.*

aggressive	confused	playful	shocked
amused	enthusiastic	respectful	unhappy

🄲🄳1 ③② Excerpt One

1. How does the interviewer feel? _____

2. The interviewer disagrees with Dr. Carskadon.　　　　T　　　F

🄲🄳1 ③③ Excerpt Two

1. How does the interviewer feel? _____

2. The interviewer admires Dr. Dement.　　　　T　　　F

🄲🄳1 ③④ Excerpt Three

1. How does the student feel? _____

2. The student knows why he is so sleepy.　　　　T　　　F

🄲🄳1 ③⑤ Excerpt Four

1. How does Dr. Dement feel? _____

2. Dr. Dement thinks 10 minutes is a reasonable amount
   of time.　　　　T　　　F

◖ EXPRESS OPINIONS

Work in a small group. Take turns reading the opinions. Then say whether you agree or disagree, and why.

1. Now that we know that teens are sleepier in the morning and less sleepy in the evening, high schools should change their schedules. They should start and finish much later in the day.

2. Sleep deprivation could have serious consequences for some workers, such as those in factories, hospitals, or airports. Managers should be able to require their workers to get enough sleep.

3. Sleep deprivation is a much more serious problem now than it was 50 or 100 years ago.

4. Different people need different amounts of sleep. Some people only need five or six hours a night, and others need as much as nine or ten hours a night.

Like teenagers, parents of small children are sleep-deprived, too. You will hear part of an interview from *Satellite Sisters,* a radio talk show featuring a conversation among five sisters who live on five continents. Lian, one of the sisters, is talking with Dr. Joyce Walsleben, director of New York University's Sleep Disorder Center.

1 ᶜᴰ ⁷ 🔘36🔘 *Listen to the interview and circle the correct answer.*

1. Lian complains about being constantly tired. What reason does she give?
   a. She can't fall asleep at night.
   b. She has small children.
   c. She wakes up in the middle of the night.

2. According to Dr. Walsleben, what do we need to do to combat sleep deprivation?
   a. We should make sleep a priority.
   b. We should not try to combine careers and motherhood.
   c. We should make sure our days are active.

3. Dr. Walsleben mentions the accident that happened to the Exxon *Valdez* oil tanker. What do some people suspect about the causes of the accident?
   a. The captain was sleep deprived.
   b. The mate had been working for too many hours.
   c. The crew was sleeping when the accident occurred.

4. How does sleep deprivation affect Lian?
   a. She's too tired to see her parents.
   b. She makes bad parenting decisions.
   c. She can't decide what to eat.

5. How do most people feel about the effects of sleep deprivation?
   a. They think they don't have them.
   b. They accept them.
   c. They think they aren't serious.

6. What happens to many workers by the end of the workweek?
   a. They accumulate a large sleep debt.
   b. They often need to take Fridays off work.
   c. They can no longer get things done at work.

7. About how many hours of sleep are many people missing by Friday?
   a. four
   b. five
   c. seven

2 Work in a small group. Discuss the questions.

1. What are some ways the parent of a young child could get more sleep?

2. What should drivers do when they feel sleepy? Why do you think people continue to drive if they feel sleepy?

3. Not everyone agrees with the viewpoints you have heard: in fact, some researchers claim that too much sleep is also bad for you. How much sleep do you think the average person needs?

C INTEGRATE LISTENINGS ONE AND TWO

◖ STEP 1: Organize

Work in a small group. Use information from Listening One about teenagers and Listening Two about the parents of young children to fill in the chart.

	TEENAGERS	PARENTS OF YOUNG CHILDREN
Causes of sleep deprivation	• melatonin is released at a different time in teens than it is in adults	• their children may sleep a little and wake up a lot
Symptoms of sleep deprivation		
Dangers of sleep deprivation		
Recommendations from professionals		

◀ **STEP 2: Synthesize**

Work in groups of three. One of you is a sleep doctor, one is a teenager, and one is the parent of a young child. The sleep doctor asks the others questions to find out the causes and symptoms of their sleep deprivation. Then the doctor describes the dangers of sleep deprivation and recommends solutions. Use the information from the chart in Step 1.

Example

DOCTOR: What causes your sleep deprivation?
TEEN: I can't fall asleep at night. Then I have to get up early for school. I'm yawning all day!
DOCTOR: Well, one cause of that is a hormone called melatonin, which . . . Not getting enough sleep is dangerous for you because . . .
PARENT: In my case, it's because my child wakes up a lot during the night. I . . .

③ FOCUS ON SPEAKING

A **VOCABULARY**

◀ **REVIEW**

Recent research has identified a number of sleep disorders. They are more common than most people realize.

Read the magazine article. Then match the bold words with the synonyms. Write the correct numbers in the blanks on page 50.

Sleep Disorders: Are You a Victim?

Many people are absolutely exhausted a lot of the time. Tiredness can leave you feeling frustrated and **(1) miserable**. The solution is simple: Get more sleep!

However, if your tiredness **(2) accumulates** and you can't seem to get enough sleep over a long period of time, you may be suffering from a sleep disorder.

Sleep disorders are more common than you might think. Here is some information about common sleep disorders and their effects. If you **(3) suspect** you have a sleep disorder, see a doctor. **(4) Chronic** lack of sleep can lead to some very serious problems.

Insomnia
If you have insomnia, you have difficulty falling asleep or you wake up in the middle of the night. Studies show that at least 50

(continued on next page)

percent of people have this problem. Here are some possible symptoms of insomnia:

- You have a (5) **surge** of energy in the middle of the night and can't sleep.
- You lack (6) **alertness** during the day.

Apnea

Apnea is a blocking of normal breathing during sleep. Here are some symptoms of apnea:

- You (7) **snore** very loudly in your sleep and sometimes wake yourself up.
- You are very (8) **cranky** in the morning.

Restless Legs Syndrome

Restless Legs Syndrome (RLS) is an uncomfortable, painful feeling in your legs that makes you kick your legs while asleep. If you suspect you have RLS, make it a (9) **priority** to visit your doctor. Here is some important information about RLS:

- It can lead to (10) **fatigue**. This can be dangerous if you operate machinery or drive.

Sleepwalking

The lights are (11) **dim**. Everything is peaceful. But sleepwalkers have an unusual, (12) **spontaneous** reaction: They get out of bed while they are still asleep and walk around. If you see somebody sleepwalking, don't panic. This behavior is probably nothing to worry about. Here is some advice:

- Let the person continue to sleep.
- Talk quietly and gently. In a (13) **subtle** way, try to get the person back to bed.
- Later, suggest that the person get a physical/checkup, just to be safe.

Daydreaming

It's the middle of the day. You begin to yawn and (14) **blink** a lot, and your mind wanders. Here's how to tell if you have a tendency to daydream:

- People often tell you you're "in another world."
- You become distracted, and you lose concentration on what is going on around you.

Nightmares

Everyone has bad dreams from time to time. Unless you often have serious nightmares, don't worry if you experience the occasional scare in the middle of the night! Here is some advice:

- It is safe to go back to sleep. You probably won't have the same nightmare again.
- Try to (15) **do without** caffeine in the afternoon and evening. You might sleep more peacefully.

_____ a. very unhappy

_____ b. extreme tiredness

_____ c. believe to be true

_____ d. always present

_____ e. adds up

_____ f. breathe noisily while sleeping

_____ g. sudden increase

_____ h. happening without planning

_____ i. easily irritated or annoyed

_____ j. low, not bright

_____ k. indirect

_____ l. most important thing to do

_____ m. open and close your eyes quickly

_____ n. not have

_____ o. focus and concentration

MetroNaps is a company that designs sleep pods—small "energy pods" designed to let employees take short naps at their workplaces.

Look at the expressions and their definitions. Then read the conversations below between an employee and his boss, and then between the boss and his wife. Complete the conversations with words from the box and then practice the conversations with a partner.

burn the midnight oil: work very late at night

catch 40 winks: to go sleep for a very brief amount of time

irritable: getting annoyed quickly or easily

naps: short periods of sleep

nod off: to fall asleep by accident

power nap: a short sleep in the middle of the working day that helps you to have more energy, do your job better, and make better decisions

run by: have someone consider

shut-eye: sleep (informal)

Conversation 1

irritable	naps	power nap	run by

WILL MARTIN: Uh, Mr. Rogers? Could I have a word?

JACK ROGERS: Sure. Come on in. What's up?

WM: Well, a few of us had an idea that we wanted to

_____ you. I was kind of, well, elected, to tell you
    1.
about it. We've thought of a way you could increase productivity and

make your employees, well, us, really happy at work. Sleep pods!

JR: Sleep pods? I'm not following you. What are you talking about?

WM: Sleep pods! They're private, reclining chairs that allow employees

to take short _____. Here, take a look at this
    2.

brochure . . .

(continued on next page)

JR:	Hmmm. They look expensive . . .
WM:	But they would practically pay for themselves. Think about it, sir. Everyone would work more productively. Everyone would be nicer, too. You know how some of us get _____ by Friday and start snapping at each other? Well, that's because we're all so tired. **3.**
JR:	Well, I'll think it over, but really, to pay people to sleep on the job?
WM:	That's not it, sir. It's more like taking a _____, **4.** something executives do to restore themselves so they can work harder and longer. Just 10 minutes and a person can feel refreshed and ready to work again.
JR:	Heh, heh. Very clever. As I said, I'll think about it. By the way, do you have that report I needed?

Conversation 2

burning the midnight oil	caught 40 winks	nodded off	shut-eye

Later that night, Mr. and Mrs. Rogers are out for an evening.

HELEN ROGERS:	Psst, wake up! You've been snoring, and Act II is about to begin.
JACK ROGERS:	What? Oh . . . sorry. I must have _____. **5.**
HR:	But at the opera?! You must be exhausted. Last night you were _____ again at your desk. What time did you get to **6.** bed?
JR:	Not until 2 A.M. I just have so much work these days. I was hoping to get some _____ today before the show, but I **7.** didn't have enough time to get home first.
HR:	Guess you could have used one of those sleep pods your employees were telling you about! Then you could have _____ at the office. **8.**
JR:	You know, you might be right. Maybe I'd better reconsider their suggestion.

CREATE

Work with a partner. Follow the steps.

Student A, read question 1 aloud.

Student B, listen and respond to your partner. Answer in detail, using at least one of the vocabulary items in the box. Use the words in any order.

Student A: Check (✓) the word(s) that Student B uses. Then switch roles. Continue until you have checked all the words.

Example

A: Does reading in bed keep you **alert** or help you relax?
B: If the book's really exciting, it keeps me **awake**. I often **burn the midnight oil** with a good book.

accumulate	chronic	miserable	rub (your) eyes
alert	do without	naps	run by
awake	drowsy	nod off	shut-eye
burn the midnight oil	fatigue	power nap	snore
catch 40 winks	irritable	priority	yawn

1. Does exercising before going to bed keep you awake?

2. Does drinking coffee, tea, or cola keep you from sleeping?

3. Do you feel better or worse after a nap?

4. The research says that most of us need a lot more sleep than we get. What do you think?

5. Do you ever try to sleep late on weekends?

6. Do you think it is a good idea to sleep while on a bus or train?

B GRAMMAR: Present Unreal Conditionals

1 *Work with a partner. Read the conversation and then answer the questions.*

PATIENT: I'm exhausted. I just can't keep my eyes open during the day.
DOCTOR: It seems that you are quite sleep-deprived and don't get to bed early enough. **If you went to sleep earlier, you would feel a lot better.**
PATIENT: There's only one problem, doctor: I can't go to bed early. I work the night shift, and I don't get home until 10:00 or 11:00 P.M.
DOCTOR: Well, perhaps you could take naps instead. **If you took regular naps, you'd feel less sleepy.**

1. What two suggestions does the doctor make?

2. In which two sentences does the doctor offer his advice? Notice the construction of those sentences.

PRESENT UNREAL CONDITIONALS

A **present unreal conditional** sentence has two clauses: the **if-clause**, which states the condition, and the **result clause**, which states the result. Use the present unreal conditional to talk about something that is untrue, impossible, or imagined.

To form the present unreal conditional, use the *past form* of the verb in the *if*-clause. Note that the sentence is not in the past tense, however.	If I **didn't work** at night, I **could go** to bed early. (I work at night, so I can't go to bed early.)
Use *would* + **base form** of the verb in the main clause to describe a definite result.	If Lian **didn't have** such a hectic lifestyle, she **would spend** more time asleep. If more people **paid attention** to their sleep habits, the problem **would not be** so serious.
Use *might* or *could* to describe a possible result.	If people **knew** more about the dangers of sleep deprivation, they **might treat** their sleep habits more seriously.
To make a question, use question order in the main clause.	If you **were sleep-deprived, would you be** able to tell?
The *if*-clause is not needed if the condition is understood by the listener.	How **would you be** able to tell?
For the verb *be*, use *were* for all subjects.	If I **were** a doctor, I would tell my patients about sleep debt.
You can begin the sentence with either the *if*-clause or the main clause. When writing, put a comma between the clauses in sentences that start with the *if*-clause.	**If I went to bed earlier,** I would feel better. (comma) I would feel better **if I went to bed earlier.** (no comma)

2 *Read the interviews. Complete the sentences using present unreal conditionals. Then work with a partner. Read the conversations aloud with expression in your voice.*

Interview between a Sleep Researcher and a Medical Worker

SLEEP RESEARCHER: Thank you for taking the time to share your experience with me.

Can you tell me about the sleep problems that medical workers have?

MEDICAL WORKER: Well, one of the problems is that medical residents and interns can work up to 100 hours a week. They can get really overtired. If they

_____worked_____ less, they _____ so tired.
1. (work)   2. (not / get)

SLEEP RESEARCHER: And does this fatigue cause serious problems in the health profession?

MEDICAL WORKER: Sure. Just think about your own work. How well

_____ your job if you _____ only five or six hours
3. (do)   4. (sleep)
a night?

SLEEP RESEARCHER: Aren't there any rules about how much you can work?

MEDICAL WORKER: Yes, but they are not strict enough. For example, if interns

_____ for work for six days and _____ for 16
5. (show up)   6. (work)
hours, they _____ following the regulations, as long as they
7. (be)

_____ less the following week.
8. (work)

SLEEP RESEARCHER: That's terrible! What can be done to make getting sleep a priority?

MEDICAL WORKER: We need to raise public awareness. For example, surgeons and medical technicians can be on call for many nights every week. If they

_____ to do that, there _____ fewer problems.
9. (not / be allowed)   10. (be)

Interview between a Sleep Researcher and a Pilots' Association Official

SLEEP RESEARCHER: Hello there. I'd like to ask you about sleep regulations in the airline industry.

PILOTS' ASSOCIATION OFFICIAL: Well, luckily there have been several studies about the importance of adequate sleep. Sleep is important for everyone, but pilots, in particular, cannot be tired or distracted. Can you imagine what

_____ if a pilot _____ asleep on the job?
11. (happen)   12. (fall)

(continued on next page)

SLEEP RESEARCHER: Asleep? I can't imagine that!

PILOTS' ASSOCIATION OFFICIAL: Well, many people take what we call "microsleeps," which last from five to 10 seconds. But if a pilot _____ one of
13. (take)
these little naps during takeoff or landing, the results _____
14. (be)
disastrous.

SLEEP RESEARCHER: I see. So you need to make sure pilots are awake and alert.

PILOTS' ASSOCIATION OFFICIAL: Yes, alert is the right word. For example, if you
yourself _____ adequate sleep, your reaction time
15. (not / get)
_____ affected. The same thing _____ to a pilot
16. (be)   17. (happen)
who _____ enough.
18. (not / sleep)

SLEEP RESEARCHER: Are all pilots made aware of the dangers of sleep deprivation?

PILOTS' ASSOCIATION OFFICIAL: Certainly. The number of accidents
_____ significantly if we _____ some serious
19. (increase)   20. (not / enforce)
regulations about sufficient sleep.

3 *Work with a partner. One of you works for the Satellite Sisters radio talk show, and one of you is calling to get advice about a sleep problem. Take turns describing the problems and making suggestions using the present unreal conditional.*

Example

CALLER: My schedule changes from day to day. Sometimes I go to bed
                     early, sometimes late, depending on how much homework I have
                     to do. When I finally do go to bed, I can't sleep.
SATELLITE SISTER: Why don't you take a bath before going to bed? If you took a
                     warm bath, you would find it easier to go to sleep.

1. I have trouble sleeping in warm weather. I often wake up feeling really hot and cranky.

2. My husband / wife / roommate gets home from work at nine o'clock every evening, so I have dinner very late.

3. I get really tired in the evenings. I usually drink a coffee after dinner, but then I can't fall asleep at night.

4. I fall asleep in the living room with the TV on. I usually wake up at two or three o'clock in the morning, go to bed, and can't fall asleep again.

5. I get home from sports activities at 9:00 P.M. Then I go online and chat with my friends. I usually don't get to bed until after midnight.

6. I get a surge of energy late at night. I keep remembering things I need to do for the next day, so I stay up until two or three o'clock in the morning taking care of them.

C SPEAKING

PRONUNCIATION: Contrastive Stress

- In some sentences, you want to contrast information. Native speakers contrast information by using heavy stress and high pitch. In the following example, the speaker wants to contrast *body* with *brain* and *classroom* with *pillow*:

  My BOdy's in the CLASSroom, but my BRAIN's still on the PILlow.

1 CD 7 *Listen to the sentences. As you listen, underline the contrasted words. Then repeat* 37 *the sentences with a partner.*

1. I need to go to bed, but I'm feeling energetic.

2. Adolescents wake up late, but children wake up early.

3. Lian is fast asleep, but her children are awake.

4. My husband has insomnia, but I need to sleep.

5. I'm sleepy in the morning, but I'm wide awake at night.

2 *Work in pairs. Look at the contrasting information in columns A and B. Using contrastive stress, create and say sentences that emphasize the information.*

Column A	Column B
Example	
What are some obvious effects of sleep deprivation? (absenteeism) *ABSENTEEISM is an OBVIOUS effect of sleep deprivation.*	What are some subtle effects of sleep deprivation? (emotional problems) *EMOTIONAL problems are a more SUBTLE effect.*
1. When is melatonin secreted in adults? (evening)	1. When is melatonin secreted in adolescents? (late at night)
2. When does melatonin "turn on"? (evening)	2. When does melatonin "turn off"? (morning)
3. Why do adults think that teenagers stay up late? (because they are having fun)	3. Why do teenagers say they stay up late? (because they are night owls)
4. How do many parents feel on Monday morning? (tired)	4. How do many parents feel by Friday night? (absolutely exhausted)

3 *Complete the survey and compare your answers with a partner's. Then report your findings back to the class using sentences that contrast your partner's response and your own. Use contrastive stress to indicate your comparisons. The stress will depend on the information you have found.*

Example

I OFTEN wake up at night, but JOE NEVER does.

OR

I NEVER wake up at night, and JANE doesn't EITHER.

	You	Your Partner
1. Do you often wake up at night?		
2. Do you snore?		
3. Do you daydream?		
4. Do you take naps?		
5. Do you use an alarm clock?		
6. What time do you wake up in the morning?		
7. How much coffee do you drink?		

◖FUNCTION: Interrupting to Ask for Clarification

At times, you may need to interrupt a speaker to ask a question to make sure you understand what the person said. This is particularly important when you need to clarify factual information. You may not have heard the information clearly because it was spoken too fast, because of background noise, or because of poor pronunciation.

Example

A: Joelle, I heard some horrifying statistics—over 30 percent of traffic accidents are caused by sleepiness! People should be more careful!
B: **What was that you said?** Thirteen percent?
A: No, I said over 30 percent. That's a lot, don't you think?
B: Thirty percent! I see what you mean! Wow! That's a very high figure.

Here are some expressions that can be used to interrupt a speaker when you do not understand something. Use rising intonation for the questions.

REQUESTS TO CLARIFY INFORMATION

Excuse me? What was that you said?

What? (*informal*)

Sorry?

I'm sorry, I didn't catch that. Could you say that again?

Could you repeat that?

Sorry, I didn't hear you. What was that?

Could you say that another way?

Work with a partner.

Student A: Read each statement aloud. Speak too softly or too quickly, or mispronounce an important word, so that Student B won't understand what you say and will have to ask you a question.

Student B: Listen to your partner. Interrupt to ask a question or to ask your partner to repeat any information you didn't understand. Use one of the expressions in the box above when you interrupt.

Example

A: I read that 17 percent of Americans are insomniacs!
B: **Sorry, could you repeat that?**

Student A

1. There are about 1,500 sleep-disorder clinics in the United States.

2. Almost 20 percent of Americans are shift workers, meaning that they often have changes in their work schedules.

3. During the winter, there can be 14½ hours of darkness in some parts of the United States. There's no excuse for not sleeping!

Now switch roles.

Student B

4. Even if a person is seriously sleep-deprived, he or she can get back on a regular pattern of sleep after only three weeks.

5. If rats are completely deprived of sleep for 2½ weeks, they die.

6. Sleeping pills first became popular in the United States in the 1970s.

◖ PRODUCTION: A Hospital Role Play

In this activity, you will **_role play a meeting about sleep deprivation_** between hospital administrators, medical interns, and members of a patients' rights group. You will study a situation at the fictional Hilldale General Hospital and then try to resolve some problems through discussion. The situation is based on real cases at many hospitals. Try to use the vocabulary, grammar, pronunciation, and language to ask for clarification that you learned in the unit.*

Read the situation. Then divide the class into three groups. Each group will study one of the roles to prepare for a meeting to establish hospital policies on how long medical personnel can work until rest is required.

Situation

Two weeks ago, a ten-year-old boy was admitted to a private hospital for some routine surgery. In preparation for the operation, he was accidentally given an overdose of his medication. He became very ill for several days, but fortunately he recovered and was not seriously affected. Investigations revealed that both the intern who ordered the medication that night and the nurse who administered it were seriously sleep-deprived. They had both been on duty for 15 hours when the boy received his medicine. The intern had worked ten hours per day for the previous eight days, while the nurse had worked the same shifts for six days in a row. Just before checking on the boy and ordering his medicine, the intern and the nurse had spent five hours in the operating room working on victims of a car accident emergency. The story appeared in the local newspaper, and the hospital received a general review.

In addition to this latest case, Hilldale General Hospital is having serious financial problems. The only other hospital in the community of Hilldale closed down two years ago due to lack of funding, leaving Hilldale General to cope with too many patients and too little money.

---

*For Alternative Speaking Topics, see page 62.

Roles		
A. *Hospital Administrators:* You are worried. There is so little money to operate the hospital and you are seriously understaffed. Your staff works long hours to cover all the shifts and keep the emergency room open 24 hours a day. Doctors' shifts cannot last longer than 16 hours a day, with one continuous 24-hour period off every week. You do what you can for your staff, but you know it's not enough. Hilldale General is in serious financial trouble.	**B.** *Interns:* You are worried. You are dedicated professionals. You work long, hard hours for very little pay, but you are committed to helping the community of Hilldale. You know that sometimes you don't perform well because you are sleep-deprived, but you don't feel you have a choice. There is no one else to take your place.	**C.** *Patients' Rights Group:* You are concerned about the patients. You fear that someone will be hurt because the hospital staff is overworked and sleep-deprived. You want the administration to take action. Other hospitals in the country are using innovative ways to prevent mistakes from happening, such as using videotapes to assess staff performance and using computers to regulate doses of medicine.

Procedure

Step 1: Work with your group to clarify your viewpoint on the issue. Make a list of points you want to discuss.

Step 2: Divide into groups of three, with one student representing each of the roles (A, B, and C). Role play a meeting. Try to reach some solutions that will satisfy everyone.

Example

HOSPITAL
ADMINISTRATOR: We are seriously understaffed. **If we had** more staff members, we **would not be** so concerned about sleep deprivation among the interns.

INTERN: Yes, that's true. For example, there are only two of us on the ward at night. **If** my partner and I **didn't show up** for work one evening, there **would be** no one available to help incoming patients.

PATIENTS' RIGHTS
GROUP MEMBER: **Excuse me?** Did you say there were only two people on the ward?

Step 3: Report to the class. Share your answers to the following questions:
- What are the causes of the crisis at Hilldale General Hospital?
- What are some possible solutions?
- Who should be responsible for addressing the problems?

(continued on next page)

Then discuss these additional questions with the whole class.

- Does this problem exist in other places?
- What can be learned?
- What steps should be taken?

ALTERNATIVE SPEAKING TOPICS

Work in a small group. Discuss the questions.

1. When teenagers get enough sleep, they are in better moods and tend to do better in school. Should schools redesign their schedules to help teenagers sleep more? How? What would be some advantages and disadvantages to a school schedule that let teens sleep later?

2. Interns and residents (doctors-in-training), as well as drivers, pilots, and factory workers, are often sleep-deprived, which leads to accidents. Should there be laws to require that these professionals get a certain amount of sleep? How could these laws be administered and enforced?

RESEARCH TOPICS, see page 219.

Animal Intelligence

① FOCUS ON THE TOPIC

Ⓐ PREDICT

1 *Work with a partner to write the name of the animal under the correct picture above.*

chimp (chimpanzee)	dolphin	parrot	seagull
crow	killer whale	scrub jay	

2 *Discuss the question with a partner or small group.*
- Do animals have feelings? Do animals reason? Explain your answer.
- How could a scientist show that an animal does or doesn't think?

1 *Discuss the questions with a partner or small group.*

    1. Which of the animals on page 63 have you seen before? Where?

    2. Which of these animals do you think are the smartest?

2 *Recently, scientists have discovered some interesting information about animal intelligence. What do you think they have found? Take this quiz. Circle the answers. Then check your answers at the bottom of the page. Talk to a partner about any answers that surprise you.*

Some animals can . . .	
1. create words and symbols	True / False
2. do simple math like addition	True / False
3. recognize themselves in a mirror	True / False
4. play tricks on humans in order to get something	True / False
5. show a sense of humor	True / False
6. show grief at the loss of a loved one	True / False
7. lie to others	True / False

CD 1
38 *Read and listen to the introductory lecture to a course on animal intelligence. Pay attention to the bold words. Then use the information in the lecture to help you match the words and phrases to their definitions.*

Good morning. Today we'll consider whether animals are "intelligent" in the same way that humans are. Why do we say humans are intelligent? Is it because we create and use language, create art, and use tools? Because we have emotions? Because we are **(1) socialized** to a particular cultural environment? Because we lie and **(2) deceive** others? Do other animals do these things as well? Let's look at some recent research.

gorilla

First, humans are conscious beings. When we look into a mirror, for example, we know we are seeing our own image. Can animals do the same? Well, when some apes look into a mirror for the first time, they **(3) spontaneously** examine their teeth. In fact, some researchers put paint on chimps' faces when they were asleep. After waking, the chimps looked into a mirror and tried to get the paint off. Scientists say this shows self-awareness.

Answers: All items are true.

Second, we've also learned some **(4) intriguing** things about the ability of animals to communicate, both with each other and with humans. Of course, most animals don't have the ability to **(5) vocalize** words. However, some animals raised in captivity have learned to communicate with humans through computers or gestures. Actually, some apes learn hundreds of words. While some people claim that this is just **(6) rote memorization**, and not true communication, studies have shown that they can ask and answer questions they have never heard before and even create new "words." For example, a gorilla named Koko saw a picture of a mask for the first time and called it an "eye hat."

What other abilities are unique to humans? Well, humans can **(7) categorize** objects by color, size, shape, and so on. And humans **(8) figure out** answers to complex problems and apply their answers in a different **(9) context**. However, there are also many examples of animals solving complicated problems, too. For instance, we have filmed crows stealing from fishermen by pulling the fishing line out of the water inch by inch until they get the fish.

Can animals deceive as well? At one zoo, an elephant secretly learned how to open his cage, but only did so at night when the humans were gone. Every night he opened his own cage and the cages of the other elephants so they could all walk outside to eat grass.

Finally, let's look at emotions. Can animals show sadness or distress? Are we the only animals who understand death? Well, when Koko's pet kitten was killed by a car some years ago, and Koko was told about the death, she made quiet crying sounds and wouldn't eat for days.

So we have to wonder if animal intelligence is really so different from our own. And if animals can categorize, perform simple mathematics, intentionally deceive others, and communicate with us, then what kind of relationship should we have with them? We'll look at these questions next.

_____ 1. socialized

_____ 2. deceive

_____ 3. spontaneously

_____ 4. intriguing

_____ 5. vocalize

_____ 6. rote memorization

_____ 7. categorize

_____ 8. figure out

_____ 9. context

a. interesting because it's unusual or unexpected

b. make someone believe something that is not true

c. in a way that is not planned

d. conclude, realize

e. the situation, events, or information related to something

f. trained to behave in a way that is acceptable to others in your group

g. make a sound with the voice

h. put objects into groups according to what kind, color, size, etc. they are

i. learned from repeating and not from thinking

2 FOCUS ON LISTENING

A ⬛ LISTENING ONE: The Infinite Mind: Animal Intelligence

Exciting new research is changing our view of animal emotions and animal intelligence. Listen to three professors discuss their experiments in a radio interview.

Dr. Sally Boysen, professor of psychology, Ohio State University
Dr. Stan Kuczaj, professor of psychology, University of Southern Mississippi
Dr. Irene Pepperberg, University of Arizona

CD 1 39 *Listen to the introduction and write the three types of animals you will hear about.*

1. _____

2. _____

3. _____

◀ LISTEN FOR MAIN IDEAS

CD 1 40 *Now listen to the interviews. What did the animals do? Check (✓) the correct picture.*

1.

2.
 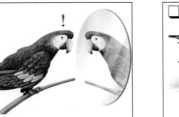 

3.

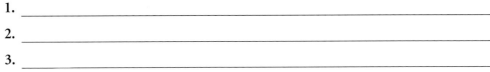

◖ LISTEN FOR DETAILS

 *Listen to the interview again. Write **T** (true) or **F** (false) for the each statement. Correct the false statements. Then discuss your answers with a partner.*

_____ 1. Sara, the older chimp, helped the new, injured chimp by giving her some food.

_____ 2. This is remarkable to Dr. Boysen because Sara has not been socialized with other chimps.

_____ 3. Alex the parrot uses a computer to communicate.

_____ 4. Alex can answer questions about what he wants to eat and do.

_____ 5. Dr. Kuczaj's killer whale used fish to attract seagulls.

_____ 6. Dr. Pepperberg says that talking to Alex the parrot is like talking to a very young human.

_____ 7. Dr. Pepperberg doesn't call Alex's talk "language"; she calls it "two-way communication."

_____ 8. When Alex answers questions, he doesn't seem to understand the questions; instead, he is answering in a rote manner.

◖ MAKE INFERENCES

Listen to the excerpts again and answer the questions.

⟨42⟩ Excerpt One

1. How did Dr. Boysen feel about Goodwin's question?
   a. She was surprised.
   b. She was pleased.
   c. She was not happy.

2. What might Dr. Boysen be thinking?
   a. "I'm not ready to speak first."
   b. "I don't know the answer to that question."

⟨43⟩ Excerpt Two

1. What is Dr. Boysen's attitude towards Sara's behavior?
   a. She's impressed by it.
   b. She's confused by it.
   c. She's saddened by it.

2. What might Dr. Boysen say about this example?
   a. "This shows that animals have emotions and feelings."
   b. "This shows that animals can teach each other."

 **Excerpt Three**

1. What does the commentator think about the example?
    a. He is impressed by what the bird did.
    b. He can't believe the behavior really happened.
    c. He doesn't believe the behavior shows intelligence.

2. What might Dr. Pepperberg say about what the bird did?
    a. "He is easily confused by new situations."
    b. "He understood that we were trying to trick him."

 **Excerpt Four**

1. How does Dr. Pepperberg speak to the bird?
    a. As if he has difficulty hearing her.
    b. As if he were a small child.
    c. As if he were not very smart.

2. What does Dr. Pepperberg believe about the bird?
    a. That he can count.
    b. That he can use the telephone.

◖ **EXPRESS OPINIONS**

Work in a small group. Discuss the questions.

1. Look at the questions in Predict again. Have you changed your mind about any of your answers? Explain.

2. Do you think the research shows that these animals are intelligent? Why or why not?
    • Sara, the chimp
    • Alex, the parrot
    • the killer whales

B **LISTENING TWO: What Motivates Animals?**

Other scientists have added to our knowledge of large ape and bird intelligence. In this radio interview, science newswriter Liz Pennisi discusses some new research on animal cognition. Liz writes for *Science Magazine*.

1 Listen to the interview. Check (✓) your answers.

The speakers say that apes and / or birds can . . .	YES	NO
1. understand when a human is watching.	❏	❏
2. manipulate humans to get what they want.	❏	❏
3. operate robots.	❏	❏
4. teach what they've learned to their offspring.	❏	❏

5. remember.	❑	❑
6. create works of art.	❑	❑
7. plan.	❑	❑
8. anticipate the future.	❑	❑
9. judge what someone else might be doing.	❑	❑
10. deceive others who might steal their food.	❑	❑

2 *Discuss the question with a partner. Then share your answer with another pair or the whole class.*

In both reports, you have heard research that investigates the meaning of intelligence. In your opinion, what is the best definition of "intelligence"?

C INTEGRATE LISTENINGS ONE AND TWO

◀ STEP 1: Organize

How did the animals you heard about show their intelligence? Complete the chart with information from Listenings One and Two.

ANIMAL	THE INFINITE MIND	WHAT MOTIVATES ANIMALS?
1. Chimps	• One chimp understood that another chimp was disabled and helped the disabled chimp	
2. Birds	Parrot:	Scrub jays and crows:
3. Killer whales		

STEP 2: Synthesize

Work in groups of three. Each of you is an animal scientist in a special area. Select your category of specialization: chimpanzees, birds, or killer whales. Present examples of recent research and explain how this research shows animal intelligence. First study the chart for your specialty. Then take one or two minutes to tell your colleagues about your research. Then, change groups and animals and repeat the presentation.

Example

My research focuses on large apes. We have seen many examples of intelligence. In one case, . . . In another case, . . .

③ FOCUS ON SPEAKING

Ⓐ VOCABULARY

REVIEW

Work with a partner. Say the words aloud. Then circle the two words that are related to the word on the left. Use a dictionary if necessary.

Example

	remarkable	(incredible)	insignificant	(intriguing)
1.	ape	gorilla	parrot	chimpanzee
2.	aware	mindful	conscious	careful
3.	in captivity	free	protected	restricted
4.	cognition	emotion	understanding	perception
5.	intriguing	irrelevant	fascinating	mysterious
6.	manipulate	pull	handle	use
7.	prevailing	current	established	past
8.	research	experiment	study	lecture
9.	socialized	tame	friendly	wild
10.	spontaneous	thoughtful	instant	unplanned

1 *Work with a partner. Read the script of a radio talk show as a host answers comments from three callers.*

HOST: I've asked our listeners about problems they're having with animals in their communities. We've got calls from all over. Yes, hello, Lin, you're on the line.

LIN: Hi . . . Well, the **pests** that create the most problems where I live are crows . . . you know, because they open the garbage cans and make a big mess. But what I can't believe is that people actually kill them! I think that's really **unethical**. I've read that crows are really intelligent . . . like, they've discovered that crows make tools to get food.

HOST: That's true. They may be small, but they're pretty smart!

LIN: Right, so these are intelligent creatures, so I think we have to treat them with **compassion**. I mean, they can think . . . just like us. So I think they have rights, too.

HOST: Thanks, Lin. OK, Kim, Are you there? You have **the floor.**

KIM: Hi, uh, I'm on the air? . . . OK, well, let me give you an example **off the top of my head**. Most people in my neighborhood think squirrels are a terrible **nuisance**. For example, they dig up people's plants, and they've totally destroyed my attic.

HOST: I don't **get it.** Do you mean they've gotten into your attic?

KIM: Yes. They made a hole under my roof and built a nest in the walls of my house! It cost me a lot of money to get rid of them. And I think squirrels carry **diseases**, don't they? We really need to keep them under control.

HOST: Thank you. All right, we have time for one more caller . . . Pat?

PAT: Uh, yeah, hello. And, uh, well I was going to give you the example of deer. They're a real **hazard** for drivers. When they run across the road at night, they cause a lot of accidents. I know people say we have to treat animals in a **humane** way, but after all, humans are **superior** to animals, and it's not as if deer are **endangered** or anything! I think we should get rid of all the deer. Just, you know, kill them.

HOST: Kill them? All of them? I don't know, Pat, that's sort of **pushing the envelope**. But it's true they're dangerous on the roads.

squirrel

2 *Match the words and phrases on the left with the definitions on the right.*

_____ **1.** pest

_____ **2.** unethical

_____ **3.** compassion

_____ **4.** (give someone) the floor

_____ **5.** off the top of (someone's) head

_____ **6.** nuisance

_____ **7.** get it

_____ **8.** diseases

_____ **9.** hazard

_____ **10.** humane

_____ **11.** superior

_____ **12.** endangered

_____ **13.** push the envelope

a. animals that create a disturbance or bother people

b. better than

c. kindness

d. go beyond accepted boundaries

e. allow someone to speak

f. threatened with extinction

g. without thinking about it in advance

h. kind; gentle

i. immoral

j. sicknesses

k. danger

l. understand

m. something that bothers or annoys

◖ **CREATE**

Work with a partner. Take turns asking each other these questions. Use words from Expand in your answers when possible. Before you begin, look at the questions and write a few notes to help you speak.

1. What is your reaction to the comments of these speakers?
   - Lin, who doesn't think people should hunt animals
   - Kim, who believes that animals can be **pests**
   - Pat, who believes that people are superior to animals

2. What other animals, in addition to the ones above, do some people consider **pests**? Are they just a **nuisance**, or are they a **hazard**?

3. Do you think the animals mentioned in the interview—crows, squirrels, and deer—are intelligent? Why or why not?

4. **Off the top of your head**, would you say that humans are **superior** to animals? In what ways? Are there ways in which animals are superior to humans?

5. Do you think people sometimes treat animals in **unethical** ways? What examples can you think of where animals are not treated in a **humane** way?

6. Should people be prevented from using animals in scientific experiments or from eating them, or is that **pushing the envelope**?

1 *Work with a partner. Read the conversation and answer the questions.*

A: I just did the assignment about animal communication. The article reported that some parrots could recognize themselves in a mirror.

B: Yeah, and it said they **were able to** string three or four words together, too. Actually, my professor told us that he **had just written** a paper on how parrots learn language. He said he **was going to** publish it next month.

A: What did the paper say?

B: Well, apparently it warned that researchers **had to** study animal intelligence more carefully before drawing conclusions.

1. Do we know the exact words of the article and the professor?

2. Why do you think speaker B chose not to quote the article and the professor directly?

REPORTED SPEECH

Reported speech (also called indirect speech) reports what a speaker said without using his or her exact words.

Use words like *said (that), told, indicated, mentioned, reported*, etc., to show that you are reporting information that someone else said.

When you are reporting what a speaker or article said, "backshift" the verb in the indirect speech statement.

Original: "We **are conducting** some interesting research with chimps."
Reported: The scientist explained that she **was conducting** some interesting research with chimps.

The verb in the reported speech has shifted back in time, in this case from the present continuous to the past continuous. See more examples in the chart below.

NOTE: If you are reporting a person's unchanging beliefs or a general truth, rather than an event, it is not necessary to change the tense of the original verb.

Original: "Many animals **are** remarkably intelligent."
Reported: The zoologist **told her students** that many animals **are / were** remarkably intelligent.

COMMON VERB CHANGES

	Direct Speech	Indirect Speech
Change **present tense** to **past tense**.	"I'm doing research on their use of tools."	The zoologist said (that) she **was** doing research on their use of tools.
Change **present progressive tense** to **past progressive tense**.	"I'm **conducting** an experiment on crows."	She said (that) she **was conducting** an experiment on crows.
Change **past tense** and **present perfect tense** to **past perfect tense**.	"The crows **made** a hook to get food from a tree."	The researcher reported (that) the crows **had made** a hook to get food from a tree.
	"We **have** never **studied** this behavior before."	She said (that) they **had** never **studied** this behavior before.
The modals **will**, **can**, and **may** change form in indirect speech.	"I **won't** be at the meeting."	She explained (that) she **wouldn't** be at the meeting.
	"I **can** ask my colleague to take notes."	She said (that) she **could** ask her colleague to take notes.
	"I **may** be able to send my secretary."	She mentioned (that) she **might** be able to send her secretary.
Change **must** to **had to**.	"I **must** find a way to repeat my experiment."	She said (that) she **had to** find a way to repeat her experiment.
Do not change the modals **should**, **could**, **might**, or **ought to**.	"I **should** publish my results."	She said (that) she **should** publish her results.
Change the pronouns, possessives, and time words to keep the original meaning.	"**I** can't access **my** computer because it broke down **yesterday**."	The student claimed (that) **she** couldn't access **her** computer because it had broken down **the day before**.

2 *Work with a partner.*

Student A: Read statement 1 aloud.

Student B: Cover Student A's statements. After Student A reads each statement, restate it using indirect speech. Use a variety of reporting verbs. Follow the example.

Student A: Check Student B's response. The correct response is in parentheses.

Example

A: I'm reading an article about Jane Goodall.
B: You **mentioned** you **were reading** an article about Jane Goodall, right?
A: That's right.

Student A

1. Jane Goodall is the world authority on chimpanzees.

   (B: You said she was the world authority on chimpanzees.)

2. She has studied chimpanzees for over 45 years.

   (B: You said she had studied chimpanzees for over 45 years.)

3. She discovered toolmaking among chimps.

   (B: You explained she had discovered toolmaking among chimps.)

4. Her work will affect generations of people.

   (B: You told me her work would affect generations of people.)

Now switch roles.

Student B

5. I'm reading about a dolphin research center.

   (A: You said you were reading about a dolphin research center.)

6. I'm going to visit the center in August.

   (A: You indicated you were going to visit the center in August.)

7. I've always wanted to swim with dolphins.

   (A: You claimed you'd always wanted to swim with dolphins.)

8. The dolphins at the center are used to interacting with humans.

   (A: You reported that the dolphins at the center were used to interacting with humans.)

3 *Work with a partner. Role play a conversation between A, who believes that animals are quite intelligent, and B, who does not. A and B each use information and reasons they've heard (see page 76) to support their positions.*

Example

A: My college professor **told me** that a recent study **had shown** that an ape **had learned** to use sign language to communicate.
B: Well, my uncle, who is a zookeeper, claimed that when the chimp he worked with **made** signs, he . . .

Support for A's Position	Support for B's Position
College professor: "A recent study showed that an ape learned to use sign language to communicate."	**Uncle who is a zookeeper:** "When the chimp I work with makes signs, he is just copying humans. He doesn't know what he is doing."
Radio report: "Crows have been filmed carrying clams high into the air. They drop the clams, and the clam shells break. Then the crows pick up the food."	**Teacher:** "Some dogs can be trained to do tricks. That doesn't prove that they are intelligent."
Neighbor: "I have a cat who can open doors and windows. My cat knows how to answer the phone, too."	**Parents who have had cats for years:** "Some people think their pets are smart. But pets that we've seen can't understand even basic ideas."
Friend: "Animals have feelings, too. When I returned home after a short vacation, my dog was waiting by the door."	**Roommate:** "Animals don't feel love for people. They're only motivated by food. No pet will ever be able to experience human emotions."

C SPEAKING

◖ PRONUNCIATION: Questions with *or*

Some YES-NO questions with **or** *ask the listener to make a choice. Listen to this question. How would you answer it?*

 Is communication more complex in humans or animals?

Some YES-NO questions that include an **or** *phrase are true YES-NO questions. They are asking the listener to say "Yes" or "No," not to make a choice. Listen to this question. How would you answer it?*

Can animals communicate about the past or the future?

PRONUNCIATION OF *YES-NO* QUESTIONS WITH *OR*

Asking choice questions with *or*

- The words joined by *or* are in different thought groups.

- Intonation rises on the first choice and falls on the second.

Is communication more complex

in humans or animals?

(The speaker is asking the listener to indicate which of the two choices, humans or animals, has more complex communication.)

Asking true YES-NO questions with _or_	
• The _or_-phrase is pronounced as one group.	Can animals communicate about the past or future?
• Intonation rises smoothly over the _or_-phrase.	(This question is asking if animals can communicate about things that are not happening now, in the present.)
Answering questions with _or_ Sometimes the answer to a choice question and a true YES-NO question can be almost the same.	**A:** Did Jane Goodall study chimps or apes? (The speaker wants the listener to indicate which choice is correct.) **B:** She studied chimps. **A:** Did Jane Goodall study plants or birds? (The speaker is asking if Jane Goodall studied those things or not.) **B:** No. She concentrated on chimps.

1 CD _Listen to the questions and repeat them. The questions are all true YES-NO questions. Say the words in the or-phrase in one group. Your voice should rise smoothly over the or-phrase._

1. Do you have a cat or a dog?

2. Do you like to visit zoos or parks?

3. Do chimps communicate with sounds or gestures?

4. Can your dog shake hands or roll over?

5. Can that parrot ask or answer questions?

6. Did the speaker talk about the intelligence of cows or horses?

7. Have you read about seagulls or crows?

8. Do you have a fur coat or a leather jacket?

2 ⓒᴰ₇ 🔵50 *Listen to the questions on page 77 again and repeat them. This time the speaker is asking choice questions. Say the words in the or-phrase in two groups. Your voice rises on the first choice and falls on the second.*

3 *Work with a partner. Read the questions below. Some of the questions make more sense as choice questions, some make more sense as true yes-no questions, and some could be either choice questions or true YES-NO questions. Have short conversations using each question. Take turns asking and answering the questions. Group words carefully and use intonation clearly.*

1. Can animals manipulate or deceive?
2. Are you a meat-eater or a vegetarian?
3. Do pets prefer human food or pet food?
4. Are you afraid of snakes or spiders?
5. Would you like to see a tiger or a lion?
6. Should people wear fur or leather?

◀ **FUNCTION: Giving and Asking for Examples**

1 *Read the conversation between two students.*

A: Elephants have an amazing capacity for memory.
B: Really? **What do you mean**?
A: Well, **off the top of my head** . . . Female elephants remember hundreds of other elephants. I read an article about this.

GIVING AND ASKING FOR EXAMPLES	
Giving Examples	**Asking for Examples**
Let me give you an example: . . . For instance, . . . Well, what I mean is . . . One example is . . . . . . , such as . . . Well, let's see . . . Well, off the top of my head . . .	Could you give me an example? What do you mean? Such as? Could you give me some more details? Like what, for instance?

2 *Read the conversations. Fill in the blanks with phrases to give examples or ask for examples. There can be more than one correct answer.*

1.
A: You know, a lot of people are against circuses because they treat elephants so badly.
B: Why? How do they treat them? _____?
A: The elephants don't exercise enough and they have too much stress, so they often get sick. _____, many of them develop skin diseases. And sometimes the elephants get hit, too.

2.

A: We have to become more aware of the problems elephants face.

B: _____?

A: Well, _____. African elephants are hunted for ivory and many hundreds of them are killed every year. And Asian elephants are losing their natural habitat because of humans.

3.

A: I read that female elephants find several "babysitters" to help them raise their babies. The babysitters help with all kinds of things.

B: _____?

A: Well, _____ they protect the young elephants when the group moves from place to place.

3 *Work in small groups and share information about types of animal intelligence. Each person selects one square in the box and reads the corresponding information. Then take turns explaining the finding to the other members of the group, giving and asking for examples. Use reported speech to restate the words of the researcher.*

PERSON A: **Expression of Emotions** **Research finding:** Chimps recognize and express emotions such as happiness and fear. **Researcher statement:** "We showed them TV scenes of other chimps playing and fighting. We used thermometers to measure their brain temperature. We found that the chimps had physical reactions to the other chimps' feelings."	**PERSON B:** **Self-Recognition** **Research finding:** Dolphins are able to recognize themselves in mirrors. **Researcher statement:** "Our research team used markers to draw lines on the bodies of two captive dolphins. Once the dolphins felt the marker, they used mirrors to inspect various parts of their body."
PERSON C: **Problem-Solving** **Research finding:** Crows are creative problem-solvers. **Researcher statement:** "I filmed crows in urban Japan. They dropped nuts on the road and waited for cars to run over them and crack the shells. Then the crows went back to eat the nuts."	**PERSON D:** **Language**  **Research finding:** Prairie dogs use complex "language" to communicate. **prairie dog** **Researcher statement:** "Well, we showed that prairie dogs make calls to warn other animals if a predator is approaching. The calls are different for different species, size, color, and speed of travel of the predator."

In this activity, you will work with a group to *identify arguments for and against a position related to animals and their relationship to people*. You will then present the issue to the class. Try to use the vocabulary, grammar, pronunciation, and language for giving and asking for examples that you learned in the unit.*

Step 1: Divide the class into enough groups so that each one can choose a different topic. Then each group selects its topic from the list or proposes a new one. Consider the question in terms of whether animals are intelligent or not.

1. Should animals be kept in zoos?

2. Should people eat animals?

3. Should people conduct experiments on animals?

4. Should people be allowed to hunt animals?

5. Should people pass stricter laws to protect endangered species?

Step 2: Study the example outline. Then organize your ideas in the outline on page 81. Be sure to think of reasons and examples for both sides of the argument.

Topic: Should people wear fur or leather?

I. People should not wear fur or leather.	II. People should be allowed to wear fur or leather.
A: Killing animals for fur is cruel.	
1. Animals raised for fur are kept in inhumane conditions.	A: Animals are raised specifically for fur.
2. They are killed before they reach old age.	1. Many rabbits wouldn't be alive unless people bred them for their fur. They weren't wild animals that were shot.
B: Fur is not necessary for people.	2. Example:
1. They can wear other materials.	B: Reason:
2. Example:	1. Example:
	2. Example:

*For Alternative Speaking Topics, see page 81.

Topic:

I. One side of the argument:	II. Other side of the argument:
A: Reason:	A: Reason:
1. Example:	1. Example:
2. Example:	2. Example:
B: Reason:	B: Reason:
1.	1.
2.	2.

Step 3: Choose one person in your group to present the group's arguments and examples to the class. Then conduct a class vote to see which side of the issue they support.

ALTERNATIVE SPEAKING TOPICS

Work with a small group and read the quotations. Paraphrase each quotation and then choose one that you agree with and explain the meaning to the class.

1. *Man is the only animal for whom his own existence is a problem which he has to solve.* (Erich Fromm, 1900–1980, psychologist and philosopher)

2. *Non-violence leads to the highest ethics, which is the goal of all evolution. Until we stop harming all other living beings, we are still savages.* (Thomas Edison, 1847–1931, inventor)

3. *If an animal does something we call it instinct; if we do the same thing for the same reason, we call it intelligence.* (Will Cuppy, 1884–1949, author)

4. *The time will come when men such as I will look upon the murder of animals as they now look on the murder of men.* (Leonardo Da Vinci, 1452–1519, artist and scientist)

(continued on next page)

5. *The greatness of a nation and its moral progress can be judged by the way its animals are treated.* (Mohandas Gandhi, 1869–1948, statesman and philosopher)

6. *The soul of man is divided into three parts, intelligence, reason, and passion. Intelligence and passion are possessed by other animals, but reason by man alone.* (Pythagoras, about 569 BC–about 475 BC, mathematician and philosopher)

7. *When it comes to having a central nervous system, and the ability to feel pain, hunger, and thirst, a rat is a pig is a dog is a boy.* (Ingrid Newkirk, 1949–, animal rights activist)

8. *Some people are uncomfortable with the idea that humans belong to the same class of animals as cats and cows and raccoons. They're like the people who become successful and then don't want to be reminded of the old neighborhood.* (Phil Donahue, 1935–, TV talk show host)

RESEARCH TOPICS, see page 220.

Longevity:
Refusing to Be Invisible

1 FOCUS ON THE TOPIC

A PREDICT

Discuss the questions with a small group or the whole class.

1. These photos show the same person at age 5, 25, 50, and 75. Describe the photos to a partner.

2. *Longevity* means the length of a person's life. Look at the title of this chapter. What do you think it means?

1 *Work with a partner. You will analyze some information about longevity.*

Step 1: Each partner selects one graph.

Step 2: First complete the statements in the graph and add some statements of your own. Then describe the graph in as much detail as you can to your partner.

Graph 1

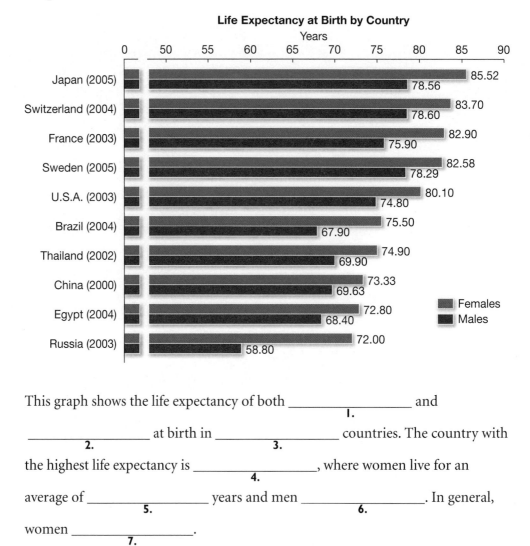

Life Expectancy at Birth by Country

This graph shows the life expectancy of both _____ and
                                                    1.

_____ at birth in _____ countries. The country with
         2.   **3.**

the highest life expectancy is _____, where women live for an
                                         4.

average of _____ years and men _____. In general,
              5.   **6.**

women _____.
           7.

Graph 2

Proportion of Elderly Population by Country
(aged 65 years and over)

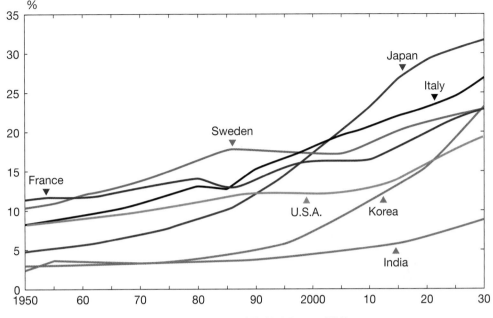

Source: Statistics Bureau, MIC; United Nations; Ministry of Health, Labour and Welfare.

This graph shows the increase in the proportion of elderly people (people aged

_____) in _____ countries from the year
      8.   **9.**

_____ to _____ . The country with the highest
      10.   **11.**

proportion in the year 2000 was _____ . In 2030, _____
                                         12.   **13.**

_____ .
      14.

2 *Discuss the questions with another pair. Use the information you learned from Graphs 1 and 2.*
- What can you predict about the number of older people worldwide in the next 50 years?
- What challenges do you think older people might face in the future?

More and more publications cater to the growing population of older people. Seniors may need information and ideas because they are living longer than their parents did.

 CD 2 *Listen to and read the news magazine. Pay special attention to the words in bold. Then use the information in the news magazine to help you match the words and phrases to their definitions.*

Senior Weekly: Your News Magazine
Vol 23, 19

Tip of the week: Don't **go in for** being alone? Be **bold**! Join your local senior group!

Inside: Elderly Alert

*The rising price of medical care is a major crisis among our oldest citizens, who have expressed anger and **bitterness** over the price of prescription drugs. If you want to express your **solidarity** with their protests, turn to page 3.*

With their wide-brimmed hats, feather boas and colorful **ensembles**, a **chapter** of the Red Hat Society posed for a recent photograph in northern California. Have you ever seen such **gorgeous**, **flamboyant** seniors?

Life Expectancy at Birth

Less than 55
55-64
65-69
70-74
75 or more
No data

Map not to Scale
Copyright © 2008 www.mapsofworld.com

Some places in the world (Costa Rica, Sardinia, Okinawa, and Loma Linda, California) are "longevity hotspots," where people seem to live for a very, very long time! What's their secret? Read more inside . . .

Did you know . . . ?

• This century, the world is expected to experience an unprecedented aging of the human population worldwide. Seniors—people aged 65 and above—will soon make up 15% of the world's population.

• There are 4.2 million Americans over the age of 85, and this number will grow as the baby boom generation gets older.

• The oldest people in the world include Edna Parker of the U.S., Maria de Jesus of Portugal, and Bertha Fry of the U.S. They were all born in 1893.

Stories to make you smile . . .

Angus Davis has a lot to **brag about**: He's 100 today! Happy Birthday, Angus! What's his secret? Angus says, "Enjoy life! Don't waste time feeling anxious and stressed."

Eighty-five-year-old Sheila Smith lives in an **assisted living facility** in Ohio. She says, "I might be getting old, but I'm very big on **self-improvement**.

That's why I've begun to study Spanish."

Annie Wilson, a dedicated home care attendant, got a big surprise when the elderly widow she cared for passed away. Still mourning her friend's death, Annie learned that the friend had left her a large sum of money in her will.

Looking for a **nurturing** caregiver? Call Joanne at 796-8000.

_____ **1.** go in for	**a.** beautiful, attractive
_____ **2.** bold	**b.** a place where seniors sometimes live, similar to a nursing home
_____ **3.** bitterness	**c.** showy, loud, colorful
_____ **4.** solidarity	**d.** outfit (clothing)
_____ **5.** ensemble	**e.** local group of an organization
_____ **6.** chapter	**f.** resentment, anger
_____ **7.** gorgeous	**g.** boast, show off
_____ **8.** flamboyant	**h.** brave, courageous
_____ **9.** brag	**i.** support; agreement
_____ **10.** assisted living facility	**j.** want to, do something with pleasure
_____ **11.** self-improvement	**k.** offering kind, supportive care
_____ **12.** nurturing	**l.** working hard to become better

②FOCUS ON LISTENING

Ⓐ LISTENING ONE: The Red Hat Society

CD 2 ③ *In this radio report, you will hear about an international organization of seniors. Listen to the introduction. Then answer the questions.*

1. The Red Hat Society is . . .

   _____

   _____

   _____

2. Why might women want to join an organization like this? Make some predictions.

   _____

   _____

   _____

◖ LISTEN FOR MAIN IDEAS

CD 2
4 *Listen to the report and answer the questions.*

1. How did the Red Hat Society start? What is its purpose?

   _____

   _____

2. How do the participants feel about the Red Hat Society?

   _____

   _____

3. What do the Red Hatters' clothes symbolize?

   _____

   _____

◖ LISTEN FOR DETAILS

CD 2
5 *Listen to the report again. Circle the best answer to complete each statement.*

1. The Red Hatters are riding on a _____.
   a. wagon
   b. bus
   c. cart

2. Red Hatter Society members wear _____ clothes.
   a. orange
   b. purple
   c. red

3. The women are throwing _____ to the children.
   a. pennies
   b. candy
   c. flowers

4. The Red Hat Society takes its name from a poem written in _____.
   a. 1906
   b. 1916
   c. 1961

5. When women this age were younger, they usually _____.
   a. worked hard to establish their careers
   b. joined clubs with other women
   c. dedicated their lives to their children

6. There are now over _____ chapters of the Red Hat Society.

    a. 35

    b. 350

    c. 3500

7. Red Hatters believe in _____.

    a. solidarity

    b. volunteering

    c. political activity

8. The women do NOT report feeling _____.

    a. anger

    b. jealousy

    c. fear

◖ MAKE INFERENCES

*Listen to excerpts from the report. Choose one or more adjectives from the box that describe the speaker's tone of voice and write them on the line. Then circle whether the person would agree (**A**) or disagree (**D**) with the statement. Explain your choices to a partner.*

concerned	humorous	playful	thoughtful
emphatic	informative	serious	worried

CD 2 ⑥ Excerpt One

    1. Tone of voice: _____

    2. "I feel embarrassed wearing colorful clothes."   A   D

CD 2 ⑦ Excerpt Two

    1. Tone of voice: _____

    2. "You can't generalize about seniors. They all feel   A   D
differently about aging."

CD 2 ⑧ Excerpt Three

    1. Tone of voice: _____

    2. "I regret that I spent so much time with my family."   A   D

CD 2 ⑨ Excerpt Four

    1. Tone of voice: _____

    2. "I feel more comfortable in a group of similar people."   A   D

Work in a small group. Discuss the questions.

1. What do you think of the Red Hat Society? Would your mother or grandmother join it?

2. Are elderly people invisible where you live? Give examples to explain your answer.

3. Look at the cartoon below. What attitudes is it showing? Do you agree or disagree with them? Do you think men and women age in a similar way?

Pickles

4. Make a graph showing how you believe people's behavior changes as they grow older. For each of the six items on the list, draw a line showing the strength of the item at each of the ages shown. Label the lines 1–6. Compare your graph with that of a partner and discuss the similarities and differences. Line 1 is drawn as an example; draw another line if you have a different opinion.

1 Competition with your peers

2 Getting together with your peers (socially)

3 Having a positive self-image

4 Joining clubs

5 Putting your family ahead of your own interests

6 Wearing flamboyant clothes

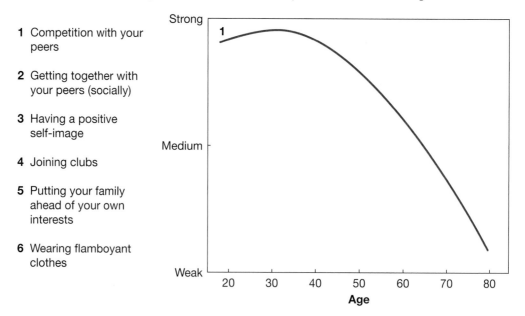

Some young people are eager to learn from the elderly, especially their relatives. In this radio interview, a young woman looks for lessons in the very long life of her grandmother.

1 CD 2 🔟 *Listen to the interview and circle the best answer to complete each sentence.*

1. Ms. Gibson was born in _____.
   a. Mississippi
   b. California
   c. Alabama

2. Susie Potts Gibson had _____ secrets to longevity.
   a. two
   b. three
   c. five

3. She drank a lot of _____ juice.
   a. pickle
   b. orange
   c. carrot

4. She soaked her feet in _____.
   a. hot water
   b. pickle juice
   c. vinegar

5. She rarely _____.
   a. took medicine
   b. exercised
   c. left her house

6. When she was 106, Susie Potts Gibson _____.
   a. moved into an assisted living facility
   b. began to play the piano
   c. bought a cell phone

7. According to the interview, Ms. Gibson was _____.
   a. wise, caring, and smart
   b. healthy, stubborn, and independent
   c. funny, loving, and talented

2 *Work in a small group. Discuss the questions.*

This report raises the question of where elderly people should live; for example, on their own, in an assisted living facility, or with family members.

• How are most elderly people cared for in your country or community?

• Where do you think you would like to live when you are a senior citizen?

INTEGRATE LISTENINGS ONE AND TWO

Views of older people vary a great deal. How are they seen? How do they see themselves? Compare the Red Hatters and Susie Potts Gibson. Fill in the chart with information from the two listenings.

◀ STEP 1: Organize

	RED HATTERS	SUSIE POTTS GIBSON
Age	• 50 years old and older	• lived to be . . .
In the eyes of other people		
In their own eyes		
Examples of their behavior		

◀ STEP 2: Synthesize

Work with a partner and perform a role play. One person plays Susie Potts Gibson, who loves her independence. Another person plays a member of the Red Hat Society, who believes that socializing in a group is important for older people. The Hatter tries to persuade Susie to join. Use as much information from the chart as you can.

③ FOCUS ON SPEAKING

Ⓐ VOCABULARY

◀ REVIEW

Read the calls made to the Elderly Hotline radio program on the next page. Complete the statements with the correct word.

Caller 1

Hi . . . uh . . . my name's Yukiko, and I'm from Japan. I'm _____*anxious*_____ about my mother.
1.

You know, my father died last year, and my mom's been _____ his death for
2.
several months. Even though there is a strong sense of family in my country, women of her _____ depended on their husbands
3.
so much. I've been trying to get her to go out sometimes to a local seniors' club. But she says she doesn't _____ that kind of
4.
thing. I've read that _____
5.
improves if a person is happy. What do you think I should do?

Caller 2

Hello, can you hear me? This is Chin here, from China. Well, I'm calling about my father. He's a(n) _____ man, you know, and I
6.
think he should move to an assisted living _____. I tried to talk about this to
7.
him, but he didn't want to hear it. I think he feels _____ about the idea. You
8.
know, his _____ is pretty
9.
independent. But I just think he'd be safer if he lived with some kind of _____. But
10.
I live too far away, and I can't _____ him myself.
11.

1. (anxious)   ~~jealous~~

2. nurturing   mourning

3. generation   chapter

4. go in for   brag about

5. life expectancy   solidarity

6. elderly   senior

7. hotspot   facility

8. bold   bitter

9. generation   population

10. attendant   citizen

11. get together with   take care of

1 *Work with a partner. Read a doctor's advice to Yukiko, the first caller. Fill in the blanks with a word or expression from the list.*

bunch of	keep an eye on	sit on the sidelines
face (verb)	pass away	the ripe old age of
it's a different story	physician	widow

Hi, Yukiko. Thanks for calling. I'm Dr. Bailey, a visiting _____. I can
                                                                                                1.

see that you're facing a difficult situation here, because it's hard to

_____ doing nothing while your mother is obviously so lonely. This
              2.

is a common situation that people _____ when their spouses
                                                                  3.

_____, so I do sympathize with you. But listen: Try to get her out of
              4.

the house. I mean, it's no secret that if you are with a _____ friends,
                                                                                                   5.

you usually enjoy yourself. A senior's club would provide her with some company.

Actually, you know—my mother's also a _____, who's reached
                                                                          6.

_____ eighty-five, and she has so much fun with people her own age.
              7.

When she's with my husband and me, _____. She tends to act much
                                                                        8.

more quietly. Of course, you'll need to _____ your mother for quite
                                                                    9.

some time. It's good to have friends, but there's nothing like having family around!

Anyway, thanks for calling!

2 *Work with a partner to role play the radio call-in show. Student A, read the phone call from Yukiko in A on page 93. Student B, read the response from Dr. Bailey above. Then discuss possible responses to Chin's phone call. Then take turns reading Chin's phone call on page 93 and giving a response from Dr. Bailey.*

1 Work in groups of three to role play a radio show. Each student should think of one problem faced by a senior citizen or the relative of a senior citizen. Think about problems with health, transportation, money, independence, living arrangements, or use your own ideas.

2 Take turns calling the radio show to ask for advice. The other two students role play people giving advice. You can give the same advice or different opinions.

CALLER: Hello, I'm Marie from Montréal.
HOST 1: Hi, Marie. What's your senior's problem?
CALLER: Well, I'm anxious about her health.
HOST 2: Can you give us an example?

Use the vocabulary items from Review and Expand. Check (✓) each word or expression you use. The first person to use 15 vocabulary items "wins"!

anxious	elderly	it's a different story	population
attendant	face (verb)	jealous	senior
bitter	facility	keep an eye on	sit on the sidelines
bold	flamboyant	life expectancy	solidarity
brag about	generation	mourning	take care of
bunch of	get together with	nurturing	the ripe old age of
chapter	go in for	pass away	widow
citizen	hotspot	physician	

B GRAMMAR: Tag Questions

1 CD2 Listen to a conversation about the Red Hat Society. Pay attention to the intonation of the bold words. Then read the conversation aloud with a partner. Try to use the same intonation.

A: You heard that story about the Red Hat Society, **didn't you**?
B: Yes, that sounds like an amazing group, **doesn't it**?

TAG QUESTIONS

In spoken English, people commonly end sentences with **tag questions**.
There are two types of tag questions:
- **question type**
- **comment type**

Question Type	Examples
• Asks for information or seeks to confirm information the questioner is not sure about • Uses rising intonation	**A:** The Red Hatters don't do any specific activities, **do they**? **B:** No, not really. Their main purpose is solidarity. **A:** My appointment for the volunteer interview is at 6:00 P.M., **isn't it**? **B:** Yes, that's right.
Comment Type	Examples
• Makes a comment • Is used when the questioner assumes the listener agrees • Uses falling intonation	**A:** The Red Hat Society is an interesting organization, **isn't it**? **B:** Yes, it is. **A:** Susie didn't live with her family, **did she**? **B:** No, she didn't.

Tag questions have two parts: a **statement** and the **tag**, an added question.

- If the verb in the statement is affirmative, the tag is negative:

  *The Red Hat Society **is** an American organization, **isn't** it?*

- If the verb in the statement is negative, the tag is affirmative:

  *Susie Potts Gibson **didn't** live alone, **did** she?*

- Tags always use a form of **be**; or the auxiliary verbs **do**, **have**, or **will**; or a modal verb such as **can**, **could**, **should**, or **would**. Like a verb, the tag must agree with the subject.

  You're late for the meeting, isn't you? **aren't** you?

Answering Tag Questions	Examples
Answer tag questions the same way you answer *yes* / *no* questions. You can agree with a tag question (comment type), or you can answer a tag question (question type) by giving the correct information.	**A:** The poem made a big impact, didn't it? (comment type) **B: Yes, it certainly did.** **A:** The Red Hat Society doesn't include men, does it? (question type) **B: No, it doesn't. It's an organization just for women.** **A:** The Red Hat Society includes men, doesn't it? (question type) **B: Actually, it's an organization just for women.**

2 *Work with a partner.*

Step 1: Complete the conversation with the appropriate tags.

A: You've heard about the Red Hat Society, ___haven't you___ ?
1.

B: Yes, I have. It's an amazing story, _____?
2.

A: They don't have organizations like that in other countries, _____?
3.

B: Of course they do. You've heard about the International Federation of Women,

_____?
4.

A: No, what is it?

B: They promote lifelong education for women. They also try to create positive change and peace in the world. It's an international network of women graduates from all cultures. That's a great idea, _____?
5.

A: Yeah, it sounds very inspiring. They don't have any chapters in Latin America,

_____?
6.

B: Yeah, I think they have a lot of groups throughout Latin America, as well as in Asia and Europe. Why do you ask?

A: Well, because my family's from Latin America. You knew that,

_____?
7.

 Step 2: Listen to the conversation and mark each tag question with a rising or falling tone. Then take turns reading the conversation using correct intonation.

3 *Practice asking and answering tag questions.*

Step 1: Read the statements about the Red Hat Society and Susie Potts Gibson below. Work alone and circle the correct words to complete the sentences. Don't check your answers yet!

1. The Red Hat Society members (wear / don't wear) red dresses.

2. The Red Hat Society (has operated / hasn't operated) for about a century.

3. Men (can / can't) join the Red Hat Society.

4. Red Hatters (feel / don't feel) very bitter about their lives.

5. The Red Hat Society (has / doesn't have) only members age 50 or over.

6. Susie Potts Gibson (died / didn't die) at the age of 106.

7. She (was / wasn't) born in Los Angeles.

8. She (believed / didn't believe) in the power of garlic.

9. The interviewer (said / didn't say) what Susie died of.

10. Her granddaughter (was / wasn't) worried about Susie living on her own.

Step 2: Work with a partner. Take turns asking tag questions to check the information in Step 1. If you are sure your statement is correct, use falling intonation. If you are not sure, use rising intonation. When you are finished, if you are still not sure about the answers, check back through this unit to find the correct information.

Example

A: The Red Hat Society members wear red dresses, don't they? (rising intonation)
B: Actually, no, they don't. They wear purple dresses (or: They wear red hats).

OR

A: The Red Hat Society members don't wear red dresses, do they? (falling intonation)
B: No, they don't. They wear purple dresses (or: They wear red hats).

C **SPEAKING**

◀ PRONUNCIATION: Recognizing Word Blends with *You*

CD 2 Native speakers often blend words together when they speak. Listen to the bold
-13- words in the conversation.

A: **Who did you** go to the movies with?
B: My 80-year-old grandmother. **You know**, she's **a lot of** fun.

RECOGNIZING WORD BLENDS WITH *YOU*	
The pronoun *you* often has a short, reduced sound in informal speaking situations.	See **yə** later. (See you later.) I'll call **yə**. (I'll call you.)
When *you* follows common words that end in a /t/ or /d/ sound, for example, words like *what* or *did*, there is often a blend of that word and *you*.	**Didjə** see the parade? (Did you see the parade?) You'll come with me, **wontchə**? (You'll come with me, won't you?)

It is not necessary for you to blend words together when you speak. However, using blends when you speak will make it easier for you to recognize them when you hear them, and native speakers use them often.

1 CD 2 *Listen to the conversation and notice how the bold words sound. Then practice the*
🄺 *conversation with a partner. Blend the bold words.*

A: **What did you** do last night?
B: Nothing special. My roommate and I rented a movie. **How about you**?
A: We went to the parade. I called to see **if you** wanted to come, **but your** cell phone was off.
B: Yeah, I turned it off during the movie. How was the parade? **Did you** see anything interesting?
A: Yeah. There were a **bunch of** older women wearing some pretty colorful clothes.
B: Oh—the Red Hat Society. You've heard of them, **haven't you**?
A: No. **But you** know, I heard people at the parade talking about the red hats.
B: It's an organization of women who led pretty conservative lives when they were young. The parade **gives them** a chance to be bold and dress in bright colors.

2 CD 2 *Listen to the sentences in Column 1 and repeat them. Then listen again. Complete*
🄺 *the questions in Column 1 with phrases from Column 2.*

Column 1

1. ____Why did you____ go there?
2. _____ see at the parade?
3. You can come, _____?
4. They won't _____ in without an ID card.
5. _____ get there?
6. _____ live?
7. You can't come, _____?
8. _____ go after class?
9. _____ think about that?

Column 2

a. how do you
b. can you
~~**c.**~~ why did you
d. where did you
e. can't you
f. where do you
g. let you
h. what do you
i. what did you

Longevity: Refusing to Be Invisible   **99**

1 *Work with a partner. Read the conversation between two college students. Underline the suggestions that A makes.*

A: Would you like to come to the movies tomorrow?

B: I would love to, but I can't. I promised to visit my grandmother.

A: I see. Why don't we ask her if she would like to join us? She'd probably love to come.

B: Probably not. She can't walk very well.

A: Well, how about taking a cab to the theater?

B: That's a good idea. I'll ask.

MAKING SUGGESTIONS

Why don't you ... Why doesn't he ... don't we ... (+ base form)
You / he / we could ... (+ base form)
How about ... (+ -ing)
You / she / we could consider (+ -ing)
What about ... (+ -ing)

---

2 *Read the suggestions. Cross out the one that is grammatically incorrect.*

1. **a.** You could take some aspirin.

    b. You could to take some aspirin.

2. **a.** What about to go to the doctor?

    b. What about going to the doctor?

3. **a.** He could consider to do more exercise.

    b. He could consider doing more exercise.

4. **a.** How about come to visit me next week?

    b. How about coming to visit me next week?

3 *Work with a partner. Take turns telling your partner about the situations. Your partner will make suggestions about what to do.*

1. My father is retired and is less active than he used to be. Now he's putting on too much weight.

2. My neighbor is in his 70s, and I've noticed he's not driving as well as he used to.

3. I'd like to spend more time with my grandfather. I'm not sure what we could do together.

4. A new chapter of the Red Hat Society is opening in my city. I want to encourage my grandmother to go.

5. My mother is considering plastic surgery because she wants to look younger than she is.

6. The woman who lives next door is really deaf. She can't hear a single thing people say to her.

◖ PRODUCTION: A FAMILY MEETING

In this activity, you will **role play a family meeting about how to best take care of a family member**. Students will take the roles of different family members with different points of view. Try to use the vocabulary, grammar, pronunciation, and language for making suggestions you learned in the unit.*

Step 1: Work in groups of three. Consider this situation: You are concerned about George, your 80-year-old relative whose wife died six years ago. George is independent and stubborn and likes to live alone. However, his physical and mental health is declining, and you are worried about his future. Choose one of the roles below, for George's daughter Lisa, Lisa's husband Ray, or George's son Josh, and study the information. Think about what you would like to recommend for George and how you will try to convince other family members that your ideas are good.

LISA (George's daughter)	RAY (Lisa's husband; George's son-in-law)	JOSH (George's son)
• Lives with Ray and their two children ages two and four; doesn't work	• Lives with Lisa and their two children ages two and four; works full-time	• Lives alone in a large apartment with an extra bedroom; works full-time and travels a lot
• Would like George to live with her family	• Believes their house is too small to accommodate another person	• Is worried about his father's health and believes he needs professional care
• Wants to see her father frequently and make sure he is getting good care	• Is worried his wife will not be able to take care of an elderly parent, the house, and their children	• Thinks his sister is good at taking care of people
• Wants her children to get to know their grandfather	• Is worried about having enough money to help Lisa's father	

*For Alternative Speaking Topics, see page 102.

Step 2: Now role play a meeting among Lisa, Ray, and Josh. Discuss each of these options for George, and evaluate their advantages and disadvantages. Then choose one option or think of your own idea.

- George could continue to live alone.
- He could live in his own house, but with a nurse either living in with him or visiting frequently.
- He could live with Josh.
- He could live with Lisa and Ray.
- He could move to an assisted living facility.

Step 3: Present your decision to the class. Discuss how this situation might be handled by your family.

ALTERNATIVE SPEAKING TOPICS

1 *Work in a small group. Discuss the questions.*

1. In your opinion, what can people do to help them live long, healthy lives? How many of those things are you doing now? Does where you live make a difference to how long you will live? Why or why not?

2. As the baby boom generation gets older, the world's elderly population will continue to grow. What problems could this cause? Can you suggest solutions to any of those problems?

3. Do you think that countries should try to increase the number of young people?

2 *Work in a small group. Do you agree or disagree with the statements? Explain your ideas.*

- Older people should behave in a quiet way.
- People of all ages want solidarity with their peers.
- When you are young, you put your family's needs ahead of your own.
- Older people need their independence, just like younger people.
- The keys to youth are good food and good company.
- People often become stubborn when they get older.

RESEARCH TOPICS, see page 220.

UNIT 6

Giving to Others:
Why Do We Do It?

"I contributed a lot to charity when I thought I was going to die."

1 FOCUS ON THE TOPIC

A PREDICT

Look at the cartoon and the title of the unit. Then discuss the questions with a partner or small group.

1. A charity is an organization that helps people who need it—often people who are poor or ill. Where do you think charities get their money from? What kind of people give money to charities? Why do they give?

2. Look at the cartoon. What does it mean? Why did the man give money to charity when he thought he was going to die?

3. What are some things that wealthy people do with money they don't plan to spend while they are alive? What do you think wealthy people should do with their money?

1 *Work with a partner. Philanthropy and charity both refer to the practice of giving money or goods, or volunteering services to individuals or groups. People and organizations may choose to give to others who need help, or to support particular social programs and political ideas. Study the word forms below and take turns reading them aloud.*

A PERSON	AN ORGANIZATION	AN ADJECTIVE	A VERB
a **philanthropist** (– –) a **volunteer** a **donor**	a **philanthropy** a **charity** (– –) (– –)	a **philanthropic** organization a **charitable** organization a **volunteer** job a **donated** car	(– –) (– –) to **volunteer** to **donate**

2 *Work in a small group. Look at the graphs. Discuss the questions.*

- What do the graphs show? What is the trend in donations and volunteering? In what year(s) was the biggest change?
- What could be some reasons behind this trend?
- Do you think there is a similar trend in your culture? Why or why not?
- Have you ever volunteered your time to help other people (for example, at school or community organization)? If you have, describe what you did and how you felt about it. Have you ever donated money? If so, to whom, and why?

Graph A: Billions of Dollars Contributed by Individuals to Charities

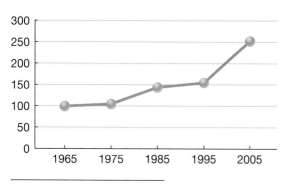

Source: Giving USA Foundation

Graph B: Percentage of the Population Who Volunteer

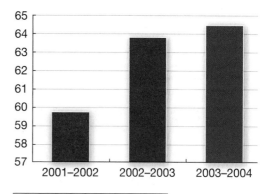

Source: Bureau of Labor Statistics, U.S. Department of Labor

1 CD 2 16 *Read and listen to the information in the news magazine feature. Pay special attention to the words in bold.*

People in the News:
Our featured "Special People" this year have done special things in a big way.

Karen Pittelman

Karen Pittelman inherited a fortune when she was 21. She is one of a growing number of young, wealthy Americans who believe in some sort of social **(1) cause**. They are challenging each other to act according to their **(2) moral** values.

Newly wealthy young people sometimes feel ashamed or confused, trying to hide the fact that they are different because they are wealthy. If they give, they may do so **(3) anonymously**. "When I was younger, I wanted to wash my hands of all the money, pretend I had never even known it existed," says Pittelman. Now she's **(4) motivated** to guide other young people to use their money to benefit others.

Warren Buffett

As one of the wealthiest men in the world, Warren Buffett made the largest philanthropic **(5) donation** in history. He decided to **(6) contribute** most of his fortune to the Bill and Melinda Gates Foundation. The magnitude of his gift, $37 billion, has doubled the Gates Foundation's resources to $60 billion.

Although Buffett's children will **(7) inherit** some of his money when he dies, Buffett doesn't believe in leaving too much money to one's children.

Buffett says he made his money because other people trusted him to invest money for them. He has known Bill and Melinda Gates for many years, watching them do their philanthropic work with true **(8) passion**. Now, he says, it's his turn to trust others. He believes Bill and Melinda Gates are the best people to help decide how to give his own money to good causes.

Bill and Melinda Gates

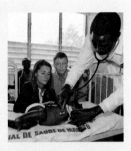

Bill Gates, founder of Microsoft and the wealthiest man in the world for years, now feels it's **(9) mandatory** to spend his wealth to help others. He and his wife, Melinda Gates, believe every life has equal value. In 2000, they created the Bill & Melinda Gates Foundation to improve living conditions for the poor around the world. Thanks to the **(10) generosity** of Warren Buffett, the resources of the Gates's charitable foundation have grown tremendously. This powerful foundation invests in the research and treatment of killer diseases around the world and gives money to many other causes.

Bono

Bono, the Irish lead singer and organizer for the band U2, has organized major concerts that benefit charities and philanthropic organizations. As a **(11) fundraiser** for various organizations, he has helped in the areas of children's causes, disaster relief, AIDS treatment and other health issues, human rights, hunger, women's issues, world peace, and poverty. Bono's fame allows him to easily meet with and make **(12) appeals** to top entertainment and political leaders, including the German chancellor, the U.S. president, and U.S. senators. He has won numerous awards for his philanthropic work, including *Time* magazine's Person-of-the-Year. As far as doing good things in the world, Bono says he's "tired of dreaming" and more concerned with "doing."

2 *Work with a partner. Match the words on the left with the definitions on the right.*

_____ 1. cause

_____ 2. moral

_____ 3. anonymously

_____ 4. motivated

_____ 5. donation

_____ 6. contribute

_____ 7. inherit

_____ 8. passion

_____ 9. mandatory

_____ 10. generosity

_____ 11. fundraiser

_____ 12. appeals

a. a gift

b. to receive something from someone who has died

c. related to principles of what is right and wrong

d. doing something without letting anyone know your name

e. a strongly felt emotion

f. very eager to do or achieve something

g. something that is required or that must be done

h. a principle or aim that a group of people support or fight for

i. an attitude or behavior of giving things to others, or of helping others

j. requests, often for money or help

k. a person or event whose purpose is to collect money for charity

l. to give money, help, or ideas

2 FOCUS ON LISTENING

A LISTENING ONE: Why We Give

Why do people donate money and time? The reasons are as varied as the people. You will hear a radio interview by Alex Goodwin, of the program *The Infinite Mind*. He speaks with Stacy Palmer, editor of the *Chronicle of Philanthropy*, a highly regarded publication for people interested in the world of philanthropy.

CD 2
17 *Listen to the introduction.*

Who wants to know why people donate time and money? Check (✓) the answer.

❑ Other rich people

❑ People who raise money for charities

❑ University researchers and sociologists

◖ LISTEN FOR MAIN IDEAS

CD 2
18 *Read the motivations for giving. Then listen to the interview and number the motivations in the order in which they are mentioned.*

_____ tax benefits

_____ required by school

_____ prevent something bad from happening

__1__ passion for the cause

_____ family tradition

_____ desire to repay someone for something

_____ see the direct effects of what they're doing

◖ LISTEN FOR DETAILS

CD 2
19 *Listen to the interview again. As you listen, circle the letter of the answer that best completes each statement.*

1. About _____ percent of people give money.
   a. 65   **b.** 75   **c.** 85

2. When a cause has an enemy or a threat, people tend to _____.
   a. give more   **b.** give the same as usual   **c.** give less

3. Most people seem to feel _____ about giving money than about giving time.
   a. better   **b.** worse   **c.** the same

4. _____ percent of the population say they have volunteered at some point.
   a. 50   **b.** 70   **c.** 80

(continued on next page)

5. Though the facts are not clear, most economists feel that less wealthy people give _____ wealthy people.

    a. proportionately more than
    b. about the same amount as
    c. considerably less than

6. One problem with the information on philanthropy is getting people to be _____ about how much they give.

    a. modest
    b. honest
    c. anonymous

7. Givers are often different from non-givers because they want to _____ society.

    a. give back to
    b. leave
    c. become known in

8. Many teachers and parents feel that giving to others _____.

    a. cannot be taught
    b. is hard for young children to understand
    c. stays with children all their lives

9. In some high schools, community service is _____.

    a. necessary to graduate
    b. carried out in academic classes
    c. paid like a job

◀ MAKE INFERENCES

*Listen to the excerpts again. Pay attention to the speakers' tone of voice. Then circle whether the statements are true (**T**) or false (**F**).*

CD 2
20 Excerpt One

The interviewer believes that the rich and the poor give proportionately the same amount of money.   T   F

CD 2
21 Excerpt Two

Ms. Palmer believes the examples she gave should be counted as charitable giving.   T   F

CD 2
22 Excerpt Three

Ms. Palmer believes that some people say they gave more money to charity than they really did.   T   F

CD 2
23 Excerpt Four

Ms. Palmer believes that families are better than schools at teaching children to give to charity.   T   F

Work in a small group. Take turns reading aloud the comments of donors and volunteers. Then discuss the questions.

A.
I'm 23. I give money to an international environmental organization. I really think we all have to play a part in solving the world's problems and not just think about our own city or country.

B.
I'm a high school senior. In order to graduate, we have to do 40 hours of mandatory community service, things like picking up trash on the streets, teaching reading to younger students after school, or helping disabled people. I don't think that's fair. Community service has nothing to do with school.

C.
I'm a businessman in my 40s. I think everyone should donate a small portion of their income to a good cause. My donations usually go to international relief efforts after a flood, earthquake, or hurricane.

D.
I have two young children. I'd like to help out in my community, but I really don't have time. I have to take care of myself and my own family before I can think about helping others.

E.
I'm in my 50's. I volunteer quite a lot. I serve meals in a homeless shelter, read stories to young children at the library, and once a month I help pick up trash in local parks. I think it's important to contribute to the community you live in.

- Do you understand these people's points of view? Do you share their views?
- Which person is most like you? Which person is least like you?

Some people who donate money and want to be publicly noticed and thanked; others, such as the Mystery Donor, prefer to donate quietly and anonymously. This radio report explores her reasons for how and why she gives.

1   *CD 2* *Listen to the interviews and circle the correct answer to complete each statement.*

1. The Mystery Donor started giving to charity after her _____ died.
   a. husband
   b. mother
   c. daughter

2. She donates _____ of her income every year.
   a. 10 percent
   b. 25 percent
   c. 50 percent

3. She gives anonymously because she _____.
   a. is worried people will think she didn't give enough
   b. is embarrassed about how much money she has
   c. doesn't want to change her relationships with the receivers

4. One motivation she has for giving to single mothers is that she _____.
   a. was the child of a single mother
   b. was a poor single mother herself for a while
   c. is most interested in children's causes

5. Philanthropists like the Mystery Donor _____ large foundations.
   a. push their political beliefs on
   b. give most of their donations to
   c. are more flexible and responsive givers than

6. The Mystery Donor _____ if the donation was received.
   a. calls to see
   b. doesn't ask
   c. is always told

2 *Work in a small group. Discuss the questions.*

1. Both listenings refer to causes that people feel strongly about. Which of the following causes do you think is most important?
   - Education
   - The environment
   - Natural disasters
   - Health care
   - Homelessness
   - Other (your own idea): _____

2. If you had time or money to donate, what would you do for this cause? Would you want to remain anonymous?

◀ STEP 1: Organize

Work with a partner or a small group. Complete the chart with information from Listening One, describing general information about who gives money and why, and Listening Two, which describes the specific case of one philanthropist.

	WHY WE GIVE	THE MYSTERY DONOR
1. Who volunteers or donates money?	• ½ of all Americans volunteer • 75% . . .	• A woman called the "Mystery Donor" from Seattle
2. Why do people give?		
3. What background factors cause people to give?		
4. Who receives the money or time?		
5. How does the giver feel?		
6. Does the donor prefer to be public or anonymous?		

STEP 2: Synthesize

Role play an interview between a reporter from the Chronicle of Philanthropy *and the Mystery Donor. The reporter interviews the Mystery Donor about each question in the chart, giving information about typical volunteers and donors. The Mystery Donor says whether she is similar or different. Then switch roles.*

USEFUL REPORTER PHRASES	USEFUL MYSTERY DONOR PHRASES
The typical / average American . . . Most / some people . . . . . . How about you? . . . Do you feel the same way? . . . Do you do the same thing?	Yes, I do, too. I feel the same way. Well, I feel differently. Not really. I . . . instead.

Example

REPORTER: The typical American donates money to charity. How about you?
MYSTERY DONOR: Yes, I do, too. I donate hundreds of thousands of dollars every year.
R: Some Americans volunteer their time. Do you do the same thing?
MD: Well, no. I prefer to be anonymous, so I contribute money instead.

3 FOCUS ON SPEAKING

A VOCABULARY

◖ REVIEW

Complete the chart with the different forms of the words. Then compare your answers with a partner's.

NOUN	VERB	ADJECTIVE
anonymity	X	
	X	catastrophic
charity	X	
		contributed
donation, donor		
generosity	X	
inheritance		
	motivate	
	moralize	
passion	X	
philanthropy, philanthropist	X	
	X	wealthy

1 *Below is a speech by the president of the board of directors of a philanthropic organization, the Tsunami Relief Fund. He's speaking to an audience of wealthy business people and retired executives.*

*Complete the sentences with a **different** form of words from the box. Then with a partner, take turns practicing the speech.*

anonymous	charity	generosity	moral	passionate
catastrophe	contribute	inheritance	motivation	wealthy

Tsunami Relief Fund
Helping others in times of crisis

Good evening. I'm Ron Prosperi. The film clips you have just seen of tsunami disasters speak for themselves. We all know that people around the world suffer from such _____ events every year.
1.
I'm not here to _____; I'm here to tell you that my
2.
involvement with the Tsunami Relief Fund has enriched my own life.

You and I are among the fortunate. We have the _____
3.
to help others, because we worked hard or because we

_____ it from our parents. Even a small donation will help
4.
so many others.

Our staff are working people like you, using their time and their skills to build homes, feed the hungry, treat the sick. Our volunteers are _____ to help these victims by rebuilding homes.
5.
They work with _____ and commitment, far from their
6.
families, so that other families have a second chance. But they can't do it without your help.

Listen, I'll be brief: _____ work is life-changing.
7.

Please make a major _____ tonight. Write a
8.

_____ check. Help with our next volunteer project. Your
9.

life will be richer for it. You can even give _____ if you
10.

prefer. Either way, I know you won't regret it.

I thank you for your important support.

2 *Now read the memo written by one of the audience members who is a friend of the speaker. Complete the memo with words from the box.*

appeal	cause	fundraiser	under the radar
benefactors	freelance	rewarding	

Subject: Great speech!
From: Bob Beddes
Date: December 30, 2008
To: Ron Prosperi

Hey,

Nice job! That was a great (**1.**) _____ you made at the (**2.**) _____ last night. I hope you found some wealthy (**3.**) _____ in the audience! Seriously, though, you did a great job, Ron. I can understand why you're so passionate about that (**4.**) _____. It must be very (**5.**) _____ to work for an organization like that.

By the way, last week I ran into Sam Ludlum from our college days. He's a big photographer in D.C. now. Doesn't work for any particular magazine, you know, he's (**6.**) _____. Anyway, apparently he inherited some money when his uncle died last year, and now he wants to volunteer for a charity like yours. He's a little embarrassed by his new wealth, but I told him he could easily fly (**7.**) _____ by remaining anonymous. I gave him your email address—I hope that's OK.

That's it for now.
See you at the game Friday,
Bob

CREATE

Work with a partner or a small group. Imagine you have $1 million to give to charity. Read the website information about different organizations and discuss each one. Decide which ones you would contribute to and how much you would give. You can give all of the money to one organization or divide it among the organizations. Each time you use a vocabulary word from Review or Expand, check it off (✓) in the box. Then share with the class how you divided the money and why.

anonymity	cause	freelance	morality	rewarding
appeal	charity	fundraiser	motivation	under the radar
benefactor	contribution	generosity	passion	wealth
catastrophe	donation	inheritance		

http://yourfavoritecharity.com

The Nature Conservancy

The mission of The Nature Conservancy is to preserve the plants, animals and natural environment of life on Earth by protecting the lands and waters. The Nature Conservancy works with corporations, traditional communities, and other partners to develop ways for people to live and work without hurting the natural world around them. The Nature Conservancy also raises money to buy fragile land from developers.

The International Committee of the Red Cross

The ICRC is an independent, non-political organization that protects human life. The ICRC does not support or oppose governments, but tries to protect the lives of people who are victims of war and internal violence. It gives medical aid and other assistance. Its main office is in Geneva, Switzerland, but the ICRC has bases in 80 countries and has a staff of more than 12,000.

Habitat for Humanity International

Habitat for Humanity International helps reduce poverty and homelessness throughout the world. Habitat invites people of all backgrounds, races, and religions to build houses together with families who need them. Volunteers give money, materials, or their own work to build simple but good houses side by side with the new owners. The new owners buy the homes at no profit, and Habitat provides them with low-cost loans.

Amnesty International

Amnesty International (AI) is a worldwide movement of people who work toward human rights around the world. AI does not support or oppose any government or political system. It tries to work with governments to protect the basic human rights of all individuals by helping to prevent discrimination and physical and mental abuse.

1 *Work with a partner. Read the paragraph aloud and answer the questions.*

Sting is a popular British musician **who is actively involved with humanitarian and environmental causes**. With the support of his wife and a native leader, Sting established the Rainforest Foundation, an organization **whose goal is to help save the world's rainforests**. Although at first it operated only in Brazil, **the country where it was founded**, the organization now operates in other countries, too. In fact, a frog **that is native to Colombia** has been named after Sting to honor his contributions to the environment.

1. Which nouns do the bold phrases describe?

2. Which word in the bold phrases indicates which noun is being described?

RELATIVE PRONOUNS IN ADJECTIVE CLAUSES

Adjective clauses (also called relative clauses) are used to identify or add information about nouns. Usually, the adjective clause directly follows the noun it refers to. These clauses are introduced by a relative pronoun, such as *who*, *that*, *which*, *whose*, *where*, or *when*.

An **identifying adjective clause**, sometimes called a restrictive clause, gives essential information about the noun it refers to. No commas surround the identifying adjective clause. It is set off in a written sentence by commas.	Sting is the person **who helped establish the Rainforest Foundation**.
A **non-identifying adjective clause**, or non-restrictive clause, gives extra information about the noun it refers to. It is set off in the sentence by commas. Pronunciation note: In speaking, people often pause and lower their tone of voice to say the words in the non-identifying relative clause.	The Rainforest Foundation, **which was founded in 1989**, is working to protect forests around the world.
Who refers to people. It can be the subject or the object of an adjective clause. In spoken English, *who* is usually used instead of the more formal *whom*, even when it is the object of an adjective clause.	Sting is a musician **who** *[subject]* is concerned about the environment. There are many hundreds of young people **who (or whom)** *[object]* he has inspired.
That and *which* refer to places and things. They can be the subject or object of an adjective clause.	The Rainforest Foundation is a group **that / which** he founded to protect the world's natural resources.

(continued on next page)

That cannot be used in a nonidentifying adjective clause (sometimes called a nonrestrictive clause) or after a preposition. You must use **which**.	The foundation, **which** is working with human rights groups, raises money to protect tropical rainforests.
In identifying adjective clauses (or restrictive clauses), English speakers often delete the relative pronoun when it is the object of the verb.	This is an organization **(that)** many young people are interested in.
Whose refers to people's possessions. It can be the subject or object of an adjective clause.	People living in the area are those **whose** lives are most affected.
Where refers to a place; **when** refers to a time. They can be the object of an adjective clause.	Brazil is one of the countries **where** the foundation's efforts have been successful.
	The foundation was started at a time **when** many people were unaware of the environmental problems we face.

2 *Work with a partner. Fill in the blanks with **who, that, which, whose, when,** or **where**. Then take turns reading about the projects aloud.*

The *Hole in the Wall* is a project _____ began several years ago in New Delhi, India. Dr. Sugata
                                       1.

Mitra was a computer scientist _____ had the innovative idea of helping the children in the
                                2.

neighborhood _____ he worked. In the wall outside his office, he installed a computer,
              3.

_____ was connected to the Internet and available for neighborhood children to play with.
4.

Within minutes, children began to touch the computer, a machine _____ many of them had
                                                                  5.

never seen before. Now there are many children, both boys and girls, _____ lives have been
                                                                      6.

touched by Mitra's generosity and _____ have gained a high level of computer literacy.
                                   7.

Orbis International, _____ is the name of an innovative humanitarian organization, operates out
                      8.

of an airplane. The plane is equipped as a flying eye hospital, a kind of hospital and training facility

_____ flies all over the world to deliver medical assistance and training to local doctors.
9.

Bangladesh, China, Ethiopia, India and Vietnam, _____ are the priority nations for the project,
                                                 10.

employ local health professionals _____ receive special training and support from the Orbis
                                   11.

group. The 27.5 million people ________ (12.) have been helped in over 70 nations of the world include both adults and children. The world surgeons ________ (13.) donate their time and the volunteers ________ (14.) form the backbone of the organization share a single goal: to save people's sight worldwide.

CAMFED, ________ (15.) stands for the Campaign for Female Education, was launched in 1993 with the goal of fighting poverty and disease in rural Africa. That was a time ________ (16.) families ________ (17.) could not afford to educate all their children gave priority to boys, but the group's founders knew that women ________ (18.) are educated are more likely to become leaders in their communities by encouraging others to get jobs and raise healthy children. Now, over 500,000 young women ________ (19.) lives were transformed by the campaign are giving back to the organization by making their own contributions. CAMFED, ________ (20.) members include actor Morgan Freeman, has won many international awards to continue its work. The small program ________ (21.) was first developed has now expanded to numerous countries.

3 *Work with a partner. Student A, your instructions are on this page. Student B, your instructions are on page 214.*

Student A

Complete the adjective clauses in the sentences. Read the sentences aloud. Student B must identify the item, time, person, or place you described. Then reverse roles. Listen to Student B's sentences and identify the thing, time, person, or place described.

Example

A: They're people **who** donate time or money to others.
B: Philanthropists?
A: That's right.

1. Name a charity ________________ you've learned about in this chapter. (for example, the Bill & Melinda Gates Foundation, Orbis International, etc.)
2. It was the year ________________ the Bill & Melinda Gates Foundation was established. (2000)

(continued on next page)

3. It's the continent _____ the CAMFED organization began.
(Africa)

4. He's a musician _____ work focuses on saving the world's rainforests.
(Sting)

5. These are some reasons _____ inspire people to help others. (to make a difference, to feel appreciated, etc.)

6. It's a word _____ means "rich."
(wealthy)

C SPEAKING

◀ PRONUNCIATION: Intonation in Lists

When we list items or talk about a series of items, we use a special intonation depending on whether the list is finished (everything has been listed) or unfinished (there are more items in the list that aren't mentioned).

For the items in a finished list, the speaker's voice rises on every item except the last one. The speaker's voice falls on the last item.

The Nature Conservancy works with **corporations**, **communities**, and **non-profit organizations**.

For the items in an unfinished list, the speaker's voice rises on every item, including the last one mentioned.

People who volunteer with the Nature Conservancy include **students**, **local businesspeople**, **nature lovers** . . .

(25) *Listen to the conversation. Then answer the questions.*

JOSÉ:	My neighbor said you could help me find some volunteer work. I'd really like to work with people.
MS. JOHNSON:	Great. We're looking for volunteers at **the Senior Center, the library, the after-school program**.
JOSÉ:	What's available in the after-school program? I like working with kids, but I'm taking classes myself, so my schedule is a little tight.
MS. JOHNSON:	Well, let's see, the teacher of the youngest group needs an assistant on **Monday, Tuesday**, and **Friday**.

1. Ms. Johnson tells José about volunteer positions at the Senior Center, the library and the after-school program. Do you think Ms. Johnson has other volunteer positions available?

2. Does the teacher of the youngest group in the after-school program need help on Wednesday? How do you know?

INTONATION IN LISTS

Lists that are finished (closed lists) Your voice rises on the first items and falls on the last item. Falling intonation tells the listener your list is finished. The word *and* is usually used in closed lists.	Monday, Tuesday, (and) Friday
Lists that are not finished (open lists) Your voice rises on the first items but doesn't fall on the last item. When your voice doesn't fall, you are telling your listener that there are other possibilities. The conjunction *and* is not usually used in closed lists (but can be).	Monday, Tuesday, Friday

1 CD 2 26 *Listen to the sentences. Write **F** in the blank if the speaker has finished the items or ideas in the list. Write **U** in the blank if the list is unfinished. Underline the words or ideas that are being listed.*

1. The World Wildlife Fund works with <u>governments</u>, <u>local communities</u>, <u>non-profits</u>. __U__

2. How can you help? You can help by giving your time, your money, and your ideas. _____

3. Communities where adults vote regularly, parents are active in schools, children play on sports teams, usually have lower levels of crime. _____

4. I need a vacation—I'm tired of waking up early, spending hours on the road, working at night. _____

5. If you volunteer at the senior center, you'll feel good about yourself, meet new people, and learn more English. _____

6. Americans give a lot between Thanksgiving and Christmas: There are food drives, coat drives, toy drives. _____

2 *Work with a partner. Read the sentences in Exercise 1 to your partner. Decide whether you want to read the lists as finished lists or unfinished lists. Use appropriate intonation. Your partner will say "finished" or "unfinished." Then switch roles.*

3 $\overset{C^{D}2}{\textcircled{27}}$ *Listen to the conversation. Underline the words or ideas that are in lists and draw intonation lines over the items in the lists. Then practice the conversation with a classmate.*

A and B are first-year college students who live in the same dormitory. They are discussing the upcoming Thanksgiving Day holiday.

A: Are you having a big Thanksgiving dinner at your house?

B: Actually, every year we spend Thanksgiving at a homeless shelter. We decorate the shelter, help with the cooking, serve the guests, and talk to them. Would you like to come?

A: Yes, I really would. For a long time, I've been thinking about volunteering—at a school, the library, a retirement home. But, you know, I never end up doing anything.

B: Great. We can pick you up here Thursday morning, around 10.

A: Should I bring anything?

B: Just your hands, your energy, and a smile. The shelter supplies everything else.

4 *Work in small groups. Think of three things that ordinary people could do to help your school, your town, or your country. Describe them to members of your group. Speak clearly and use intonation carefully.*

◀ **FUNCTION:** Prioritizing or Ranking Ideas

Work with a partner. Read the conversation between two students who are working on a project together.

A: OK, so let's get started and get this philanthropy research paper finished. **Our top priority** is selecting the right topic, don't you think?

B: Yeah. But **it's also important** to make sure we can get the information we need for the research. Then there's the writing and then the editing . . .

A: Well, I think **our lowest priority** right now is the writing. We can only do that when we have everything else we need first.

When people are discussing more than one task or idea, it helps to prioritize or rank them to indicate the most important and the least important. Here are some useful expressions:

PRIORITIZING OR RANKING IDEAS		
Highest Priority	**Also a Priority**	**Lowest Priority**
Our top priority is . . . First of all, . . . First and foremost, . . . Above all, . . .	But it's also important . . . In addition, . . . Another consideration is . . . Aside from that, . . .	Least important is . . . Of least concern is . . . The lowest priority is . . .

Step 1: Read the ads for volunteer jobs with nonprofit organizations.

WANTED

Part-time worker at neighborhood animal shelter. Help find homes for abandoned animals. Help with feeding, walking, and taking care of animals. Some contact with the public and experience in office work necessary. Volunteers needed at least eight hours per week: daily 8 A.M. to 10 P.M.

POSITION

Volunteer fundraiser for charitable healthcare organization. Responsibilities include helping to find new donors and raise money for yearly budget. Responsible for helping with black-tie fundraising dinner. Handle correspondence and telephone fundraising drive.

VOLUNTEER HELP NEEDED

Hospital worker. Volunteer needed to be a companion to ill patients. Read aloud to patients, take them for walks, offer a shoulder to lean on. Our motto: "A friend when you need one." Call 555-5863 or email us at *www.we-care.org*.

VOLUNTEERS NEEDED

Public radio station needs volunteer telephone representatives for one week during our Phone-a-thon Appeal. Answer calls, encourage donations, and take credit card information for payment. Your time will be spent on a good cause.

Step 2: Work with a partner. Read the personal qualities listed. Discuss which qualities apply to each job, and add other qualities that may apply. Then prioritize the qualities. Use expressions from the Function section and when possible, use adjective clauses.

be able to	finish tasks work long hours get along with people	
be	flexible cheerful clean	assertive patient
have	good listening skills good communication skills good office skills compassion	emotional strength experience (with _____) a sense of humor a stylish appearance

Example

STUDENT A: **First and foremost**, volunteers at the animal shelter must love animals.
STUDENT B: Of course. **But it's also important** for them to have good communication skills, don't you think?
STUDENT A: Yes, you're right. And **aside from that**, I think the animal shelter will want **a person who** has good office skills for the administrative work.

◀ **PRODUCTION: A Public Service Announcement**

> In this activity, you will **create and present a public service announcement, or PSA.** A PSA is a short announcement aired on the radio or television that educates people about an important cause or encourages them to donate money or volunteer time. Try to use the vocabulary, grammar, pronunciation, and language for prioritizing or ranking ideas that you learned in the unit.*

Work with a partner. Follow the steps.

CD 2
28 **Step 1:** Listen to the PSA. Then answer these questions.

- Which organization sponsored the PSA?
- What is the PSA encouraging people to do?
- Do you think the PSA is persuasive? Why or why not?

*For Alternative Speaking Topics, see page 126.

Step 2: Select a not-for-profit organization from the following list, find one of your own on the Internet at www.charitynavigator.org, or use one of the organizations you learned about in this unit.

The Nature Conservancy

The Red Cross

World Wildlife Fund

Doctors Without Borders

NPR (National Public Radio)

Orangutan Foundation International

Habitat for Humanity International

The Union of Concerned Scientists

Amnesty International

Greenpeace

UNICEF

Other: _____

Step 3: Make notes in the chart for your PSA.

Define your audience: Who should be listening to your appeal? College students? Middle income workers? Higher income people? Stay-at-home parents?

Define the method for your announcement: How will your PSA be announced? On a TV station? On a radio station? If so, what kind of radio station? A rock music station? Classical music station? Public radio station? Talk radio station?

Select a time for your PSA to air: Think about when your audience is listening or watching. What is the best time for your PSA to be aired? After school? At rush hour?

Define your request: What do you want people to do? Volunteer? Give money? Call your organization to discuss ways to help?

Audience:	
Method:	
Time to air:	
Request:	

Step 4: Write a one-minute PSA. Explain what the organization does and why people should donate time or money to it. Make your PSA motivating and convincing by explaining to people why they should help.

Step 5: Record or film your PSA and play it in class.

Step 6: Listen to all the PSAs. Then choose one organization to which you wish to donate money or volunteer time. Have the class show by raising their hands which organizations they plan to help.

ALTERNATIVE SPEAKING TOPICS

Work in a small group. Read the three different viewpoints about high school students and volunteering. Then discuss the questions.

STUDENT A: "High schools should require community service in order for students to graduate. It's just as important for students to learn to be good citizens as it is for them to learn math, history, and science. Even students who didn't like the idea at first would probably change their minds after they spent some time volunteering."

STUDENT B: "Service opportunities should be available for students who are interested, but they shouldn't be required. Students should have some choice about what they want to do in high school, but I think it would be great if volunteering could be part of that choice. They could get credit for service the same way they do for art, music, or gym classes."

STUDENT C: "Students should decide whether to volunteer on their own, and not as part of a school program. Requiring students to serve or trying to get them to serve by offering class credit goes against the very spirit of the word 'volunteer.' "

1. Which student's viewpoint is most like your own?

2. For high school students, what are some benefits of volunteering? What are some drawbacks?

3. How many hours a week should students volunteer?

4. Should teenagers be required or encouraged to volunteer when they are not in school? (for example, after school or on weekends, or during vacations)

5. What kinds of organizations would be best suited for teenage volunteers?

RESEARCH TOPICS, see page 221.

What's the Use of Homework?

"I don't have my homework, Miss Flynn—my parents forgot to do it."

1 FOCUS ON THE TOPIC

A PREDICT

Look at the cartoon and the title of the unit. Then discuss the questions with a partner or small group.

1. What is the message of the cartoon? Do you think it is believable?

2. How much help do you think parents should give their children with schoolwork?

3. How much time should a child spend on homework every night in elementary school, in middle school, and in high school?

1 *Work with a partner. Read the descriptions of the assignments. Then do tasks (a) and (b) for each assignment.*

    a. Decide whether the assignment is appropriate for students in elementary school (ages 5–10), middle school (11–13), or high school (14–18). Check (✓) all that apply.

    b. For each level that you checked, write the approximate length of time you think the assignment should take (in minutes, hours, or days).

ASSIGNMENT		LEVEL		TIME REQUIRED
Math Do a page of 10 math problems, writing out the answers in a notebook.		E	❏	
		M	❏	
		H	❏	
English Write an essay about an experience that changed the way you feel about other people.		E	❏	
		M	❏	
		H	❏	
Science Research an endangered species and prepare a report to present in class.		E	❏	
		M	❏	
		H	❏	
Social Studies Make a replica of an important discovery or invention that had a significant impact on your country, such as the Sputnik satellite.		E	❏	
		M	❏	
		H	❏	
History Make a timeline of a sequence of important events; for example, from the arrival of the *Mayflower* in North America to the American war for independence.		E	❏	
		M	❏	
		H	❏	

2 *Explain your answers to other classmates. Discuss any differences in your answer choices.*

C BACKGROUND AND VOCABULARY

1 CD 2
🔵29 *Read and listen to the short lecture on the history of homework in the U.S. Then work in groups of three. Each student chooses a different paragraph and figures out the vocabulary in bold. Then share your answers by first explaining the paragraph in your own words and then explaining the vocabulary.*

A History of Homework in the United States

A In the 19th century, homework was not a daily **(1) ritual** because many students did not even go to high school. In the early 20th century, there were not many **(2) advocates** of homework. Actually, homework was considered illegal in many places. Homework was not seen as a **(3) foundation** for learning. Even in the mid 20th century, there were no national homework standards, so the amount of homework **(4) fluctuated** from school to school.

B In the late 20th century, educators saw that homework had **(5) tangible** benefits, and they linked good homework habits to strong **(6) self-esteem**. Children were expected to be obedient to their parents and to **(7) sacrifice** so that they could make academic progress. Doing substantial amounts of homework was considered a student's **(8) duty**.

C In the early 21st century, teachers began to assign more homework and more **(9) demanding** assignments, and parents began to **(10) monitor** their children's work. Standardized tests became more common, and teachers were held **(11) accountable** for the students' progress. Today, some children have so much homework that they become **(12) distraught** when they can't complete it. Even some parents think that the amount of homework that is expected is over the top.

A
1. ritual: **a.** problem; disturbance **b.** something you do on a regular basis

2. advocates: **a.** teachers; tutors **b.** supporters believers of one side of a controversy

3. foundation: **a.** basis; an idea from which a system develops **b.** building; school

4. fluctuated: **a.** changed from one level to another **b.** increased steadily

(continued on next page)

B

5. tangible: **a.** real; something that can be measured   **b.** uncertain; not proven

6. self-esteem: **a.** motivation   **b.** feeling good about yourself

7. sacrifice: **a.** give up something you want or enjoy   **b.** ask for help; beg

8. duty: **a.** something you must do   **b.** reward

C

9. demanding: **a.** difficult; challenging   **b.** frequent; common

10. monitor: **a.** complete; finish   **b.** carefully check or examine

11. accountable: **a.** praised   **b.** considered responsible

12. distraught: **a.** bored; uninterested   **b.** very upset

2 *Work with the same group. Use the information you learned to make a graph showing the amount of homework assigned to school children in the U.S. where 0 = no homework, 4 to 6 = some homework, and 10 = a lot of homework.*

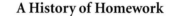

A History of Homework

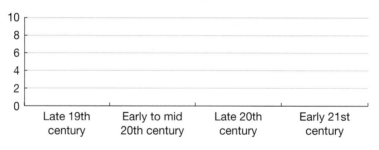

②FOCUS ON LISTENING

A **LISTENING ONE: Effects of Homework on Family Life**

CD 2 *Listen to a radio report on the effects of homework. Listen to the first part and* 🔊30 *discuss the questions with a partner.**

1. According to the report, what are thousands of families doing?

2. How do you think families might feel about this? Predict what you will hear in this report.

---

*Tracks 30–32 include the complete radio report. Listen to Track 30 to answer the introduction questions. Listen to Track 31 for Listen to Main Ideas and Listen for Details (page 131).

◀ LISTEN FOR MAIN IDEAS

CD 2
31 *Listen to the report. Draw a line from the person to his or her idea.*

1. Kaitlyn Oloya, student

2. Ms. Cecilia Bluer, mother

3. Margot Adler, news reporter

4. Joyce Epstein, sociologist

5. Gary Natriello, sociologist

6. Steven Russo, administrator

a. Students spend more time in school than workers spend at their jobs.

b. Students who do homework do better in school than those who do not.

c. Children get really tired doing all their homework and sometimes get little sleep.

d. It's not just children who have to do homework. Their parents have to help, too.

e. The amount of homework teachers give has fluctuated over history, but these days, children and their families are doing lots of homework.

f. Young children get so much homework that they must stay up late and get up early to finish it.

◀ LISTEN FOR DETAILS

CD 2
31 *Listen to the report again. Circle the letter of the correct answer.*

1. Which of the following homework assignments is NOT mentioned?
   a. making a replica of the *Mayflower*
   b. doing an Internet search
   c. drawing the costume of a historical character

2. Which of the following statements is NOT true?
   a. Hands-on projects are more common than they used to be.
   b. Homework is pretty minimal until high school.
   c. These days, homework is a family event.

3. What is Kaitlyn's homework schedule, approximately?
   a. from 4:00 P.M. until 12:00 A.M.
   b. from 5:00 P.M. to 11:00 P.M.
   c. from 6:00 P.M. until 10:00 P.M.

4. What does Mr. Oloya do when his daughter starts to fall asleep?
   a. He gives her a cup of tea or coffee.
   b. He makes her go outside and run.
   c. He allows her to take a short nap.

5. What does Ms. Cecilia Bluer do when her daughter gets too tired?
   a. She lets her take days off from school.
   b. She does her daughter's homework for her.
   c. She talks to her daughter's teacher about the problem.

(continued on next page)

6. What changed Professor Natriello's mind about homework?

   a. reading that the U.S. was falling behind other countries
   b. becoming a parent and gaining a different perspective
   c. realizing that homework had long-term benefits

7. Which of the following statements about today's families is correct?

   a. Both parents often work outside the house.
   b. Parents feel that teachers are not doing a good job during school hours.
   c. Parents are grateful because they feel that today's children are learning more.

8. How many hours a week does Mr. Russo say that a 10-year-old is in school?

   a. 30 hours a week
   b. 40 hours a week
   c. 45–50 hours a week

◖ MAKE INFERENCES

Listen to the excerpts. Circle the letter of the correct answer.

 **Excerpt One**

1. How would you describe the relationship between father and daughter?

   a. supportive
   b. confrontational
   c. distant

2. What would the father probably say about the amount of homework his daughter has?

   a. "I'm resigned to helping my daughter finish her work. I don't know what else to do."
   b. "I'm totally frustrated. I'm going to go and see my daughter's teacher."

 **Excerpt Two**

1. How did Ms. Bluer's daughter probably feel about her homework?

   a. excited
   b. overwhelmed
   c. bored

2. What did Ms. Bluer probably tell her daughter?

   a. "Getting enough rest is as important as doing your schoolwork."
   b. "You might have to give up watching TV."

 Excerpt Three

1. What did Professor Natriello worry about after he became a parent?

   a. the quality of assignments
   b. how much time he and his wife had to spend on the assignments
   c. his child's ability to do the assignments

2. What might Professor Natriello say to his wife?

    a. "Over the years, I've changed my mind about the type of homework assignments kids should have."

    b. "I don't think homework helps the kids do any better on their tests."

Excerpt Four

1. What is Mr. Russo's attitude towards the amount of homework his children have?

    a. approving

    b. concerned

    c. shocked

2. What opinion might Mr. Russo express?

    a. "Children spend so much time on schoolwork that they don't have enough timeto do other activities."

    b. "It's essential that parents help their children with homework so that theirchildren can get ahead."

◀ EXPRESS OPINIONS

Work in a small group. Read the quotations and then say whether you strongly disagree, somewhat disagree, somewhat agree, or strongly agree. Give reasons and examples to explain your opinion.

| Strongly Disagree | Somewhat Disagree | Somewhat Agree | Strongly Agree |

1. "Elementary school students should have at least a little homework every night." (Ken Nakayama, parent)

2. "A good teacher should be able to teach everything necessary in class and not have to assign homework." (Luisa Montoya, parent)

3. "I think parents should help their children with their homework." (Cindy Chen, teacher)

4. "A lot of homework assignments I had in school were just "busy work," and they didn't really help me learn." (Joss Halen, student)

5. "Teachers need to assign homework because it's impossible to teach new material and give students enough practice during the school day." (Marie Martin, principal)

When she was a 13-year-old student, Ying Ying Yu wrote this commentary about her feelings on homework. She then read it on the radio.

1 🔵 *Listen to the essay. Cross out and correct the false information.*

                 China

    1. Ying Ying grew up in ~~the U.S.~~

    2. She would consider a grade less than 65 to be a failure.

    3. Ying Ying considers duty a combination of pride, fear, and self-esteem.

    4. Ying Ying wanted to do well for her family, her country, and her classmates.

    5. She used to want to be a teacher.

    6. Her parents want her to become a doctor.

    7. She doesn't want any more pressure.

    8. She believes it isn't too late to change her future.

2 *Work in a small group. Discuss the questions.*

    1. Why do you do homework? Give as many reasons as apply to you.

    2. Have you ever chosen not to do a homework assignment? Explain why. Do you think you made the right decision?

    3. Do you think your performance in school reflects on your family? your teachers? yourself? anyone else?

STEP 1: Organize

Work with a partner or small group. Complete the chart with information from Listening One, the case against homework, and Listening Two, the case for homework.

EFFECTS OF HOMEWORK ON:	WHY HOMEWORK IS HARMFUL (A PARENT'S VIEW)	WHY HOMEWORK IS IMPORTANT (A STUDENT'S VIEW)
1. Children's physical health		
2. Children's mental health		
3. Parents		
4. The relationship between parents and children		
5. Other		

STEP 2: Synthesize

Work with a partner. Role play a conversation about the value of homework and how much homework there should be. Discuss each topic in the chart. Use reasons and examples from the chart to explain your ideas. Choose one of these role plays:

- An American parent and Ying Ying
- An American student and Ying Ying's parents

3 FOCUS ON SPEAKING

A VOCABULARY

REVIEW

*Work with a partner. Read each quote aloud and circle the letter of the word or phrase that is closest in meaning to the **bold** word or phrase. Then check (✓) the person or people who most likely made the statement. Compare your choices with another pair's and discuss any differences.*

1. "Most homework has become a useless **ritual**. Teachers should assign more hands-on projects instead of exercises and drills."

   a. habit   **b.** assignment

   ○ teacher or professor   ○ student   ○ parent

(continued on next page)

2. "It's important for kids to be **obedient** at home."
   a. willing to do what is asked   **b.** hardworking
   ○ teacher or professor   ○ student   ○ parent

3. "Homework demands too much **sacrifice**. It takes time from family activities and can even make kids distraught."
   a. loss of something important   **b.** intellectual effort
   ○ teacher or professor   ○ student   ○ parent

4. "It is a parent's **duty** to see that his children's homework is correct."
   a. responsibility   **b.** choice
   ○ teacher or professor   ○ student   ○ parent

5. "Homework is important for teaching skills that are not **tangible**, like self-discipline."
   a. easy to see or touch   **b.** hidden
   ○ teacher or professor   ○ student   ○ parent

6. "The amount of homework a teacher assigns should not **fluctuate**; students should know exactly how much time to allow each night."
   a. increase   **b.** change
   ○ teacher or professor   ○ student   ○ parent

7. "Homework as punishment should really be **outlawed**."
   a. made illegal   **b.** examined
   ○ teacher or professor   ○ student   ○ parent

8. "Teachers should not be **held accountable for** their students' test scores."
   a. considered guilty of   **b.** held responsible for
   ○ teacher or professor   ○ student   ○ parent

9. "Students who complete **demanding** homework assignments will do better in their schoolwork."
   a. challenging   **b.** required
   ○ teacher or professor   ○ student   ○ parent

10. "I'm **an advocate** of less homework and longer school days."
    a. an opponent   **b.** a strong supporter
    ○ teacher or professor   ○ student   ○ parent

◖ **EXPAND**

Three college students, Chen, Kai, and Alex, are taking a course together. They were assigned to read and make a group report on comparative educational practices of 3,500 children from around the world. The students are discussing the information before they write their group report.

Look at the abstract of the article and the charts that the students found online. Then read the students' conversation on page 138 and fill in each blank with the correct term.

Abstract

A recent study involving over 40 countries worldwide was conducted under the International Association for the Evaluation of Educational Achievement (IAEEA). Overall, the study showed that well-chosen homework assignments can improve classroom performance and help all students do better. Some of the results were quite surprising. For example, there was a wide difference between the number of hours children spent on homework on a normal school day in different countries. In addition, time spent on homework assignments did not always show a clear match with students' attitudes toward their schoolwork.

This bar graph shows the amount of time students spent studying math, science, and other subjects outside of school in five different countries.

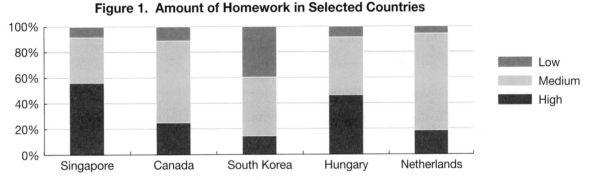

Figure 1. Amount of Homework in Selected Countries

A *high* level of homework indicates more than three hours of homework a day, *medium* indicates between one and three hours a day, and *low* indicates less than one hour per day.

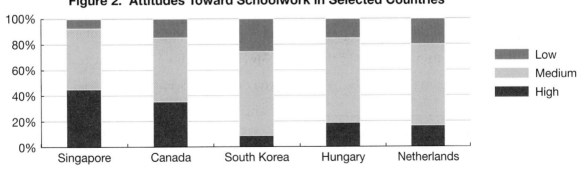

Figure 2. Attitudes Toward Schoolwork in Selected Countries

High indicates a very positive attitude, *medium* indicates a less positive attitude, and *low* indicates a fairly negative attitude.

a. **buckle down:** concentrate and do your work

b. **came to mind:** occurred to (me)

c. **conked out:** fell asleep or felt exhausted

d. **count on:** depend on, rely on

e. **a cinch:** something that is very easy

f. **hopping mad:** really angry

g. **over the top:** excessive, too much

h. **pays off:** leads to good results

i. **pull (one's) weight:** do (one's) fair share of the work

j. **had (one's) nose to the grindstone:** worked hard

KAI: Hi, guys. Did you see that research?

ALEX: Yeah, but I was so tired I almost _____ halfway
        1.
        through it. I'm exhausted! So can we only talk about Figure 1 today . . . the
        amount of homework these poor kids get? What did you think of it, anyway?

KAI: Do you think these results are accurate?

CHEN: Sure, I think we can _____ that. It's a published study
        2.
        and it's international, too.

KAI: Yeah, but . . . a fifth grader having hours and hours of homework a night.
        That sounds a bit _____ to me. What do you think—
        3.
        is that believable?

CHEN: Oh, I think so. When I was in middle school, we had to come home from
        school and immediately _____ to do our
        4.
        homework—didn't you?

ALEX: Well, no, I didn't. I got a little bit of homework, sure, but not every night.
        And it didn't take that long. Now, in high school I got some real work.
        But that was OK. Work that you do in high school really
        _____ when you get to university.
        5.

KAI: Well, getting back to the work we're doing now . . . According to this,
        children in Singapore do a lot of homework.

ALEX: Right! When I saw that, the first thing that _____ was
        6.
        a poor fifth grader surrounded by math textbooks.

CHEN: That sounds like me when I was younger! I always _____
7.
my _____. But it didn't seem to help, actually.

KAI: Oh, come on, Chen! Math is _____ for you! Anyway,
8.
guys, let's get these reports finished. Professor Lamov got

_____ last time he had to grade late papers.
9.

ALEX: Yeah, you're right. Listen, since both of you did more work on our last group

project than I did, I need to _____ my
10.

_____ more this time. How about if I write up a

summary and send it to you guys for corrections and changes?

◖ CREATE

Work with two partners and discuss the questions.

1. Look again at the study results in Figure 1. Did any of the results of the study surprise you? Why or why not?

2. If you are not from one of the countries mentioned in the study, draw a simple line graph and decide where your culture might fit in relation to the countries mentioned. Show and explain your graph. If you are from one of the countries mentioned, say whether you think the results are accurate or not.

3. Role play a second conversation between Chen, Kai, and Alex and comment on Figure 2, students' attitudes toward their school work.

Use vocabulary from Review and Expand in your comments. Use the chart below to prepare your comments.

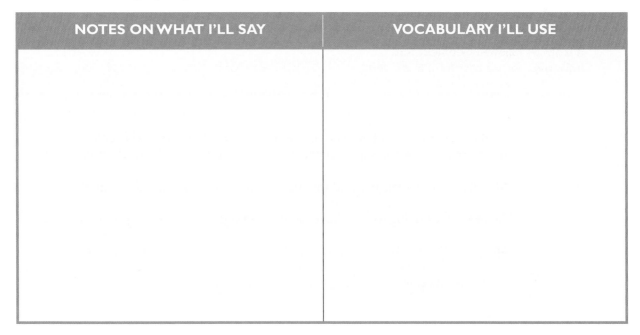

NOTES ON WHAT I'LL SAY	VOCABULARY I'LL USE

1 Work with a partner. Read the conversation. Then explain what the bold phrases mean.

A: Hey, want to come over and play some videogames after school?

B: I can't. My dad **makes me do** my homework right after school.

A: Oh, too bad! Can't you **get him to change** his mind?

B: Well, he said it's the only time he can **help me do** the math problems, and I really need his help.

MAKE, HAVE, LET, HELP, AND GET	
1. Use *make*, *have*, and *let* + object + base form of the verb to talk about things that someone can **require**, **cause**, or **allow** another person (or an animal) to do. You can also use *make* to mean *cause to / force to*.	• She **has** her kids **do** their homework immediately after school. • She **makes** them **turn off** the TV. • She **lets** them **play** computer games later.
2. *Help* can be followed by: **Object** and **base form** of the verb (more common) OR **Object** and **infinitive** The meaning is the same.	• He **helped** me **do** the homework. OR • He **helped** me **to do** the homework.
3. *Get* has a similar meaning to **make** and **have**, though it implies a less direct action by the subject of the sentence. It is always followed by **object and infinitive**, not the base form of the verb.	• The teacher **got** us to do extra homework. NOT The teacher ~~got us do~~ extra homework.

2 Read the conversation between a mother and father about their child. Complete the sentences using the verbs in parentheses. Use the correct pronouns where necessary.

MOTHER: Andre's teacher told me Andre is not doing well in school right now.

FATHER: Not doing well? What exactly is wrong?

M: He's a little lazy. I can't ___get him to do___ his homework without a
                                    1. (get / do)

struggle.

F: I'll speak to him tonight, but why can't you _____ and do it?
                                                       2. (make / sit down)

M: He has extra study classes two days a week and sports after school the other three days. When he gets home from school, he's so tired that I _____ TV or play his music. He's just a kid. You see him at
                 3. (let / watch)
8:30. He conks out on the sofa. The poor child is exhausted.

F: Well, he has to do his homework. I guess we'll have to _____ watching TV.
             4. (have / stop)

M: I think we also have to help. He says he doesn't understand the concepts in science and the problems in math are hard, too.

F: Well, then, we'll have to help. I can _____ the science. But
                            5. (help / understand)
the math . . . you're much better at that.

M: Then I'll help with the math. And when he comes home from school, maybe I'll _____ a short nap. Then studying might be
               6. (have / take)
easier for him.

F: Good idea. If all this doesn't work, we'll _____ the sports
                           7. (make / give up)
for a while.

M: OK. But if we can _____ his homework, maybe we won't
                        8. (get / do)
have to go that far.

2 *Work in a small group. Some parents are asking a school counselor for advice about their children's homework problems. Follow the steps.*

Step 1: Take turns reading the problems aloud.

Step 2: Each group member writes some suggestions from the counselor using *make, have, let, help,* or *get.* Write the suggestions on slips of paper.

Step 3: One student reads all of the suggestions aloud. Then the group votes on the best suggestion.

(continued on next page)

Example

PARENT: My son rushes through his homework, finishes quickly, and is careless.
COUNSELOR: **Have him do** one assignment at a time, and then **help him check** his work.

B.

My daughter often can't understand her homework assignments. They seem unclear to me, too.

A.

My son rushes through his homework, finishes quickly, and is careless.

C.

My kids can't seem to concentrate on their homework. They get up every few minutes and are easily distracted. Do you think it's because they eat a lot of candy while they're working?

D.

My son plays baseball, practices violin, and then does his homework. By that time, he's very tired.

E.

My children listen to music or watch TV while doing their homework. I don't know if they can really concentrate.

F.

My son always finishes his homework—but then leaves it at home or brings it to school but forgets to turn it in.

G.

My daughter always calls her friends for help with her homework. But I think they spend most of their time chatting about other things.

◖ **PRONUNCIATION: Stressed and Unstressed Vowels**

$\overset{CD\ 2}{\underset{38}{\bullet}}$ *Listen to the underlined vowels in these words. Are they stressed or unstressed? How many different vowel letters are underlined? Do the underlined letters have different sounds or the same sound?*

ago   decide   minute   office   opinion

STRESSED AND UNSTRESSED VOWELS	
Stressed Vowels Stressed vowels in English are long and loud. Sometimes they are pronounced on a higher pitch.	abōlish ādvocates
Unstressed Vowels • Unstressed vowels are short. • Unstressed vowels are pronounced /ə/, regardless of how they are spelled. • /ə/ has a special name, *schwa*. It is the sound of the hesitation word that native speakers use when they need time to think: *uh . . . uh.* • Schwa (/ə/) is the most common vowel sound in English. • Unstressed vowels spelled with the letters *i* or *e* can be pronounced /ə/ or /ɪ/. • The unstressed endings *–ow* and *-y* are not pronounced /ə/	![lips] əgō (ago) ōffəs (office) mīnət (minute) dəcīde *or* dɪcīde (decide) wīndow būsy

1 $\overset{CD\ 2}{\underset{39}{\bullet}}$ *Listen to the words and put a line over the stressed vowels to show they are long. Then practice the words with a partner. Make the stressed vowels very long.*

1. mēssage
2. optional
3. distraught
4. promotions
5. social

6. abolish
7. heritage
8. tangible
9. decision
10. responsible

2 CD 2 ⏺40 *Listen to the words and repeat them. The spellings show how the unstressed vowels are pronounced. Write the normal spelling of the words on the line. Then check your answers with a partner and practice saying the words. Use the pronunciation spellings to guide your pronunciation.*

1. mĭnəməl

   _____minimal_____

2. əcoūntəbəl

   _____

3. əchĭevmənt

   _____

4. ēksələnt

   _____

5. kəmplēte

   _____

6. əsīgnmənts

   _____

7. mōnətər

   _____

8. dəmānding

   _____

9. əgrēe

   _____

10. rədĭkyələs

    _____

11. əpĭnyən

    _____

12. əbōləsht

    _____

3 CD 2 ⏺41 *Listen to the questions and repeat them. The bold spellings show the pronunciation. Then work with a partner. Ask the questions and answer them.*

1. Do you **əgrēe** that kids today sacrifice their childhood to homework?

2. Did your parents **mōnətər** your homework?

3. Did you have **dəmānding** homework **əsīgnmənts** in school?

4. Do you think homework should be **əbōləsht** in elementary school?

◀ **FUNCTION: Restating for Clarity**

When you are explaining a concept that is difficult or complicated, your listeners might not always understand what you mean. In that case, you can restate your idea using different words. You can begin like this:

In other words, . . .

To put it another way, . . .

I mean that . . .

What I'm saying is . . .

What that means is . . .

1. Divide the class into two groups, A and B. Group A should look at the statements on the next page. Group B should look at the statements on page 214.

2. Each group reads their sentences. Work together to explain them in your own words. Make notes in the space provided.

3. Then work in pairs, with one student from Group A and one from Group B. Take turns reading the sentences and explaining them to each other using the expressions above.

Student A

Read the statements and try to explain them in your own words.

1. Schools should give students who do well special incentives, like money or prizes. This will motivate students to work harder both in and out of school.

   _____

2. The best way for parents to enforce rules about homework is through strict consequences, such as loss of privileges.

   _____

3. A study by the Public Agenda Foundation found that 25 percent of parents want more homework for their children, and only 10 percent want less.

   _____

◀ **PRODUCTION: A Town Meeting with the Board of Education**

> In this activity, you will **role play a town meeting**. The local school board has requested ideas from parents, teachers, and students about how much homework should be assigned at the local high school. Try to use the vocabulary, grammar, pronunciation, and language for restating that you learned in the unit.*

Step 1: Read the situation.

The School Board of Springview is made up of residents who have been elected to make decisions about the schools. Tonight, the Board is meeting to hear arguments and ideas about how much homework should be assigned in the town's high school. One group feels that high school students get too much homework in general, while others disagree.

Step 2: Divide the class into three groups:

- Three or five **School Board members**, who will vote on the school policy
- **Anti-homework group:** Your members think students currently do too much homework. In fact, you're not even sure homework is beneficial at all. In addition, you are concerned that parents are helping students too much with their assignments. Your members are students, parents, and teachers.

(continued on next page)

---
*For Alternative Speaking Topics, see page 147.

- **Pro-homework group:** Your members think homework is essential for success in high school and beyond. You think students should be assigned less traditional types of homework and instead do more creative, group-based projects. Your members are students, parents, and teachers.

Step 3: Make notes in the chart below.

School Board Members	Anti-Homework Group	Pro-Homework Group
How will we make our decision? What are the most important points to consider?	Arguments and ideas about • amount of homework	Arguments and ideas about • amount of homework
	• types of assignments	• types of assignments
	• whether students should do their assignments by themselves	• whether students should do their assignments by themselves

Step 4: Hold a meeting. The School Board members will call on members from both groups to explain their arguments. Then the Board will make a decision about how much and what kind of homework the high school should assign.

ALTERNATIVE SPEAKING TOPICS

Read the statements and decide whether you strongly agree, agree, are not sure, disagree, or strongly disagree with them. Mark your reaction on the line.

1. I wish I had had more homework in school. I think it would have made me more successful.

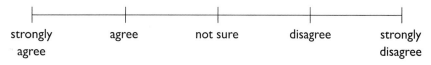

| strongly agree | agree | not sure | disagree | strongly disagree |

2. It is much easier for students to do well in school if their parents help them do their homework.

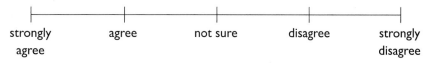

| strongly agree | agree | not sure | disagree | strongly disagree |

3. Too much homework can lead to psychological problems among high school students.

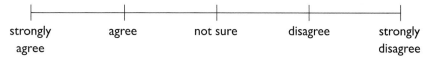

| strongly agree | agree | not sure | disagree | strongly disagree |

4. Relaxing and doing hobbies is just as important as doing homework.

| strongly agree | agree | not sure | disagree | strongly disagree |

5. Homework is more important today than it was 50 years ago.

| strongly agree | agree | not sure | disagree | strongly disagree |

RESEARCH TOPICS, see page 222.

UNIT 8 Goodbye to the Sit-Down Meal

"I just dialed 1-800-BAGUETTE."

1 FOCUS ON THE TOPIC

A PREDICT

Look at the cartoon and the title of the unit. Discuss the questions with a partner and then with the class.

1. What does the cartoon say about the couple's attitude towards meal preparation? Do you think the cartoon is supporting or criticizing their attitude?

2. Where do you usually eat breakfast, lunch, and dinner? How much time do you typically spend on each meal? How often do you eat in restaurants? How often do you buy take-out (food from restaurants to eat somewhere else)?

3. Do you think cooking and eating habits have changed in your country in the last few decades? If so, talk about how and why.

149

Work in a small group. Look at six factors that influence food trends. Then discuss the questions with your group.

1. *Economic conditions:* How does the amount of money you have affect what you eat? Is it cheaper to prepare your own food or to eat in restaurants?

2. *Faster and cheaper methods of transportation:* How do changes in the way food is transported affect the way people eat? Is locally grown food available in stores near you?

3. *Scientific research:* Have advances in science or research findings affected the way you eat? Do you think food is more or less healthful today?

Factors Influencing Food Trends

4. *Advertising:* Where are some places you see or hear ads for food? What kinds of food? Have you ever bought food or eaten at a restaurant because of an ad?

5. *World cultures:* Have your eating habits or preferences been influenced by other cultures? Are international restaurants available near you?

6. *Changes in the workforce:* How do your work or study habits affect your family's or your eating habits? Has an increase in the number of women who work full-time affected meals for anyone you know?

If you want to know how food is changing, ask a chef. These food professionals both reflect and create new trends in eating.

 Read and listen to the interview. Circle the correct meaning of the bold words.

Interviewer: Monsieur Renard, thank you for talking to me today. It's not every day I get to speak to a French chef!

Monsieur Renard: You're welcome.

Interviewer: I'd like to talk to you about changes in our eating habits over, say, the past five or ten years. I mean, lately it's been much easier to buy food that used to be expensive and hard to find—you know, **(1.) delicacies** like snails, lychee nuts, and so on . . . They've become quite a hit in a lot of American cities.

Monsieur Renard: What you're saying is quite true. As the world becomes smaller, we're **(2.) witnessing** a change in people's eating habits. People want to experiment with new tastes. If you go to any large supermarket, you'll see shelves **(3.) stacked** with food from all over the world.

Interviewer: So . . . there's been a **(4.) shift** in our eating habits, in other words.

Monsieur Renard: Oh yes, and in our cooking habits, too. You know, women make up almost 50 percent of the **(5.) workforce** these days. People like to eat at home, but it's tough to cook if you've been working outside the house all day! So buying take-out food is part of a big social change. It's a relatively recent **(6.) phenomenon**.

Interviewer: I guess people want the convenience. In fact, my neighborhood is also being **(7.) overrun** by fast-food restaurants.

Monsieur Renard: You know, what's so interesting is that food is like a **(8.) core** cultural value. Food is connected with people's entire lifestyle. In the past, preparing and eating food were **(9.) intimate** family activities. But that's changing, even in France.

Interviewer: In a way, it's sad that we're losing the tradition of a **(10.) sit-down** meal.

Monsieur Renard: Perhaps, but on the other hand, all this experimentation is leading to some really interesting new dishes. Some cooks come up with all kinds of innovations.

1. a. luxuries
   b. small things
   c. foreign items

2. a. recommending
   b. seeing
   c. hoping for

3. a. full
   b. burdened
   c. open

4. a. change
   b. improvement
   c. growth

5. a. labor force
   b. industrial workers
   c. home makers

6. a. disadvantage
   b. development
   c. habit

7. a. changed
   b. taken over
   c. improved

8. a. valuable
   b. key
   c. shared

9. a. close
   b. isolated
   c. involved

10. a. takeout
    b. more formal
    c. relaxed

②FOCUS ON LISTENING

A LISTENING ONE: French Sandwiches

France is a country that cares deeply about food. A journalist, Sarah Chayes of National Public Radio, reports from France on some recent trends in food and in society.

CD 3
🎵3 *Listen to the first part of the report and answer the questions.*

1. Which meal in France is changing? How is it changing?

_____

_____

2. Why do you think this particular meal is changing?

_____

_____

◀ **LISTEN FOR MAIN IDEAS**

CD 3
🎵4 *Now listen to the entire report. Answer the questions and then compare your answers with a partner's.*

1. According to the interview, take-out food is becoming more popular in France. Check (✓) the reasons.

   ○ Bakeries have learned to make different kinds of food.

   ○ Women's lifestyles have changed.

   ○ Men's lifestyles have changed.

   ○ France has been influenced by trends in the U.S.

   ○ People are adjusting their working hours.

2. Check (✓) the changes the bakery has made.

   ○ It serves more hamburgers than before.

   ○ It is open longer hours.

   ○ It is trying to attract different customers.

   ○ It has expanded its staff.

   ○ It offers take-out meals.

C D 3
5 *Listen to the report again. As you listen, circle the letter of the correct answer.*

1. How long did people traditionally sit down to eat lunch in France?

   a. one hour
   b. two hours
   c. three hours

2. What does the report say about the reasons for the change in eating habits?

   a. They are contradictory.
   b. They are conservative.
   c. They are complex.

3. In the past, what products did French bakeries offer?

   a. many kinds of baked goods and dairy products
   b. a few kinds of breads and pastries
   c. a selection of baked goods and general grocery items

4. How does Nicole, a worker in the bakery, feel about making all the different products she now prepares?

   a. She dislikes it.
   b. She likes it.
   c. She's confused by it.

5. How has the owner of the bakery reacted to the demand?

   a. She is being more creative.
   b. She is busier than she wants to be.
   c. She is quite unhappy.

6. In general, what do French working people now do?

   a. pay more for better food
   b. leave work earlier at the end of the day
   c. eat lunch later than usual

7. How have women contributed to the changes?

   a. Fewer women want to cook.
   b. Women are having fewer children.
   c. More women are working.

8. What is the key to the success of the bakery?

   a. The prices are low.
   b. The bakery uses only French products.
   c. The bakery serves customers quickly.

9. What just closed around the corner from Au Pain Gourmet?

   a. a French full service restaurant
   b. a hamburger place
   c. a foreign bakery

◖ MAKE INFERENCES

Listen to the excerpts. The reporter uses several words that have more than one meaning. This deliberate use of words with double meanings adds humor and interest to the report. Answer the questions with a partner.

Excerpt One

Reporter Sarah Chayes explains what happens in Au Pain Gourmet, a bakery in Paris.

1. What does the reporter mean?
   a. Nicole should continue to make sandwiches, even if she doesn't want to.
   b. The sandwiches Nicole makes are not very soft or fresh.

Excerpt Two

The reporter talks about why Nicole now makes sandwiches.

2. What does the reporter mean?
   a. Nicole will also eat the sandwiches.
   b. Making sandwiches is how Nicole earns money.

Excerpt Three

The reporter explains how the bakery owner has adapted to the new demand.

3. What does the reporter mean?
   a. The size of the sandwich was too large for most people's mouths.
   b. The sandwiches were too different from what people were used to.

Excerpt Four

The reporter describes the customers' reactions to the new products.

4. What does the reporter mean?
   a. The lines are long and frustrating, so customers in a hurry occasionally fight.
   b. The sandwiches are enormously popular with the people who go there.

Excerpt Five

A customer talks about the new trend.

5. What does the woman mean?
   a. It's difficult to eat this kind of food neatly.
   b. Take-out food has become very popular.

◖ EXPRESS OPINIONS

Work in a small group. Discuss the questions.

1. In your opinion, why is the bakery doing better than the hamburger place? What do you predict for the future of the bakery?

2. Is there an increase in fast-food products and restaurants in your area? If there is, how do you feel about it? How often do you eat fast food? What are some advantages and disadvantages to eating fast food?

What are the food trends in California? You will hear some comments from *Satellite Sisters*, a radio show featuring five sisters who live in different parts of the world and share their thoughts—via satellite—on everyday life. In this segment, Lian talks about life in California.

1 🎧 *Listen to the report and answer the questions.*

1. Why was Lian surprised in the supermarket?
    a. She found unusual food items in bowls.
    b. She thought the bowls were too expensive.

2. Why does Lian think this food-in-bowls trend is happening?
    a. People are too hurried to be careful about eating.
    b. Bowls keep food warmer than plates.

3. Lian jokes that maybe the next new eating style will be _____.
    a. eating while keeping one hand on the phone
    b. eating without using our hands

4. Lian exaggerates by using humor when she says, "just get yourself a nice *trough*, and put the lasagna in there." Why does she mention an animal food container?
    a. Many Californians are vegetarians and don't eat animal products.
    b. She thinks that people do not have good manners.

trough

5. Lian thinks that teaching children to eat with a knife and fork _____.
    a. is a parent's responsibility
    b. won't be necessary in the future

6. Lian's sister, Julie, in Bangkok, also makes a comment. What is her attitude toward the subject?
    a. She shares Lian's feelings about food in bowls.
    b. She seems to have no problem accepting food in bowls.

7. What does Lian's sister Liz, in New York, struggle with?
    a. eating food on *skewers*
    b. finding lamb in a bowl

skewers

2 *Work in a small group. Discuss the questions.*

- Do you think it's important for families to eat meals together? Why or why not? What are some reasons that families might not eat together?

- What factors are most important for you when choosing a meal: taste, price, convenience, or something else?

STEP 1: Organize

Work in groups of three. Fill in the chart with ideas from Listenings One and Two about food trends.

CATEGORIES	GOODBYE, SIT-DOWN MEAL	FOOD IN A BOWL
1. Examples of changes in eating habits (diet and style of eating)	• French bakeries are serving sandwiches now	
2. Reasons our eating habits are changing		
3. Speakers' attitudes toward these changes		
4. Speakers' tone		

STEP 2: Synthesize

Continue working with the same group and perform a role play. Student A is a reporter asking Student B (Fishlere) and Student C (Satellite Sister) questions from the categories on the left of the chart. The reporter also asks for examples and explanations. Use a tone similar to that of the speakers you heard.

Example

A: Most people seem to agree that our eating habits are changing in many ways. Can you give me some examples?

B: Yes, that's true. In France, for example . . .

C: Well, where I live . . .

A VOCABULARY

REVIEW

Read the sentences and focus on the bold words and expressions. Then circle the letter of the correct paraphrase of the underlined sentence.

1. I have to work long hours at my new job. <u>It's really **tough**.</u>
   a. It's difficult.
   b. It's unpleasant.

2. Lise said she cooked that meal all by herself. <u>That's a little **hard to swallow**!</u>
   a. It's difficult to believe.
   b. It's not a good meal.

3. I want to quit my job, but I can't. <u>Someone has to **put bread on the table**.</u>
   a. Someone has to go shopping.
   b. Someone has to earn money.

4. Have you been to my neighborhood lately? <u>It's **pizza city**!</u>
   a. There are many different kinds of restaurants there.
   b. There are many pizza restaurants there.

5. Did you hear about the new Brazilian restaurant? <u>It's really a **hit**!</u>
   a. It's not doing very well.
   b. It's very popular.

6. <u>The number of delis downtown is **exploding**.</u>
   a. Many delis are going out of business.
   b. More delis are opening all the time.

7. Did you complete that restaurant survey yet? You should. <u>Customers should make their **tastes** known.</u>
   a. Customers should try more restaurants.
   b. Customers should express their opinions.

8. <u>That man just **beaned** me with a loaf of bread!</u>
   a. He hit me with the bread.
   b. He gave me the bread.

9. Have you been to *Chicken Delight*? <u>It's a new **chain**.</u>
   a. It's a new kind of restaurant.
   b. It's part of a group of stores.

10. <u>He's really **shoveling food in**!</u> He must be very hungry!
    a. He's eating very quickly.
    b. He's working hard to earn money for food.

In English, there are many idiomatic expressions, or figures of speech, related to food. The expressions feature words related to food or eating, but are commonly used in other contexts. In many cases, English speakers no longer think about or even remember the original meaning of the expressions, and instead use them only in the figurative sense.

Here are some examples from Listening One.

- It puts bread on her table. (= It helps her make a living.)
- It was a bit hard for people to swallow. (= People couldn't believe it.)

In the sentences that follow, match each bold food expression to its definition from the list. Write the correct number in the blank.

1. Men used to be the main **breadwinners**, while women raised the children.

2. In the past, only men were responsible for the family income. Now women have to **bring home the bacon**, too.

3. Hey, there's a new DVD player out that's really great, but it's $300. That's a lot of **dough**.

4. We've got a lot of work to do outside today. Let's **get cooking** before it gets dark.

5. **There's trouble brewing** in my office. I've heard some people might get fired soon.

6. I have too much work to do right now, so I can't help you with that new project you mentioned. Let's **put it on the back burner** and see how I'm feeling in a month or two.

7. He's really hard to get along with. He always **stirs up** trouble.

8. There was an interesting show on TV last night about problems in our city. It really gave me some **food for thought**.

9. She writes books for fun, but teaching is really her **bread and butter**.

10. I love my grandmother. She's **the salt of the earth**.

11. You can't believe everything he says. You should **take it with a grain of salt**.

12. I hated that discussion we had at work yesterday. It really **left a bad taste in my mouth**.

_____ **a.** creates

_____ **b.** leave something until later; treat as less urgent

_____ **c.** earn money

_____ **d.** gave me a negative feeling

_____ **e.** money

_____ **f.** something to think about

_____ **g.** problems are developing

_____ **h.** main source of income

_____ **i.** start working

_____ **j.** salary earners

_____ **k.** be skeptical about what you hear

_____ **l.** a really good person

Work in groups of three and discuss one or more of the topics. Each time a student uses a figure of speech from the box, he / she gets one point. After five minutes, the person with the most points wins.

be (something) city	(store) chain	put bread on the table
be a hit	dough	put (something) on the back burner
be hard to swallow	exploding	
be tough	food for thought	salt of the earth
bean (someone) with (something)	leave a bad taste in one's mouth	shovel (food) in
		stir up trouble
bread and butter	let's get cooking	take (something) with a grain of salt
breadwinner	make (one's) tastes known	
bring home the bacon		there's trouble brewing

School: Talk about a challenging class and why you are having difficulties with it.

Work: Talk about some problems with your job.

Hobbies: Discuss a team sport that you play and what it's like getting along with the other team members.

TV show: Describe a popular TV show and what its characters are like. What did they do last week?

Family: Discuss a recent family vacation or get-together.

Example

A: There's **trouble brewing** in my office! My boss wants us to work overtime every day this week. That's a bit **hard to swallow**! I feel like quitting.
B: Yeah, that sounds **tough**. Still, you have to **put bread on the table** . . .

Ⓑ GRAMMAR: Phrasal Verbs

1 *Work with a partner. Read the conversation. Then explain what the bold phrases mean.*

A: In France, more and more people are buying their food at the local bakery and **taking it out**. Au Pain Gourmet has to **keep up with** the trend.
B: Well, that's because of changes in the workforce. Women now **make up** almost half of all workers. If they have young children in daycare, they have to rush to **pick them up** as early as they can.

PHRASAL VERBS

A **phrasal verb** is two or three words put together to make one verb. Two-word phrasal verbs consist of a verb and a particle (an adverb or preposition). This combination of words often has a meaning that is very different from the meanings of its separate parts.

Verb	+	Particle	Meaning
keep		up with	stay at the same level
take		out	bring food from a restaurant to another place
make		up	compose
pick		up	collect

Phrasal Verbs	Examples
Some phrasal verbs contain three words.	Au Pain Gourmet is having difficulty **keeping up with** the demand.
Some phrasal verbs are **transitive**. They take a direct object.	Parents **pick up** their children as early as possible.
Many transitive phrasal verbs are **separable**. The direct object can come between the verb and the particle, or after the particle.	Workers often **take** their lunch **out** to the park. Workers often **take out** their lunch to the park.
However, when the direct object is a pronoun, it must go between the verb and particle.	They **take** it **out** to the park. NOT They ~~take out~~ it to the park.
If the direct object is a long phrase, it always comes after the particle.	Are you going to the deli? Can you please **pick up** a sandwich with Swiss cheese, mustard, and lettuce and tomato? NOT Can you please ~~pick a sandwich with Swiss cheese, mustard, and lettuce and tomato up~~?
Other transitive verbs are **inseparable**. The direct object always comes after the particle.	Au Pain Gourmet is having difficulty **keeping up with** the demand. NOT Au Pain Gourmet is having difficulty ~~keeping the demand up with~~.
Some phrasal verbs are **intransitive**. They do not take a direct object.	Outside the store, customers were **lining up**.

2 *Work with a partner. Complete the telephone conversations using the phrasal verbs in parentheses. Use the correct pronoun and place the pronoun between the verb and the particle when necessary. Adjust the verb tense if necessary. Then practice the conversations aloud.*

MARK: Hi, Julie? It's Mark. I'm sorry to _____ just before the
1. (call up / pronoun)

math test, but you said you wanted to try that new sandwich place you

read about—Au Pain Gourmet.

JULIE: Oh, I read about it in the paper. Apparently people are lining up around the block to give it a try. It has really _____.
2. (catch on)

MARK: Yeah, I'd like to _____, too. In fact, I wanted to
3. (check out / pronoun)
_____ tomorrow morning to finish our homework
4. (ask over / pronoun)
together. Then we could walk over and get one of those baguette sandwiches.

JULIE: Mark, I don't know . . . see, Brandon was talking about getting together . . .

MARK: What was that? Oh, your friend Brandon? Well, can't you

_____? Just _____ until another time.
5. (turn down / pronoun)   **6.** (put off / pronoun)

JULIE: Well, I . . .

(An hour or two later . . .)

JULIE: Hi, Brandon? This is Julie. How are you?

BRANDON: Hey, Julie! How are you? I'm really looking forward to . . .

JULIE: Brandon, hold on a minute . . . Listen, I know you offered to cook lunch for me tomorrow, but I'm afraid I have to cancel.

BRANDON: You mean you're _____?
7. (call off / pronoun)

JULIE: Yes, I know I'm _____, but I was _____
8. (letting down / pronoun)   **9.** (think over / pronoun)
and I don't know if I can spare the time. I'm working on a big math project for school, and we have to _____ on Monday.
10. (hand in / pronoun)
Maybe some other time?

BRANDON: But Julie! Well, OK. I'll just wait until you're available since you're the only girl I want to date.

JULIE: Brandon, I'm sorry. I was hoping I could _____, but I . . .
11. (work out / pronoun)
What's that sound?

BRANDON: Oops, hang on a minute. I have another call. Could you hold for a minute?

(continued on next page)

JULIE: Well, actually, can you _____ in about an hour?
12. (call back / pronoun)

BRANDON: I can't, but we'll see each other around. I'll talk to you soon, OK?

JULIE: OK, 'bye.

(Brandon switches to the other line.)

BRANDON: Hello?

EMMA: Hi, Brandon. It's Emma.

BRANDON: Hey, Emma.

EMMA: Oh, I hear the radio in the background there. Are you listening to WYYN, too?

BRANDON Yeah, I just _____ a few minutes ago.
13. (turn on / pronoun)

EMMA: Did you hear about that new sandwich shop? Listen, why don't we

_____ tomorrow? We could go for lunch.
14. (try out / pronoun)

BRANDON: Sounds great. But what if everyone is going there? It'll be really crowded. I'm not sure if I want to hang out with everyone in the class.

EMMA: Come on, it'll be fun. As for the people from our class . . . there's no way

we will _____.
15. (run into / pronoun)

BRANDON: Cool! See you tomorrow, then!

3 *Match the phrasal verbs on the left with the definitions on the right. Use the conversations above to help you. Write the correct letter in the blank.*

Phrasal Verbs

_d_ **1.** call up

____ **2.** catch on

____ **3.** check out

____ **4.** ask over

____ **5.** turn down

____ **6.** put off

____ **7.** call off

____ **8.** let down

Definitions

a. cancel

b. investigate

c. invite to one's home

d. phone

e. become popular

f. return a phone call

g. submit work (to a teacher)

h. solve a problem

_____ **9.** think over

i. start (a machine)

_____ **10.** hand in

j. experiment to see if you like it

_____ **11.** work out

k. reject

_____ **12.** call back

l. disappoint

_____ **13.** turn on

m. postpone

_____ **14.** try out

n. meet by accident

_____ **15.** run into

o. consider

4 *Work in a group of four. Imagine that Brandon, Emma, Julie, and Mark all meet each other at the sandwich shop. Write the conversation they have, and then act it out for the class. Use the phrasal verbs you have learned in the unit.*

C SPEAKING

◖PRONUNCIATION: Spelling and Sounds—oo and o

English uses six letters (*a, e, i, o, u,* and *y*) to spell 14 vowel sounds. Some spellings are confusing, because the same spelling can be pronounced in different ways. The spellings **oo** and **o** are examples of confusing spellings. When you learn words with these spellings, pay attention to the sound of the vowel.

SPELLING AND SOUNDS—OO AND O

oo spellings are usually pronounced /ʊ/ as in **good** or /uw/ as in **school**. These vowels have somewhat similar sounds.

- Round your lips tightly as you say /uw/, the vowel in *sch**oo**l.*

- Round your lips a little when you say /ʊ/, the vowel in *g**oo**d*

o spellings can have several pronunciations:
1. /ɑ/ not, stop, hot (as in *father*)
2. /ow/ no, ago, rose (as in *hope*)
3. /ə/ some, done, Monday (as in *cut*)
4. An unusual pronunciation of the letter *o* is the vowel sound in *w**o**men.* In this word, the letter *o* is pronounced /ɪ/, like the vowel in *win.*

1 ᶜᴰ3 ⑫ *Listen and repeat the words. The bold, underlined letters show the vowel sounds. Circle the word with the different vowel sound.*

1. **o**ne, s**o**me, l**o**ck

2. f**oo**l, w**oo**l, sh**oo**t

3. b**o**dy, r**o**de, b**o**th

4. d**oo**r, b**oo**t, fl**oo**r

5. sh**oo**k, l**oo**k, b**oo**st

6. n**oo**n, c**oo**k, b**oo**m

2 ᶜᴰ3 ⑬ *The following words are all spelled with* **oo**. *Listen and repeat the words.*

blood	cook	✓food	noon
book	cool	look	too
boom	flood	noodles	tool

Now work with a partner. How is **oo** *pronounced? Write the words from the box in one of the columns. Check (✓) the words as you use them. Then read the words in each column. Your partner will check your pronunciation.*

/uw/ too	/ʊ/ good	/ə/ cut
food		

3 ᶜᴰ3 ⑭ *The words in the box are all spelled with* **o**. *Listen and repeat the words.*

come	frozen	home	oven	products
done	go	job	✓popular	shock
explode	grocery	money	possible	whole

Now work with a partner. How is **o** *pronounced? Write the words from the box in one of the columns below. Then read the words in each column. Your partner will check your pronunciation.*

/ɑ/ not	/ow/ no	/ə/ Monday
popular		

4 *Work with a partner. Take turns asking each other the questions, using words from the box in your answers. Check (✓) the words as you use them. Can you use them all? Check each other's pronunciation of **o** and **oo** sounds.*

blood	do	frozen	noodles	shock
boom	done	go	noon	too
come	explode	job	oven	tool
cook	flood	look	popular	whole
cool	food	money	possible	women

1. When it's too hot to cook, what do some people do?

2. Can you think of any popular books about technology or science fiction? What do they discuss?

3. What are some tools used around the home, and what are some of their uses?

4. When was the last time you emailed or phoned home? What did you say?

◀ **FUNCTION:** Calling Attention to a Particular Item

When you are speaking to a group of people and need to demonstrate a process or show visual material, you need to focus your audience's attention on what you are doing. Read this example from a food demonstration.

Example

Do you see what I'm holding? It's just a potato peeler. But I'm going to use this peeler to cut thin strips of carrot for a salad. **Watch me carefully** ...

Here are some expressions you can use to focus your audience's attention on a particular process or item.

CALLING ATTENTION TO A PARTICULAR ITEM

Watch me carefully ...	Have you ever seen anybody do this before?
Notice what I'm doing ...	Would you like to try it?
Watch how I ...	This ingredient is very special. Take a look at it.
See this (whisk)?	Look at what I'm holding.
Have you ever seen this before?	Can you see what I'm doing?

Work in a small group. Take turns explaining how to use one of the utensils or gadgets listed, or another of your choice. As you explain, use the expressions for calling attention to a particular item or part of an item.

Example

"Now, **see these**? They're called *chopsticks*. **Watch me carefully** and I'll show you how to use them. First you hold one like this . . . **Have you ever seen this before? Now look at** my fingers. **Notice what I'm doing** with these two fingers . . ."

chopsticks   steamer   pressure cooker   bamboo mat

whisk   cookie cutters   coffee grinder   spice grater

◀ PRODUCTION: A Cooking Show

In recent years, TV shows that demonstrate how to cook a dish or a meal have become popular in many parts of the world. In this activity, you will **create an episode of your own cooking show**. Try to use the vocabulary, grammar, pronunciation, and language for calling attention to a particular item that you learned in the unit.*

Step 1: Work with a partner. Decide what you are going to cook. Choose an interesting dish or meal: for example, something nutritious, unusual, or for a special occasion. Make sure it is relatively easy to cook.

---

*For Alternative Speaking Topics, see page 168.

Step 2: Write the script. Make your show as interesting and entertaining as possible by using humor, facts about the food, and visuals. It's easy to be funny when you use food idioms in this context. If you can, link your demonstration to a social or cultural situation.

Example

A: I'm making a four-layer sandwich, which has become a real hit in my office. And it's easy to make! Now, watch me carefully. First, I'm slicing . . . oops, I've dropped the knife. Can you pick it up for me?

B: Um . . . Can you see what I'm doing? I'm busy washing the lettuce, carrots, and green peppers. It's vegetable city here! Can't you pick it up yourself?

A: Uh oh, I see trouble brewing. My assistant doesn't want to assist? Now let's get cooking.

Step 3: Perform your cooking show for the class or videotape it and show it to the class.

Step 4: Watch the other class members' cooking shows. Rate four shows in the categories below. Write **1** for excellent, **2** for good, **3** for OK, and **4** for needs improvement.

	INSTRUCTIONS	INFORMATION ABOUT THE DISH OR MEAL	ACTING	HUMOR
Show 1				
Show 2				
Show 3				
Show 4				

ALTERNATIVE SPEAKING TOPICS

There are many new trends in food and in society. Work in groups of three. Each person should 1) Read one of the news clippings; 2) Summarize the topic in your own words; 3) React by giving your opinion about the topic. Write notes to explain your ideas. Then use your notes to report on the stories to your group.

Veganism Becoming More Popular

Vegans, people who do not consume any animal products, are becoming more and more common in many countries. A recent study estimated that about one percent of young people become vegans for a short time. Many older people express concern about this lifestyle, saying that it is unbalanced and unnatural.

Summary: _____

_____

_____

_____

Reactions: _____

_____

_____

_____

More Overweight Children

Childhood obesity, once a little known problem, is affecting increasing numbers of children in the world. Some people attribute this problem to our inactive lifestyle, while others blame it on the availability of fast food.

Summary: _____

_____

_____

_____

Reactions: _____

_____

_____

_____

The Surprising Value of a Sit-down Meal

A recent study suggested that there is a strong link between sit-down meals and school achievement. Children who grow up in families who eat dinner together on a daily basis tend to do better in school, make more friends, and have fewer social problems than those who do not.

Summary: _____

_____

_____

_____

Reactions: _____

_____

_____

_____

RESEARCH TOPICS, see page 223.

Finding a Niche:
The Challenge for Young Immigrants

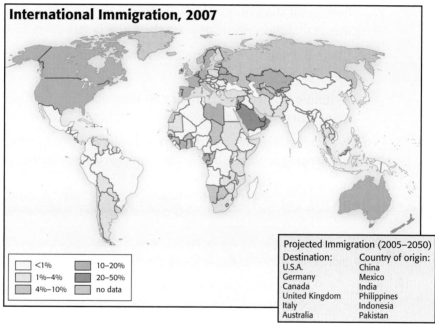

International Immigration, 2007

<1%	10–20%
1%–4%	20–50%
4%–10%	no data

Projected Immigration (2005–2050)

Destination:	Country of origin:
U.S.A.	China
Germany	Mexico
Canada	India
United Kingdom	Philippines
Italy	Indonesia
Australia	Pakistan

①FOCUS ON THE TOPIC

A PREDICT

Look at the map, the information about projected immigration, and the title of the unit. Then discuss the questions with a partner or small group.

1. Which areas of the world have the highest proportions of immigrants today? Is that likely to change in the future? Where will most immigrants probably come from in the next half century?

2. A *niche* here means a place that you fit in, or a group of people you fit in with—for example, your hometown, your family, a group of friends, a club, etc. What is a niche that you have? Why do you think it may be difficult for young immigrants to "find a niche"?

B SHARE INFORMATION

Work in a small group. Discuss the questions.

1. Have you ever moved to a different country? If so, describe the experience: How long did you live there? Why? What difficulties did you have? What did you learn? If you have never moved to a different country, do you know people who have? Describe their experience.

2. When teens immigrate, they face particular issues at school, and so do their teachers. Read these opinions. Decide whether you agree or disagree. Write **A** (agree) or **D** (disagree).

_____ **a.** One of the main responsibilities of teachers is to make sure that immigrant students maintain their own language and culture, even if it means that those students learn their new language more slowly.

_____ **b.** It is important that immigrants and non-immigrants study the same curriculum.

_____ **c.** As immigrant teens learn their new language, they become less proficient in their first language.

_____ **d.** Teenage immigrants should learn subjects like math and science in their first language, rather than in the language of their new country.

C BACKGROUND AND VOCABULARY

CD 3
🔢15 *Read and listen to the conversation between a college student and his professor. Then match the words on the left with the definitions on the right.*

TRAI: Good morning, Professor. I'd like to ask your advice about an oral presentation I'm doing on international immigration. I'm trying to narrow down my topic, and I'm thinking of concentrating on language policy. I've read that in some countries, such as the Netherlands, for example, immigrants have to take a language exam.

PROFESSOR LEE: Yes, that's right. Language policy is an interesting and controversial debate worldwide, but it involves complex legal issues, too. I'd suggest that you focus more on how language learning is connected with cultural identity. That's especially fascinating in Europe and the Middle East, which have large immigrant populations.

TRAI: Yes, and I know that there are some places in the U.S. with large immigrant populations, too. I was reading about a (**1**) **unique** neighborhood in New York City. This article said that if you walk down the street, you hear many people speaking in their (**2**) **native tongue**.

PROFESSOR LEE: Sure. Immigrant groups are **(3) flourishing** there, just like in many other states, like California, Texas, Florida, and so on. Now, some recent immigrants are not really part of the **(4) mainstream**. They tend to live in **(5) tight-knit** communities, although by the second or third generation, they will **(6) assimilate** to some extent. And, for example, the children tend to pick up English fast.

TRAI: Does their native language get **(7) suppressed**, then?

PROFESSOR LEE: Not necessarily. Actually, I came to this country as a child. I learned English, of course, but my parents also made me learn Korean. Fortunately, I was really motivated. My mother was very **(8) relieved** about that. She wanted me to be able to speak to my relatives. I haven't spoken Korean for a while now, though, so I probably need to **(9) bone up on** it!

TRAI: Did your parents learn English too?

PROFESSOR LEE: Not as well as we children did. It was kind of **(10) intimidating** for them because they were adults. They were uncomfortable and felt really **(11) uprooted** from their own country. They fit in a little better now, but their memories have **(12) set** them **apart** in some ways.

TRAI: Professor, thank you so much. This has been really helpful. I just got a great idea. I think I'll make my presentation about my cousin, who lives in France.

_____ 1. unique

_____ 2. native tongue

_____ 3. flourishing

_____ 4. mainstream

_____ 5. tight-knit

_____ 6. assimilate

_____ 7. suppressed

_____ 8. relieved

_____ 9. bone up on

_____ 10. intimidating

_____ 11. uprooted

_____ 12. set apart

a. special; individual

b. removed from; torn from

c. the common way of thinking or acting

d. not allowed to express

e. frightening

f. make someone or something different

g. growing and developing well

h. review; study again

i. adapt and adjust

j. happy that you don't have to worry about something

k. first language

l. close; connected

②FOCUS ON LISTENING

In New York City, where immigration is at a historical high, some young immigrants go to special schools, such as the International High Schools. You will hear a report by Richard Schiffman, with host Mary Ambrose, from the Public Radio International program *The World*. Schiffman interviews teachers and students at the International High School in Queens.

Students helping each other at the International High School in Queens

🎧 *Listen to the introduction and answer the questions.*
16

1. Why do you think that the approach at the International High School is successful?

   _____

   _____

2. How do you think the program differs from other high school programs that serve immigrant students?

   _____

   _____

◖**LISTEN FOR MAIN IDEAS**

🎧 *Listen to the report. Check (✓) the statements that are true about the International High School.*
17

_____ 1. Students work in groups, speaking their native languages.

_____ 2. Some students are immigrants to the United States, and others were born in the U.S.

_____ 3. Students improve both their English and their native language.

_____ 4. Teachers think that speaking two languages causes problems.

_____ 5. Students try to be assimilated quickly into American culture.

◖ LISTEN FOR DETAILS

CD 3 ⬤18 *Listen to the report again. Check (✓)whether each person is a student or teacher. List what they like about the school. Check your answers with a partner.*

PERSON BEING INTERVIEWED	STUDENT	TEACHER	WHAT THIS PERSON LIKES ABOUT THE SCHOOL
Jennifer Shenke	◯	◯	Students have a successful learning experience; they enjoy themselves
Priscilla Billarrel	◯	◯	
Aaron Listhaus	◯	◯	
Evelyna Namovich	◯	◯	
Kathy Rucker	◯	◯	

◖ MAKE INFERENCES

*Listen to the excerpts. Then write **A** if you think the speaker would agree with the idea that follows, and **D** if you think the speaker would disagree. Explain why.*

CD 3 ⬤19 **Excerpt One**

_____ "Most other high schools don't have students do group projects in class."

CD 3 ⬤20 **Excerpt Two**

_____ "American students can easily understand how we feel as new immigrants to their country."

CD 3 ⬤21 **Excerpt Three**

_____ "Students can use their native language to help learn a new language."

CD 3 ⬤22 **Excerpt Four**

_____ "Even though people speak different languages, inside, we all have the same feelings and ideas."

CD 3 ⬤23 **Excerpt Five**

_____ "American students should learn a second language too."

Work in a small group. Discuss your reaction to the comments. Which person's beliefs are most similar to your own?

1. Student: "I would love to attend the International High School. Just imagine being able to meet other students from all over the world!"

2. Parent: "I'm worried about my son studying math in our native language. In this country, only English matters. I'm afraid he will fall behind."

3. Visitor to the school: "I don't know if the teachers can control the situation when they don't understand what everyone is saying. And how can teachers be sure the kids aren't wasting time?"

4. Student: "I'm from Romania, but a lot of my classmates are Mexican. I'm not only learning English, I'm learning Spanish, too."

5. Researcher: "I think we should study the approach at the International High School closely. It might even be applicable to college education."

B LISTENING TWO: *The Words Escape Me*

This song, by Steve Coleman and the band called Gabriel's Hold, expresses some feelings from the perspective of a young person coming to live in a new country. (For more information about the music, visit www.gabrielshold.com or www.stevecoleman.org.)

1 CD 3 **24** *Listen to the song and circle the correct answer.*

1. What is the young man concerned about?
   a. learning a language
   b. finding a job
   c. getting on the right train

2. What problem does the singer have with communicating with people?
   a. They don't want to speak to him.
   b. His own pronunciation isn't good enough.
   c. They speak too quickly.

3. The singer questions a decision he made when he says, "What was I thinking?" What is he referring to?
   a. deciding to take the train in a foreign country
   b. deciding to come to the new country to live
   c. deciding to speak in a loud voice

4. What does the singer mean when he says, "I can also use your words to order only fish"?
   a. He knows how to say *fish*, so that's why he orders it.
   b. He can order food in restaurants, but not do anything else.
   c. He goes to restaurants that serve only fish.

5. Why does the singer say he doesn't "get the jokes"?

    a. Nobody will share jokes with him.

    b. He doesn't know any jokes to tell people.

    c. He can't understand jokes that people tell him.

6. Why does he feel that people think he's not smart?

    a. He can't communicate his knowledge in his new language.

    b. He does badly on examinations in his new language.

    c. He doesn't have a good job in his new country.

7. Why does the singer imagine people saying "Get out, get out"?

    a. He is late and he has to leave his house now.

    b. He is not confident around people, and he imagines they don't like him.

    c. He had a fight with someone he lives with.

8. How would you describe the singer's general tone in the song?

    a. frustrated

    b. motivated

    c. accepting

2 _CD 3 (24) Complete the song lyrics below by filling in the missing words. Compare your answers with a partner. Then listen again and check your answers._

The Words Escape Me

WORDS AND MUSIC BY STEVE COLEMAN

1   I was standing on a train platform in a _____ land.
           1.

2   I was 21 years old,

3   Excited to be involved, and to do my part, to understand everything I was told.

4   But they moved too quickly, talked too _____, moved too quickly.
           2.

5   I couldn't even catch my _____.
           3.

6   Frozen in a fast frame, action is blurred.

7   Loud, too loud, I can't understand your _____.
           4.

8   What was I thinking? I can't do this, learn this.

9   Think I'll just go home.

10   But I can't go home.

11   I worked out some bugs[1] and know where I live.

---

[1]**worked out some bugs:** solved some small problems.

(continued on next page)

12   I can also use your words to order only fish.

13   I try to eat their food; I _____ the meals from home.
                                          5.

14   I eat too little; I eat too much.

15   I'm _____ hard, but I don't get the jokes.
               6.

16   They think I'm _____; I can't tell them I'm not.
                          7.

17   Writing in this book makes me feel at home.

18   The words I can't _____, they're hiding my best, you know.
                            8.

19   What was I thinking? I can't do this, learn this.

20   Think I'll just go home.

21   But I can't go home.

22   Hey, yeah, words escape me, [repeat]

23   And I can't use my _____. [repeat]
                              9.
      I can't use it like you. [repeat]

24   *Learn the language, talk the language, learn the language, boy.* [repeat]

25   *Get out, get out, get out, get out, boy.* [repeat]

26   Oh, I'm too tired, I'm too old, it's too _____, it's too cold. I can't even . . .
                                                    10.

27   *Get out, get out, get out, get out, boy.*

28   Writing in this book makes me feel at home.

29   The words I can't escape are hiding my best, you know.

30   What was I thinking? I can't do this, learn this.

31   Think I'll just go home.

32   But I can't go home.

33   Hey, yeah, words escape me, [repeat]

34   And I can't use my tongue. [repeat]

◀ **STEP 1: Organize**

Work in a small group. Complete the chart with your ideas about how these people from Listenings One and Two would answer the questions.

TOPICS	NEW STUDENT AT THE INTERNATIONAL HIGH SCHOOL	SINGER OF "WORDS ESCAPE ME"
1. Specific problems these people face	• Inability to speak English	
2. Feelings about their new life in the United States		
3. Things that would help them to adapt better and find a niche in this country		

◀ **STEP 2: Synthesize**

Imagine that a new student at the International High School and the singer of "Words Escape Me" meet. What might they say to each other? Work in pairs and continue the conversation below. Discuss each topic in the chart, using specific information from the listenings.

Example

STUDENT: Hi, nice to meet you. Listen, I heard you just arrived, right?
SINGER: Yes, that's right. I only got here a couple of months ago. How about you?
STUDENT: I've been here for six months. It was pretty hard at first . . .

③ FOCUS ON SPEAKING

Ⓐ VOCABULARY

◖ REVIEW

Work with a partner. Look at a student's PowerPoint presentation about the experience of one young immigrant to France and read his comments. Fill in the blanks with words from the box. Then compare your answers with a partner's.

assimilate	interpret	mainstream	set her apart	tight-knit
boned up on	intimidated	niche	support	unique

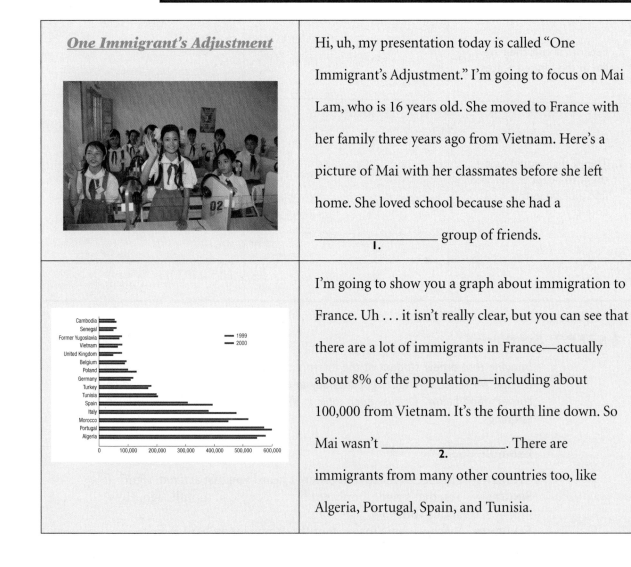

One Immigrant's Adjustment

Hi, uh, my presentation today is called "One Immigrant's Adjustment." I'm going to focus on Mai Lam, who is 16 years old. She moved to France with her family three years ago from Vietnam. Here's a picture of Mai with her classmates before she left home. She loved school because she had a

_____ group of friends.
   1.

I'm going to show you a graph about immigration to France. Uh . . . it isn't really clear, but you can see that there are a lot of immigrants in France—actually about 8% of the population—including about 100,000 from Vietnam. It's the fourth line down. So Mai wasn't _____. There are
                                   2.
immigrants from many other countries too, like Algeria, Portugal, Spain, and Tunisia.

Mai's Problems:

active, outgoing
➡️ quiet

good student
➡️ academic difficulties

Well, this was the problem: In Vietnam, Mai had been very active and outgoing. But when she went to France, it was very difficult for her to _____ 3. to her new life, in spite of the _____ 4. she got from her family. For example, although she was a very good student, she felt _____ 5. by her classes at school and couldn't seem to find a _____. 6.

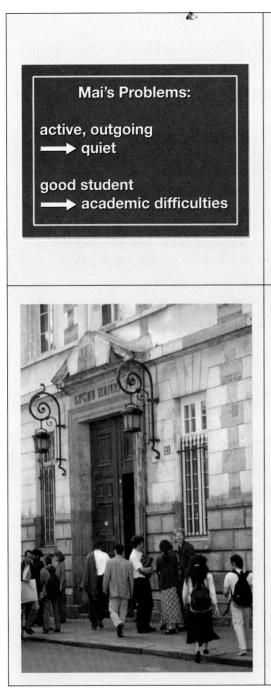

The hardest thing for Mai was that no one spoke her language and could _____ 7. for her. Not being able to express her opinions really _____ 8. from the other students.

But this story has a happy ending. After a few months, things began to get better. She _____ 9. her French, and she was able to join the _____ 10. classes with her French classmates. Mai not only made friends—she made the honor roll at school! Her parents were very proud of her. And I am, too. Mai is my cousin!

A high school with a large immigrant population put a suggestion box in its lobby, asking students to identify problems and suggest solutions.

Read the comments from the suggestion box. Pay attention to the bold words and phrases. Then match the words and phrases on the left to their definitions on the right.

Problem: There are lots of different languages and **dialects** in our school. I would like to learn more about them.
Suggestion: I think we should have some kind of information session. I'm interested in other people's cultures, and so are my classmates.

Problem: I think a lot of people **have a hard time** adjusting to high school. If they don't speak English very well, it's even harder for them to **blend in**, so there's a lot to **deal with**.
Suggestion: Could the school organize a cultural fair?

Problem: Some of the teachers talk too quickly in class for students with limited English.
Suggestion: It would be much better if we had more hands-on activities, because everyone **learns by doing**. That way, we'd be learning more and having fun **in the process**!

Problem: New students can feel left out. Some teachers try to force us to make friends with newcomers, but this doesn't work.
Suggestion: **Encouragement** works better than **punishment**. Let's have a "meet someone new" week with games and activities. Then we'll be motivated to **do our part** to improve our school community.

_____ 1. dialect

_____ 2. have a hard time

_____ 3. blend in

_____ 4. deal with

_____ 5. learn by doing

_____ 6. in the process

_____ 7. encouragement

_____ 8. punishment

_____ 9. do (your) part

a. a distinct variety of language

b. praise, support

c. at the same time, simultaneously

d. have difficulty

e. act in a similar way; not stand out or be noticed

f. do what is necessary to solve a problem

g. contribute a fair amount of the work; share the responsibility for accomplishing something

h. learn in an active, practical way

i. something that is done to make someone suffer

◀ CREATE

Work with a partner. Read the statements and decide how strongly you agree or disagree with each one. Circle a number from 1 (strongly agree) to 5 (strongly disagree). Then explain your choices to your partner. Use the words and phrases in the box and check (✓) each one as you or your partner uses it. Can you use them all?

assimilate	do (one's) part	intimidated	support
blend in	encouragement	learn by doing	tight-knit
bone up on	have a hard time	mainstream	unique
deal with	in the process	niche	
dialect	interpret	set (him) apart	

	Strongly Agree				**Strongly Disagree**

1. Adolescents have a much harder time adapting to life in a new country than adults or young children.   1   2   3   4   5

2. Sports, food, and music are among the most important areas where immigrants make an impact on their new country.   1   2   3   4   5

3. The most powerful emotion that an immigrant experiences in a new culture is fear.   1   2   3   4   5

4. After a person lives in a different country for some time, that person is never completely the same.   1   2   3   4   5

5. The experiences that immigrants first have when they get to a new country can have a crucial impact on their adjustment to their new lives.   1   2   3   4   5

B GRAMMAR: Present and Past—Contrasting Verb Tenses

1 *Work with a partner. Read the sentences and answer the questions.*

a. When **we're working** in class, we **help** each other. We**'re** all immigrants here, we all **know** what it feels like to be different, so we **support** one another.

b. Sometimes it **was** so difficult because I **didn't know** what the subject **was** all about, what the teacher **was speaking** about.

c. This project **has been** really successful. The students **have learned** a lot of math. They**'ve been working** together really well.

1. Which sentences are about actions in the present?

2. Which are about actions in the past?

3. Which sentences focus on activities in the past that are still relevant now?

PRESENT AND PAST—CONTRASTING VERB TENSES

Present Progressive and Simple Present	Examples
The **present progressive** is used to describe something that is happening right now, an action that is in progress.	The students in one group **are speaking** Polish.
The **simple present** is used to describe a general fact or habit.	The students at the International High School **speak** many different languages.
The **present progressive** can be used with the **simple present** to describe a present action that is continuing while another present action takes place.	While we**'re working** in class, we **help** each other.
The **simple present** is also used with non-action verbs to refer to states that are true at the moment of speaking.	The students **seem** to be enjoying the project they **are working** on right now.

Past Progressive and Simple Past	Examples
The **past progressive** is used to describe an action that was in progress at a specific time in the past.	The students **were designing** a temple during math class.
The **simple past** is used to describe an action that was completed in the past.	The students **finished** building their temple by the end of class.
The **past progressive** is used with the **simple past** to describe one action that was interrupted by another action.	The teacher **was walking** around the room when a student **asked** a question.
The **simple past** is used to describe two actions that happened in a sequence, one after the other.	Another student **stopped** working and **helped** her classmate with the answer.

Present Perfect and Present Perfect Progressive	Examples
The **present perfect** and **present perfect progressive** are used to talk about things that started in the past, continue to the present, and may continue in the future.	She **has lived** in the United States since her twenty-first birthday. She **has been living** in the United States since her twenty-first birthday.
The **present perfect** is used to talk about things that happened • at an unspecified time in the past; • more than one time in the past.	She **has taken** the math test. She **has taken** several math tests this year.

2 *Read the interview with Lisa Chin, a Chinese-American physician. Complete the sentences using the correct forms of the verbs. Then read the interview aloud with a partner, switching roles in the middle.*

INTERVIEWER: Dr. Chin, your mother was an immigrant. Her family was uprooted because of war. You were saying that she came to this country under very different conditions than we have now. What was it like for her as a young girl?

DR. CHIN: Well, her experience wasn't unique in those days. When my mother
_____ to this country from China, she
    1. (come)
_____, let's see, I guess about eight years old. She
    2. (be)
_____ any English. When she _____ to
  3. (not / speak)   **4. (go)**
school, there _____ any special classes for immigrants.
    5. (not / be)
Immigrant students _____ to join the regular classes,
    6. (have)
even if they couldn't speak English. My mother said this
_____ very difficult for her at first.
  7. (be)

INTERVIEWER: Did she tell you what those school days were like for her?

DR. CHIN: Oh, yes. She talks about it a lot now. On the first day of school, she
_____ anything the teacher _____ about.
  8. (not / understand)   **9. (talk)**
But when my mother _____ a friend to explain in
    10. (ask)
Chinese, the teacher _____ angry and
    11. (become)
_____ her to speak only English.
  12. (tell)

INTERVIEWER: That sounds like a lot of pressure for such a young girl.

DR. CHIN: I'm sure it was. My grandparents also _____ her to
    13. (want)
learn English quickly. They _____ that it was important
    14. (feel)
for her to blend in. They _____ that learning English
    15. (think)
would help my mother succeed. Soon, my mother _____
    16. (feel)

(continued on next page)

the same way. In fact, today she _____ Chinese very
17. (not / speak)

well at all, and she can't read or write it.

INTERVIEWER: Since then, the world _____ quite a bit. With all the
18. (change)

new technology, it _____ difficult to travel and
19. (not / be)

communicate with people all over the globe. How do you think all

this has affected your family?

DR. CHIN: That's a good question. Well, I guess we _____ truly
20. (be)

part of a global economy now. People's attitudes are different in

many ways. For example, attitudes about language

_____ a lot since I was young. Many people feel that it
21. (change)

_____ an advantage to speak two or more languages. I
22. (be)

can see that change when I _____ at my children.
23. (look)

INTERVIEWER: When you look at your children?

DR. CHIN: My kids _____ English at home all their lives, but
24. (speak)

today they both _____ a "two-way" bilingual Chinese
25. (attend)

school. That's where English-speaking children study Chinese, and

Chinese-speaking children study English. So my children are

Chinese-American, but they _____ to speak Chinese
26. (learn)

for the first time now. They _____ the school because
27. (love)

all the students _____ very good friends. They
28. (become)

_____ each other the new language. My children
29. (teach)

_____ their friends learn English, and their friends
30. (help)

_____ them Chinese at the same time.
31. (teach)

INTERVIEWER: How do you think it helps the kids?

DR. CHIN: Well, I really believe that in the future, knowing a second language will

help my children get better jobs and, well, find their niche with so

many different people . . .

INTERVIEWER: You mean sort of a multicultural society?

DR. CHIN: Yes, exactly.

INTERVIEWER: So, how is your mother doing now?

DR. CHIN: Well, she's doing really well, actually. You know, she _____
              32. (not / speak)

Chinese since she was a girl, so she _____ how to speak
                                      33. (not / remember)

it any more. Now she _____ that she hadn't forgotten it.
                      34. (wish)

In fact, she _____ language lessons recently, trying to
             35. (take)

bone up on her Chinese!

3 *Work with a partner.*

*Student A: Ask Student B the questions about the interview. Use the correct verb
tense. Listen to Student B's responses and ask follow-up questions to find out more
information.*

*Student B: Respond to Student A's questions. Use an appropriate verb tense. Some
questions are not answered directly in the interview, so you must express your own opinion
based on what you have read.*

Example

Where / be / Dr. Chin's mother born?

A: Where was Dr. Chin's mother born?
B: She was born in China.

Student A

1. How long / she / be / in the United States?

2. How / she / feel / about speaking Chinese when she was in school in the U.S.?

3. How / she / feel / about it now?

4. Why / her feelings / change?

5. What new technology / change / the way people learn other languages?

6. How / you / feel / when people speak a language you don't understand?

Now switch roles.

Student B

7. What / be / Dr. Chin's native language?

8. What / be / the benefits of a bilingual school?

9. How / the bilingual school / help / Dr. Chin's children?

10. What types of jobs / require / a bilingual person?

11. How / Dr. Chin's views about language / differ / from her grandparents' views?

12. In your opinion, what kind of school / be / best for immigrant children?

C SPEAKING

◖ **PRONUNCIATION:** *ship* /ʃ/, *measure* /ʒ/, *cheap* /tʃ/, *and* *jazz* /dʒ/

C D 3
25 *Listen to the sounds of the bold letters in this sentence.*

It's hard to mea**s**ure how immi**g**ration affe**c**ts a culture, but it's an interesting sub**j**ect.
　　　　　/ʒ/　　　　　　/ʃ/　　　　　　/tʃ/　　　　　　　　　　/dʒ/

/ʃ/ SHIP, /ʒ/ MEASURE, /tʃ/ CHEAP, AND /dʒ/ JAZZ

These four sounds are similar in some ways but different in others. The outside of the mouth looks the same for all four sounds. The lips are a little rounded and protrude (stick out) a little. Inside the mouth, the tongue pulls back from the top teeth with all four sounds.

The first sound in *child* /tʃ/ starts with /t/. The first sound in *just* /dʒ/ starts with /d/. You cannot hear the /t/ or /d/ as separate sounds, but you must say them to pronounce these words correctly.

The first sounds in *ship* /ʃ/ and *child* /tʃ/ are voiceless. The vocal chords do not vibrate. The bold sounds in *pleasure* /ʒ/ and *just* /dʒ/ are voiced. The vocal chords vibrate. When these sounds end words, do not release them strongly. Keep these sounds short at the end of a word.

Voiceless /ʃ/	Voiced /ʒ/		Voiceless /tʃ/	Voiced /dʒ/
she	plea**s**ure		**ch**ild	**j**ust
wa**sh**	bei**g**e		wa**tch**	a**g**e

Spellings: The spellings of these four sounds can be confusing.

Common Spellings		Uncommon Spellings
/ʃ/	**sh**ip, wi**sh**, na**ti**on, popula**ti**on artifi**ci**al, spe**ci**al, physi**ci**an	posse**ss**ion, **Ch**icago, ma**ch**ine
/ʒ/	(this is a rare sound in English and has a variety of spellings) deci**si**on, conclu**si**on, vi**si**on plea**su**re, trea**su**re, lei**su**re, ca**su**al bei**ge**, gara**ge** A**si**an	
/tʃ/	**ch**eck, **ch**eap, mu**ch**, ma**tch**, ca**tch**	na**tu**ral, ma**tu**re
/dʒ/	**j**azz, ed**ge**, a**ge**	gra**du**al, indivi**du**al

1 CD 3 26 *Listen to the list of words. Put a check (✓) in the column that describes the sound of the bold letters.*

	/ʃ/ SHE	/ʒ/ PLEASURE	/tʃ/ CHILD	/dʒ/ JUST
1. interna**ti**onal	✓			
2. langua**ge**				✓
3. en**j**oy				
4. ad**j**ust				
5. mea**su**re				
6. lec**tu**re				
7. tradi**ti**onal				
8. cul**tu**re				
9. u**su**al				
10. puni**sh**ment				
11. spe**ci**al				
12. sub**j**ect				

(continued on next page)

	/ʃ/ SHE	/ʒ/ PLEASURE	/tʃ/ CHILD	/dʒ/ JUST
13. **Chile**				
14. televi**si**on				
15. edu**c**ators				
16. occa**si**on				
17. communica**ti**on				
18. encoura**ge**				
19. trea**s**ure				
20a. ni**che**				
20b. ni**che**				
21. flouri**sh**				

2 *Work with a partner. Practice pronouncing /ʃ/, /ʒ/, /tʃ/, and /dʒ/.*

Student A: Read the comments or questions.

Student B: Use the words in parentheses to help you with your answers. Pay attention to your pronunciation of these sounds. Switch roles after number 6.

Example

STUDENT A: The United States attracts people from all over the world.
STUDENT B: (That's right . . . salad bowl) That's right, it's a real salad bowl.

Student A

1. Do the students seem to like the International High School?

2. Is it typical for immigrants to feel uncomfortable at first?

3. Immigrants have to learn to adjust in many ways.

4. The high school we heard about seems unique.

Student B

1. (Yes . . . enjoy it)

2. (Yes . . . usually the case)

3. (That's right . . . find their niche)

4. (Yes . . . special)

5. Do the teachers at that school often lecture?

5. (No . . . only occasionally)

6. Ms. Shenke uses an unusual approach.

6. (Right . . . doesn't lecture)

Now switch roles.

Student B

Student A

7. The report said that the school was multilingual.

7. (That's right . . . different languages)

8. Did the report mention a country in South America?

8. (Yes . . . Chile)

9. The teachers at this school don't seem to believe in discipline through fear, do they?

9. (No . . . Instead . . . encouragement)

10. Is it hard to tell how successful a new approach is at first?

10. (Yes . . . takes time to measure results)

11. Can you think of another word for *instructor*?

11. (Yes . . . *educator*)

12. It's important to talk to others when you have a problem, don't you think?

12. (Yes . . . communication)

◀ **FUNCTION: Hesitating in Response to a Question**

When you respond to a question, or when someone asks for your opinion, you sometimes need time to think about your answer and to decide what to say. Here are some expressions to use when you hesitate in response to a question.

HESITATING IN RESPONSE TO A QUESTION	
I need a moment to think about that . . .	Umm, that's a good question . . .
I'm not sure . . .	Well, uh . . .
Let me think a minute . . .	Well, let's see . . .
Hang on a minute . . .	Well, you know . . .

1 *Study the short conversation. Circle the expression that is used to show hesitation. Then practice the conversation with a partner.*

A: I just read a report about where most immigrants to the United States came from in the early twentieth century. You'll never guess where most of them came from!
B: Let me think a minute. Was it Latin America?
A: Actually, it wasn't. In fact, it was Europe.
B: Really! I'm very surprised.

2 *Work with a partner. Exchange information about the country of origin of those who immigrated to the United States from 1820–1975.*

Student A: Ask Student B the questions below the chart.

Student B: Cover the questions. Listen to Student A ask the questions. Look at the chart below to find the answer. Use an expression to hesitate as you look for the answer.

Student A

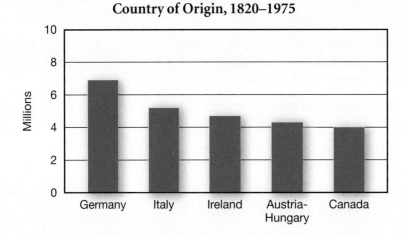

Country of Origin, 1820–1975

1. Where did most of the immigrants come from during this period?
2. Did many immigrants come from Latin America during this time?
3. What time period does the chart cover?
4. Does the chart show how old the immigrants were?

Now switch roles. You will exchange information about the country of origin of those who immigrated to the United States from 1976–1986.

Student B: Ask Student A the questions below the chart on the next page.

Student A: Cover the questions. Listen to Student B ask the questions. Look at the chart on the next page to find the answer. Use an expression to hesitate as you look for the answer.

Student B

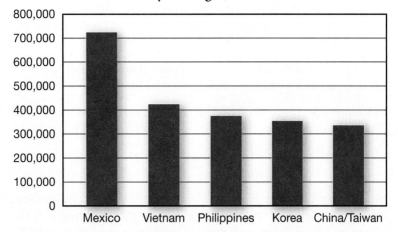

Country of Origin, 1976–1986

5. Did any of the countries in the first chart continue sending immigrants to the United States during this period?

6. What country sent the most immigrants during this time?

7. Was Europe still the continent that most immigrants came from?

8. How many immigrants came from Korea?

◀ PRODUCTION: A Town Meeting

> Many countries and cities are trying to find the best way to help immigrants adapt to their new lives. You live in a community that is currently growing as the result of immigration. In this activity, you will **hold a town meeting to discuss how to help the entire community adjust to this change**. Try to use the vocabulary, grammar, pronunciation, and language for hesitating that you learned in the unit.*

Step 1: Look at the five categories of immigrants to your town. On your own, take notes on your answers to the following questions:

- What benefits will the immigrants gain?
- What benefits will the town gain?
- What challenges will the immigrants face?
- What challenges will the town face?

*For Alternative Speaking Topics, see page 192.

Category A: Highly skilled professionals, such as doctors or engineers, with a very different culture and religion from most of the people in the town.

Category B: Elderly relatives of citizens who already live in the town. These immigrants might soon need state-supported medical care and are already past working age.

Category C: Refugees who are fleeing natural disasters or war. Many of these people do not speak the language in the town.

Category D: Young adults, who would like to attend the local college, but who may not share the political and social beliefs in the town.

Category E: Unskilled or semi-skilled workers, many of whom are willing to do low-paying or dangerous jobs.

Step 2: Work in a small group. Discuss both the benefits and challenges that the immigrants and the town will face. Then rank the categories from 1 to 5. Which group will need the most help (1) in adjusting to the town? Which group will need the least help (5)?

Step 3: Share your ideas with the whole class and expain your rankings.

ALTERNATIVE SPEAKING TOPICS

Work in a small group. Discuss the questions.

1. Do you think official printed matter, such as information about schools and hospitals, voter registration materials, legal advice, drivers' permits and so on, should be made available in many languages to help immigrants cope? Why or why not?

2. Would you like to be a teacher in a school with a large immigrant population? Why, or why not?

3. Would you prefer to learn a new language in a class where
   - everyone spoke your native language?
   - no one spoke your native language?
   - many different native languages were spoken?

4. What are the immigration issues in the country where you are living? How are they similar to or different from issues in the countries mentioned in the unit?

RESEARCH TOPICS, see page 223.

UNIT 10
No Technology? No Way!

① FOCUS ON THE TOPIC

Ⓐ PREDICT

Look at the cartoon and the title of the unit. Then discuss the questions with a partner or small group.

1. Why do you think the man is hiding from his laptop and his cell phone?

2. What do you think the title of the unit—"No technology? No way!"—means?

Work in a small group. Look at the graph and then discuss the questions.

Percentage of Technology Use in the U.S. for Adults Ages 18–64 (2006)

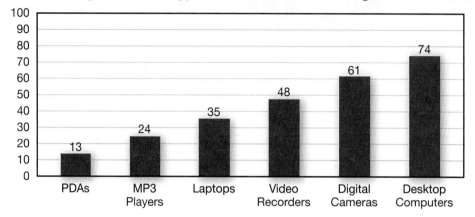

1. Draw in the bars for people in your country, based on your best guesses.

2. Look at the items in the box. Do you think they have improved or diminished the quality of our lives? In what ways?

3. Look again at the items. Circle the five which have improved your life the most, and explain your choices. Which of the items do you never use? Why not?

cell phones	MP3 players	VoIP (voice-over Internet protocol: Internet phone services such as Skype)
computer games	social networking sites (Facebook, MySpace)	
instant messaging		YouTube
Internet shopping	voice mail	other: _____

Complaining in public has become popular on the Internet. It's easy with blogs (short for "Web logs"), which are Web sites containing the personal opinions and comments of a single writer. They are usually written in diary form and updated frequently. Guests to the site may add their own comments.

The blog below chronicles one writer's daily beefs, or complaints, related to annoying sounds in everyday life.

 Read and listen to the blog and some of the comments from readers. Then circle the letter of the word or phrase below that is closest in meaning to the words in bold.

HERE'S MY BEEF!
Blogsite of Johnny Le Boeuf

Today's beef is NOISE! The **(1) sonic** pollution around here is **(2) sending me over the edge**! Is it just me, or is life getting too loud? Last night was awful for me. It didn't start out that way, mind you. In fact, I thought it was going to be a peaceful evening. My family was out shopping and I had the place to myself and was ready for a good night's sleep.

At around 10:00 P.M., the dog in the apartment downstairs started barking. And he continued to bark all night. I mean aaaalll night! The noise was really getting under my skin. After trying to reach the owners and getting no response, I started planning **(3) retaliatory** steps, like, you know, turning on my TV really loud! AHA! I thought, I'll keep THEM awake all night! Or maybe letting their dog out of the apartment. I'm not normally some kind of **(4) vigilante**, but I was getting a little crazy at this point! Anyway, it was 4 A.M. when I last saw the clock . . .

Next thing I know, I'm **(5) jolted** out of sleep when the alarm clock goes off at 6:00 A.M. And get this: the dog IS STILL BARKING! I drink some water and notice that the dog has finally shut up, so I decide to take a few extra minutes to relax before getting ready for work. But just as I lie down, the quiet is **(6) shattered** by two cars outside that start honking at each other like it's party time or something. We're talking 6:15 in the morning! By this time I am so ticked off I could have **(7) towed** both cars away—with my bare hands! Fortunately, I can now hear the **(8) wail** of a police **(9) siren**. Maybe they're coming for those honking cars . . .

All right, I've finished. I just hope I can have some peace and quiet tonight . . .

Comments posted Thursday:

9:33 A.M.
I totally agree, man! I think any loud noises in residential areas should be totally **(10) banned** before 7 A.M. Sonic pollution has become a nightmare in the city where I'm living.
Carlos

9:46 A.M.
You are so right! Reading your piece **(11) prompted** me finally to do something about my upstairs neighbors, who keep talking (loudly!) and playing music at all hours. I hate to be the cranky old woman in my building, but I've had it with the noise. So this time I actually called the police. I'm sure my neighbors are mad at me, but that shut them up, all right! At least tonight I can finally have some quiet!
Linda

10:07 A.M.
Johnny,
My beef is constant loud construction work. Workers have been constructing an ugly office building near my house for the past six months. The noise has been constant, 16 hours a day. They even work at night with lights! I can feel the **(12) vibrations** of the heavy machines right through my floor and walls. The noise is driving me crazy!
Gerard

1. **a.** noise   **b.** air   **c.** solar

2. **a.** hurting me   **b.** making me tired   **c.** frustrating me greatly

3. **a.** involving revenge   **b.** immediate   **c.** official

4. a person who . . .
     a. helps others   **b.** punishes others   **c.** is crazy

5.	a. helped	b. persuaded	c. startled; surprised
6.	a. increased	b. annoyed	c. destroyed
7.	a. removed	b. parked	c. damaged
8.	a. long loud cry	b. words	c. whisper
9.	a. officer	b. station	c. warning signal
10.	a. prohibited	b. permitted	c. requested
11.	a. reminded	b. caused	c. allowed
12.	a. sounds	b. movements	c. echoes

②FOCUS ON LISTENING

A LISTENING ONE: Noise in the City

You will hear a segment of a report from *Living on Earth* by Neal Rauch of Public Radio International. Rauch interviews several residents of a large city about their beef with one type of sonic pollution. Steve Curwood is the host of this news program.

CD 3
28 *Listen to the report and answer the questions. Compare your answers with a partner.*

1. What do you think is causing the noise you heard?

   _____

2. How do you think people feel when they hear this noise?

   _____

3. What might they do after hearing the noise?

   _____

◖ LISTEN FOR MAIN IDEAS

CD 3
29 *You will now hear the entire report. Read each statement and write **T** (true) or **F** (false).*

_____ 1. Many New Yorkers agree about banning this form of sonic pollution.

_____ 2. When an alarm goes off too often, vigilante groups sometimes do something to damage the car.

_____ 3. These gadgets are effective at preventing theft.

_____ 4. These gadgets can affect people's health.

_____ 5. There are no laws or penalties to punish drivers whose alarms go off for too long a time.

_____ 6. Police can break into a vehicle if it makes too much noise for too long.

◀ LISTEN FOR DETAILS

🎧 CD 3
30
Listen to the report again. As you listen, take notes on the opinions of the people. Then compare your answers with a partner's.

1. Judy Evans, scenic designer and artist
   a. Why are these devices such a problem at night?

   _____

   b. What usually happens when a person makes a lot of noise in public?

   _____

2. The "egg man," a music producer and composer
   a. What does he (and his neighbors) do when they hear one of these things go off?

   _____

   b. What do other vigilante groups sometimes do?

   _____

3. Lucille DiMaggio, a target of retaliation from vigilantes
   a. What happened to her car?

   _____

   b. What happened when she set off her device in the restaurant parking lot?

   _____

4. Judy Evans, scenic designer and artist
   a. What happened on a different night when she heard one of these things going off?

   _____

   b. What should happen to these types of gadgets in densely populated neighborhoods?

   _____

5. Catherine Abate, New York state senator
   a. How does the noise from alarms affect people?

   _____

   b. How can loud noise be particularly harmful to young people?

   _____

6. Neil Rauch, radio reporter
   a. How have existing laws helped cut down on noise from these devices?

   _____

   b. How would it be helpful if owners of these gadgets adjusted them to be less sensitive to vibrations?

   _____

Listen to the excerpts from the radio report. Pay attention to each speaker's tone of voice and choice of words. Evaluate how serious or humorous the speaker sounds as he or she makes a complaint or gives an opinion. Check (✓) the appropriate column.

	MOSTLY SERIOUS	SOMEWHAT SERIOUS	SOMEWHAT HUMOROUS	MOSTLY HUMOROUS
CD 3 ㉛ **Excerpt One: Judy Evans**				
Tone of voice	❑	❑	❑	❑
Choice of words	❑	❑	❑	❑
CD 3 ㉜ **Excerpt Two: Lucille DiMaggio**				
Tone of voice	❑	❑	❑	❑
Choice of words	❑	❑	❑	❑
CD 3 ㉝ **Excerpt Three: Senator Abate**				
Tone of voice	❑	❑	❑	❑
Choice of words	❑	❑	❑	❑
CD 3 ㉞ **Excerpt Four: "Egg Man"**				
Tone of voice	❑	❑	❑	❑
Choice of words	❑	❑	❑	❑

◖ EXPRESS OPINIONS

Work in a small group. Discuss the questions.

1. How serious is noise pollution from sources such as car alarms? In what ways can sonic pollution be damaging to people's health?

2. What do you think of the vigilante group in the report? Do you agree with any of their choices? Explain.

Ⓑ LISTENING TWO: The Ten Commandments of Cell Phone Etiquette

Dan Briody once wrote a column about the "Ten Commandments" (rules) of cell-phone use. The interviewer, John Gordon, discusses how Briody's article has been "passed around the blogosphere" on the Internet for several years, but the article is still current because rude, obnoxious cell phone behavior is still with us.

1 *Listen to the interview and circle the correct answer to complete each statement.*

1. Dan Briody's column first appeared _____.
   a. in the year 2000
   b. when cell phones were first invented
   c. when the Internet became popular

2. Cell phone talkers are _____.
   a. not as well behaved as they were in the past
   b. better than they were before
   c. becoming more accepting of others' habits

3. The best way not to offend people is to _____.
   a. choose classical music for your ring tone
   b. switch your cell phone off
   c. set the phone to *vibrate*

4. In public performances, people tend to _____.
   a. hear an announcement asking them not to interrupt the performance
   b. leave the theater when their phone rings
   c. fight about cell phone use

5. Cell phones are _____.
   a. no longer used as fashion statements
   b. used to impress other people with their style
   c. commonly selected for their features, not their look or color

6. The number one commandment is to not _____.
   a. subject others to your phone conversations
   b. use your phone on the train
   c. use your phone on the street

7. The problem with speaking on your phone in a public place is that it _____.
   a. creates a lack of privacy
   b. disturbs everyone around you
   c. can be dangerous

2 *Work in a small group. Discuss the questions.*

- The Ten Commandments are ancient laws about life taken from the Bible. Do you think the title of this listening is appropriate? Is the title meant to be serious? Explain.

- As more personal technology becomes available, there is an increasing risk that it will bother other people. What other examples can you give, apart from those you heard in the listenings, of one person's use of technology bothering someone else?

◀ **STEP 1: Organize**

Work in a small group. Listening One and Listening Two described problems with technology and some people's responses and solutions to those problems. Complete the chart with the problems that match the given solutions.

	PROBLEM	RESPONSE	IS RESPONSE APPROPRIATE?
Noise in the City	1.	Leave note on car saying, "Fix your car alarm. It disturbed hundreds of people last night." Break an egg on windshield. Put grease on windshield. Break windshield.	
Ten Commandments	1.	Select music that won't offend anyone. Set ring tone to vibrate.	
	2.	Make announcements that remind people to turn off phone.	
	3.	Go to a vestibule (wide passage near the door).	

◀ **STEP 2: Synthesize**

Work with a partner. One of you is a civic leader concerned about both sonic pollution and crime by vigilantes. The other of you is a citizen frustrated by the sonic pollution in your neighborhood. Take turns explaining a problem and response from the chart. Then together, evaluate the response. Is it appropriate? Would it be effective? Before you begin, take notes in the last column of the box.

3 FOCUS ON SPEAKING

A VOCABULARY

REVIEW

Work with a partner.

Student A: Look at Conversation One. Complete each statement by choosing the correct word or phrase from the box. Read the statements to Student B. Then listen to Student B's response, and check that Student B has used the word or phrase in parentheses. Continue with numbers 2 and 3. Do the same with Conversation Two.

Student B: Read the directions on page 215.

Conversation 1

banned	getting under my skin	siren
frustrated	jolts	wails

Student A:

1. My new clock radio is really _____. I wish I'd never bought it.

   (Your partner should use *prompted* in the response.)

2. Well, the alarm goes off too often! And it makes a really annoying noise. It

   _____ me out of my sleep.

   (Your partner should use *defective* in the response.)

3. It's not broken. I just can't figure out how to set it. The instructions are so

   complicated that I just get _____ and give up whenever I try to

   read them.

   (Your partner should use *frazzled* in the response.)

Conversation 2

defective	irritated	pay a fine	vigilantes
drive you crazy	offense	sirens	

Student A:

4. Hi. What's up? You look really _____.

   (Your partner should use *I've had it* in the response.)

5. Yeah. They really play their music too loud. I guess it can _____ if you hear it all day.

   (Your partner should use *retaliatory steps* in the response.)

6. You're kidding! You called the police? Are those kids breaking the law? I mean, is it really a(n) _____ to play loud music?

   (Your partner should use *disturbing the peace* in the response.)

7. If kids had to _____ for breaking the law, they would think twice about making so much noise next time.

   (Your partner should use *banned* in the response.)

8. Well, don't do anything extreme. I mean, don't turn into one of those _____.

   (Your partner should use *siren* in the response.)

9. Wow. I guess you've really had it!

   (end of the conversation)

1 *Listen to some common noises. What do you think makes each noise? Write your response in the left column of the chart.*

Noise	What Makes the Noise?	Adjectives to Describe the Noise
1. bang	_____	_____
2. beep	_____	_____
3. buzz	_____	_____
4. clang	_____	_____
5. honk	_____	_____
6. hum	_____	_____
7. rattle	_____	_____
8. ring	_____	_____
9. screech	_____	_____
10. tick	_____	_____
11. whistle	_____	_____

2 *Listen to the noises again. Choose one or two adjectives from the box to describe each noise (or use other adjectives that you know). Write them in the right column of the chart above. Then compare your answers with a partner's.*

annoying	constant	jolting	piercing	soft
awful	faint	loud	rhythmic	startling
comforting	irritating	low	shrill	

◖ CREATE

In Listening Two you heard Dan Briody discuss his "Ten Commandments of Cellphone Use." Work with a partner. Take turns creating some of your own "commandments." Talk about what sounds annoy you and your plans to stop them. Plan what you're going to say by making notes in the chart on page 204.

Example

I'm really **frazzled** by the sound of cars **honking** their horns. It's such an **irritating** sound! So my first commandment is, "Cars can only honk in a real emergency." If someone honks for an unimportant reason, they will have to **pay a fine.** My second commandment is . . .

DEVICE OR SERVICE	NOTES ON WHAT YOU WANT TO SAY	VOCABULARY TO USE
Cars		
Fax machines		
Fireworks		
Lawn mowers		
Hand-held DVD players or video games		
Trains		
Web sites that use sound		
Your idea:		

1 *Work with a partner. Read the sentences and answer the questions.*

   a. By the time I figure out how to work the remote, the news **will** already **have started**.

   b. We **will be hearing** from more listeners right after this break.

   1. Are these sentences about activities in the past, present, or future?

   2. In sentence a, which of these events will happen first:
   a. I figure out how to work the remote.   **b.** The news starts.

   3. In sentence b, which of these events will happen first:
   a. We hear from listeners.   **b.** This break (occurs).

FUTURE PERFECT AND FUTURE PROGRESSIVE

Both the **future perfect** and the **future progressive** are commonly used to speak about events in the future.

Future Perfect	Examples
The **future perfect** is used to talk about a future action that will *already have been completed* by a certain time in the future.	By the time I **figure out** how to use the remote, the news **will** already **have started**. (*or* the news **will have** already **started**)
The future perfect is used with the simple present tense to show the relationship between two future events.	
The event that will take place first uses the future perfect. The event that will take place second uses the simple present tense.	
To form the future perfect, active voice: Use *will* + *have* + **past participle**	By tomorrow evening, **I will have sent** about 20 email messages.
To form the future perfect, passive voice: Use *will* + *have been* + **past participle**	By the end of the week, about 50 email messages **will have been sent.**
Future Progressive	**Examples**
The **future progressive** is used to describe actions that will be in progress at a specific time in the future.	If the trend **continues**, and cell phones **become** more and more popular, people **will be spending** most of their waking hours on the phone.
To form the future progressive: Use *will* + *be* + **present participle**	In the future, we**'ll be using** a lot of new technology.

2 *Work with a partner. Play the "Mystery Item" game using the future perfect. Student A, look at the directions on this page. Student B, look at page 216.*

Student A: Read the clues about some common items. Fill in the blanks with future perfect forms of the verbs in parentheses. Then read the first two clues about the mystery item to Student B. If Student B cannot guess what the item is, read the third and fourth clues.

Mystery Item 1: Clues

1. By this time next year, you _____ the battery in your mystery
   (replace)
   item.

2. Small factories and workshops _____ about 80 million of these
   (produce)
   items by the end of this year, and almost everybody has at least one of them.

3. This mystery item was invented in Germany around 1500.

4. Today it is the number one jewelry item in the world.

Mystery Item 2: Clues

1. You definitely use this item; in fact, you probably _____ it once
   (use)
   or twice by the end of the day.

2. By the end of the day, these items _____ millions of gallons of
   (use)
   water around the world.

3. The modern version of this item saves a lot more water than previous versions
   did.

4. It has greatly improved since it was first invented, and now you would probably
   find it very hard to live without.

Mystery Item 3: Clues

1. There is a good chance that someone in your family _____ your
   (turn on)
   mystery item before nine o'clock tonight.

2. This mystery item will not go out of style. In fact, by the end of this century,
   this item _____ any less important than it is today for
   (not / become)
   entertainment and news.

3. Millions of people use the item every second.

4. This item was first available only in black and white.

Answers: (1) watch (2) toilet (3) TV

3 *Work with a partner. Discuss what type of technology people will be using in the next 10 to 20 years and beyond. Use the ideas below and your own ideas to make predictions about what people will and won't be doing. Use the future progressive when you make your predictions.*

Example

By the end of this decade, people **will** probably **be vacationing** in outer space.

- vacation in outer space
- use video telephones
- live past the age of 100
- select their children's genetic characteristics

- use robots to do housework
- drive electric or solar-powered cars
- do all their shopping online
- get a complete education online

C SPEAKING

◀ PRONUNCIATION: Adverbial Particles

🔊 *CD 3*
37 *Listen to the bold words in the sentences. Which word in each pair is stressed?*

Hand it **in in** an hour.

Try it **on on** Sunday.

Pick it **up up** the block.

ADVERBIAL PARTICLES

Adverbial particles like *up*, *down*, *off*, *on*, *back*, and *out* are usually stressed.
I'm fed UP!

- Stress these particles when they are used as adverbs after verbs.
  Come BACK!

- Stress them when they are part of separable two word verbs.
  Turn it DOWN.

- Do not stress these words when they are used as prepositions or as part of an infinitive.
  Turn left <u>on</u> the next street.
  I want <u>to</u> move!

- Adverbial particles that begin with vowel sounds, like *up*, *on*, *in*, *out*, and *off*, join closely to the consonant sound of the preceding word.
  Come ON!   Hurry UP!   Get OUT!

---

1 CD 3 38 *Listen to the sentences. The prepositions and particles are bold. Circle the adverbial particles that are stressed.*

  1. I tried **to** read the instructions, but then I gave **up**.

  2. I asked him **to** turn it **down**, but he said he didn't want **to**.

  3. Come **in** and sit **down**. You look really worn **out**.

  4. I want **to** buy a new car. This one keeps breaking **down**.

  5. I'm taking this new gadget **back**. I can't get it **to** work, and I'm really fed **up**.

2 CD 3 39 *Listen to the complaint about technology.*

  A *Circle the particles that are stressed.*

  I give up! I've had it with these modern appliances! I bought a new alarm clock,

  but it goes off whenever it feels like it. Last night it went off at midnight. I got up

  before I realized what time it was. First I got angry and threw it out. Then I took

  it out of the garbage and decided to take it back. I want to get my money back!

  B *Look at the words before* **up, on, in,** *and* **out**. *Draw a line from the final consonant sound of the preceding word to the vowel of the particle. Then practice reading the complaint with a partner. Stress adverbial particles and join words together smoothly.*

3 *Work with a partner. Match the comments on the left with the responses on the right. Then practice the dialogues. Stress the particles and join words together smoothly when appropriate.*

  _____ 1. When did the police show up?

  _____ 2. Do you want to go out tonight?

  _____ 3. My new alarm clock goes off all the time.

  _____ 4. I'm fed up with those new machines.

  _____ 5. Ugh! I have six new voice messages and no time to make calls.

  a. I can't. I have to get up early.

  b. I know. They're always breaking down.

  c. Why don't you take it back to the store?

  d. But they're probably new customers. You have to call them back.

  e. Forty minutes after I called them up.

◖ **FUNCTION: Expressing Frustration**

There are many ways of expressing frustration. For example, in this unit, you have heard many people complain about their problems with different types of technology. The box below presents some phrases (preceded or followed by a noun or noun phrase) that can be used to express frustration. Words such as *really* or *truly* (used in front of verbs or adjectives) or *very*, *so*, or *extremely* (used in front of adjectives) are often added to intensify the meaning.

Examples

- What's one thing about modern technology that **truly bothers you**?
- I know that a lot of people like the convenience of cell phones, but **they really send me over the edge**.
- I'm **so annoyed** with my new Web-based email account. There are too many advertisements. They're **extremely irritating**!

EXPRESSING FRUSTRATION

I'm annoyed with / by . . . . . . is annoying.	. . . bothers / annoys / frustrates me.
I'm irritated with / by . . . . . . is irritating.	. . . gets under my skin. (informal)
	. . . sends me over the edge. (informal)
I'm frustrated with . . . . . . is frustrating.	. . . drives me crazy. (informal)
I'm fed up with . . .	. . . drives me up the wall. (informal)
I'm sick and tired of . . .	. . . drives me nuts. (informal)
I've had it with . . .	

Work with a partner. Role play one of the situations between neighbors, or create your own situation in which one or both of you complains. Use expressions of frustration in your role play. Then perform your role play for the class.

Situation 1

Neighbor One: Your neighbor plays loud music (that you don't like!) during the evening. He doesn't turn it off until midnight. You have told him politely several times that you have to get up early in the morning. Each time, he gets the message and turns it down, only to do the same thing the following night.

Neighbor Two: When you get home from a long, tiring day at the office, you like to play a little soft music. You have excellent taste in music, too! Your neighbor is supersensitive and sometimes asks you to turn it down. You always do. Tonight he was banging on the wall to get you to turn it down. You think that's really rude.

Situation 2

Neighbor One: Your neighbor has an air conditioner that hums and clanks loudly all night. You can't sleep with the constant noise. You've mentioned it casually to your neighbor before, but your neighbor hasn't gotten the message. You've decided to be more direct to solve the problem.

(continued on next page)

Neighbor Two: Your neighbor mentioned your noisy air conditioner once before, but you explained that a new one is very expensive, and you can't buy one right now. It's been hot lately, and you can't sleep without air-conditioning. You thought that your neighbor understood your situation after you explained it. Everything seemed OK until today.

Situation 3

Neighbor One: Your neighbor has a loud car alarm that plays several musical tunes. It goes off all the time, even if no one is near the car. You can't stand it anymore. You are going to your neighbor's apartment to say something.

Neighbor Two: Your car alarm seems to be a little defective. Sometimes it goes off when it's not supposed to. You've taken it to be repaired, but it still seems to be a little too sensitive.

◀ **PRODUCTION:** A Technology Fair

In this activity, your class will **hold a technology fair to introduce some new inventions**. Each pair of students will present one invention at the fair that solves a problem that people have with some kind of new technology. Try to use the vocabulary, grammar, pronunciation, and language for expressing frustration that you learned in the unit.*

---

*For Alternative Speaking Topics, see page 212.

Step 1: Work in a small group. Choose one item from the list or use your own idea. Take notes on the problem(s) that people have with the item and propose an invention to solve the problem(s). Be as creative as you can!

ITEM	PROBLEMS	SOLUTION
Cell phones	• May not work if are not used in correct network—this drives people crazy! • •	• Have a universal network for hand-held device • •
Computers	• • •	• • •
Online shopping	• • •	• • •
Printers	• • •	• • •
Television	• • •	• • •
Your idea:	• • •	• • •

Step 2: Hold a technology fair in class. Circulate among other class members and tell them the item you chose, the problem(s) you identified, and how your invention will solve the problem(s).

Step 3: List all of the inventions on the board. Have the class vote on their two favorites. Discuss why these inventions were chosen as the most popular.

ALTERNATIVE SPEAKING TOPICS

1 *Modern life is full of noises, and many of them we hardly notice. Close your eyes for one minute and sit quietly. Concentrate on the sounds around you. Then write down all the sounds you have heard. Are they pleasant or irritating? Did you notice anything new? Then do the same thing in another place—at home, at work, on a bus or train, in a park. Discuss your observations and reactions with a small group or the whole class.*

2 CD3 40 *Technology might be a big part of modern life, but it is clear that its impact is still controversial. Work in a small group. Listen to this excerpt from an essay. Take turns reading the lines aloud. Then discuss the questions with a partner or small group.*

The Paradox of Our Times
by Bob Moorehead

The paradox of our time in history is that we have taller buildings, but shorter tempers; wider freeways, but narrower viewpoints.

We spend more, but have less; we buy more, but enjoy it less. We have bigger houses and smaller families; more conveniences, but less time.

We have more degrees[1], but less sense; more knowledge, but less judgment; more experts, but more problems; more medicine, but less wellness.

We drink too much, smoke too much, spend too recklessly, laugh too little, drive too fast, get too angry too quickly, stay up too late, get up too tired, read too seldom, watch TV too much, and pray too seldom.

We have multiplied our possessions, but reduced our values.

We talk too much, love too seldom, and hate too often.

We've learned how to make a living, but not a life; we've added years to life, not life to years.

We've been all the way to the moon and back, but have trouble crossing the street to meet a new neighbor.

---

[1]**degrees:** credentials given to those who complete courses of study at a university

1. This essay includes many words that contrast with each other, such as *taller* and *shorter* in line 2. Underline the contrasting words in each line. A *paradox* is a statement or situation that contains two opposing ideas. How do the contrasts in the essay show a paradox? What is meant by "the paradox of our times"?

2. Does the essay express the way you feel sometimes? Explain your answer.

3. Select one or two lines that seem most interesting to you. Read them aloud. Discuss with the group what they mean and whether you agree with them.

4. The author effectively uses comparisons of unlike things for emphasis. Can you point out some examples? What else makes the poem effective?

5. Can you think of any similar comparisons or paradoxes? Could you add another line to the essay?

3   **CD 3 / 40**   *Listen again and enjoy the language.*

RESEARCH TOPICS, see page 224.

STUDENT ACTIVITIES

UNIT 6: Giving to Others: Why Do We Do It?

Exercise 3, Page 119

Student B

Complete the adjective clauses in the sentences. Then listen to Student A's sentences and identify the thing, time, person, or place described. Then read your sentences aloud. Student A must identify the item, time, person, or place you described.

1. Name a philanthropist _____ you've learned about in this chapter. (for example, Bill Gates, Warren Buffet)

2. It's a time _____ many people give money. (for example, Christmas, Easter, holidays)

3. It's a country _____ the flying eye hospital operates. (for example, Bangladesh, China, Ethiopia, India, or Vietnam)

4. It's a word _____ means "money that you give to others." (donation)

5. It's the noun _____ corresponds to the adjective "poor." (poverty)

6. It's an innovative project _____ helps others. (for example, Orbis International, the Hole in the Wall project, etc.)

UNIT 7: Giving to Others: Why Do We Do It?

◀ **FUNCTION, Page 144**

Student B

Read the statements and try to explain them in your own words.

1. Some people believe that too much studying and reading is very unhealthy for children, and that more time should be spent doing some kind of physical activity.

   _____

2. Teachers should be rewarded when their students do well on standardized tests, and should have consequences, such as loss of promotions or salary raises, if their students do poorly.

   _____

3. Some teachers believe in the "10-minute rule," which says that teachers should give ten minutes of homework per grade level every day.

UNIT 10: No Technology? No Way!

◖ REVIEW, Page 201

Student B: Look at Dialogue One. Complete each statement by choosing the correct word or phrase from the box. Listen to Student A, who will begin a dialogue. Check that Student A has used the correct word or phrase in parentheses. Then read item 1 to Student A, who will check your answer. Continue with items 2 and 3. Do the same with Dialogue Two.

Dialogue One

banned	defective	frazzled	go off	offense	pay a fine

1. Why? Doesn't the alarm _____ when it should?

   (Your partner should use *getting under my skin.*)

2. Maybe it's broken. Why don't you take it back? Most stores will give you your money back if a product is _____.

   (Your partner should use *jolts.*)

3. (frustrated) Well, you sound really worn out. If you get too _____, you might get sick. You need to get some sleep.

   (Your partner should use *frustrated.*)

Dialogue Two

banned	frustrated	I've had it
disturbing the peace	getting under my skin	siren

4. I am. In fact, _____ with the neighborhood kids and their boom boxes.

   (Your partner should use *irritated.*)

5. And all night. I've already called the police. They tried to calm me down and told me not to take _____.

   (Your partner should use *drive you crazy.*)

6. Actually, it is. Playing loud music is _____, which is against the law.

(Your partner should use *offense*.)

7. You're right. Who needs them? Boom boxes should be _____ from public places.

(Your partner should use *pay a fine*.)

8. Honestly, I wouldn't mind walking around with my own _____, so I could scare kids into thinking there's a police car coming!

(Your partner should use *vigilantes*.)

Exercise 2, Page 206

Student B: Read the clues about technological items that are common today. Fill in the blanks with future perfect forms of the verbs in parentheses. Be sure to use the correct structure, active or passive. Student A will read you two sentences about a mystery item. Try to guess what item is being described. If you need more clues, Student A will read you two more sentences. Continue until you have guessed three mystery items.

Then read the first two clues about Mystery Item 4 to Student A. If Student A cannot guess what the item is, read the third and fourth clues.

Mystery Item 4: Clues

1. Most kids love these. It is likely that your children _____ you to
(ask)
buy them one of these items by the time they are five or six years old.

2. Now these items are made with 18 or 21 gears. Maybe by the mid-twenty-first century, a new version with 100 gears _____.
(invent)

3. A Scottish blacksmith first came up with the idea for this item. That is surprising, because there are so many hills in Scotland that these items are difficult to use there.

4. This mystery item usually has two wheels, and you ride it.

Mystery Item 5: Clues

1. Most likely, by the time you retire, you _____ to buy a pair.
   (have)

2. At present, they are made mainly of glass, metal, and plastic, but it's likely that

   by the mid-21st century, manufacturers _____ other materials.
   (introduce)

   Despite the design changes, they will probably still look the same.

3. In the late Middle Ages, they were worn as ornaments for the face.

4. They first appeared in Italy, in the late 13th century, and were used in China

   around the same time.

Mystery Item 6: Clues

1. By 8:00 A.M. tomorrow, your mystery item _____.
   (turn on)

2. By 8:00 A.M. tomorrow, millions of Americans _____ one on for
   (switch)

   the news and weather.

3. You listen to this mystery item.

4. It usually gets both FM and AM frequencies.

Answers: (4) bicycle, (5) glasses, (6) radio

RESEARCH TOPICS

UNIT 1: Information Overload

Watch the news on TV or listen to it on the radio or the Internet. Select one day or several days in a row. List the stories that are reported. Complete the chart for each news story. Discuss your results with the class.

NAME OF PROGRAM / DAY / TIME	TOPIC	GOOD NEWS OR BAD NEWS?	PROBLEM	SOLUTION

UNIT 2: The Achilles Heel

1   *Many movies have been made about the heroism and achievements of people who have overcome obstacles. Some examples are: I am Sam, Benny and Joon, The Eighth Day, Shine, My Left Foot, Sound and Fury, The Mighty, Simon Birch, Girl Interrupted, The Color of Paradise, The Gift, The Hero, The Keys to the House, The Little Girl Who Sold the Sun, and Oasis. Work in a small group. Research the movies that are available to you and choose one to watch. Describe the movie to the rest of the class. Focus on how one of the characters in the film overcomes an obstacle.*

2   *Work in a small group and research a singer, actor, athlete or other celebrity who has a disability of some kind. Prepare a short biography about him or her. Here are some possibilities:*

   - Bethany Hamilton, teen surfing champion, who has one arm
   - Marlee Matlin, actress, who is deaf
   - Sirimit Boonmul, lawyer, who is blind
   - Michael J. Fox, actor, who has Parkinson's Disease
   - Hyang-suk Jang, politician and human rights activist, who has polio and uses a wheelchair
   - Simona Atzori, artist and dancer, who was born without arms
   - John Stossel, broadcast journalist, who stutters
   - John Cougar Mellencamp, singer/songwriter, who has spina bifida
   - Jim Abbott, retired major-league baseball pitcher, who has one hand
   - Ved Mehta, author, who is blind

UNIT 3: Early to Bed, Early to Rise . . .

Choose one of these topics to research. Then present your findings to a small group or the whole class.

1. You know that sleep deprivation can be dangerous. Research to find more information about the negative effects of sleep deprivation. How long does it take to recover from sleep deprivation? What should a person who is sleep deprived do in order to recover as quickly as possible?

2. Travelers who cross time zones frequently experience *jet lag*. What is jet lag? What causes it? What are the results of jet lag? How can travelers prevent it or cope with its effects?

UNIT 4: Animal Intelligence

Research one of these topics. Then discuss your findings with a small group or the whole class.

1. Watch the *Jane Goodall's Wild Chimpanzees* or search "Nature PBS" and select some animal videos to watch. Report to the class on what you learn.

2. Research one of these famous animals. Find out what the animal was able to learn, and what the scientists who worked with the animal thinks that means. Give your own opinion: Do you think the animal is (or was) intelligent? In what way (i.e., able to speak, use sign language, understand mathematical concepts)? Present your research and opinions to the class.
   - Akeakamai, a dolphin
   - Clever Hans, a horse
   - Kanzi, a Bonobo ape
   - Kosik, an elephant
   - Washoe, a chimpanzee

UNIT 5: Longevity: Refusing to Be Invisible

1 *Choose one of the following topics to research by yourself or with a small group.*
   - What images of older men and women are presented in advertisements? What kinds of products do they advertise? Why?
   - What privileges do seniors have in different communities around the world? For example, do they enjoy discounts, medical care, and so on? At what age should a person be considered a "senior"?
   - What are the retirement ages and customs of senior citizens in different countries around the world?

2 *Present your findings to the class.*

Investigate and report on a philanthropic organization or a philanthropist.

Step 1: Choose a non-profit organization or a philanthropist you would like to know more about. Select from the groups or people in this unit, choose from the box below, or think of your own.

Some Philanthropists*

Hasso Plattner	Tan Tock Seng
Joan Kroc	Oprah Winfrey
John D. and Catherine T. McArthur	Victor Fu
Brooke Astor	Zainab Salbi
George Soros	Charles F. Feeney
John Kluge	David Geffen
Oveta Culp Hoby	Robert Wood Johnson
Carol F. Sulzberger	John D. Rockefeller
Pierre Toussaint	Ted Turner

Step 2: Prepare a short report on the organization or person you chose. Try to answer these questions:

- What is the mission of the organization?
- What are some examples of its activities?
- How effective is it?
- Would you donate time or money to this organization?

Present your report to the class, and listen to your classmates' reports.

---

*You may need to look up the name as a foundation (for example, Robert Wood Johnson Foundation).

UNIT 7: What's the Use of Homework?

Conduct a survey about homework among people outside the class.

1. Set up a questionnaire like the one below. Choose the people you would like to interview. Write a brief description (age, sex, nationality, etc.) of each person you interview.

	ELEMENTARY SCHOOL STUDENT OR PARENT	MIDDLE SCHOOL STUDENT OR PARENT	HIGH SCHOOL STUDENT OR PARENT	COLLEGE OR UNIVERSITY STUDENT
Questions	Description	Description	Description	Description
1. About how much homework do you (or your child) get a week? Do you think it is the right amount?				
2. Describe an assignment that was really good.				
3. Describe an assignment that was really bad.				
4. What factors should teachers or professors think about when they assign homework?				
5. Other question (your choice)				

2. Interview 2–3 people about their opinions on homework. Aim to speak to each one for about 3–5 minutes.

3. Share your results with the class.

UNIT 8: Goodbye to the Sit-Down Meal

Choose a supermarket and analyze the food trends in your area.

Step 1: Conduct the research. Like Lian, the Satellite Sister, wander through the frozen food aisles or another section in the supermarket. Answer the following questions.

- What types of foods are most plentiful? For instance, are there several brands of one particular product?
- Which types are at the best eye level for sales? Check whether the "specials" are clearly visible.
- What trends can you identify? For example, look at the diet foods or foods from certain areas of the world. See if you can tell what is becoming more popular and what is losing popularity.

Step 2: Present your findings to the class. You can be academic and analytical, like Claude Fishlere, or funny, like the Satellite Sisters.

Step 3: Present your report to the class. Tell your classmates what you saw and what trends you spotted. Listen to the reports of other groups.

UNIT 9: Finding a Niche: The Challenge for Young Immigrants

Interview someone who has lived or is now living in a country where he or she had to learn a new language or adjust to a new culture.

Step 1: Before you conduct your interview, write questions that address each of the topics below. Make sure everyone in your group asks the same questions of the people they interview.

- reasons for living in the other country
- reaction to the new language
- reaction to some traditions in the new culture
- reaction to working or going to school in the new culture
- other aspects of the experience
- what is missed from the home culture

Step 2: After completing your interview, compare what you learned with your class. Discuss the similarities and differences among the experiences of all the people you interviewed.

Work with a partner to investigate recent developments in technology.

Step 1: Visit the library or do some research online. Investigate recent developments in one of the following areas:

- Nanotechnology
- Cloning
- Robotics
- Genetic engineering
- Personal electronics
- Artificial intelligence

    Your idea: _____

Include the following in your report:
- history of the development
- ways the development has affected and will affect your culture and/or your life

Step 2: Present a summary of your findings to the class. Be prepared to answer questions about your project.

GRAMMAR BOOK REFERENCES

NorthStar: Listening and Speaking Level 4, Third Edition	Focus on Grammar Level 4, Third Edition	Azar's Understanding and Using English Grammar, Third Edition
Unit 1 Passive Voice	**Unit 18** The Passive: Overview	**Chapter 11** The Passive: 11-1, 11-2
Unit 2 Gerunds and Infinitives	**Unit 9** Gerunds and Infinitives: Review and Expansion	**Chapter 14** Gerunds and Infinitives (1) **Chapter 15** Gerunds and Infinitives (2) 15-2
Unit 3 Present Unreal Conditionals	**Unit 23** Present and Future Unreal Conditionals	**Chapter 20** Conditional Sentences and Wishes: 20-1, 20-3
Unit 4 Reported Speech	**Unit 25** Direct and Indirect Speech **Unit 26** Indirect Speech: Tense Changes	**Chapter 12** Noun Clauses: 12-6, 12-7
Unit 5 Tag Questions	**Unit 7** Negative Yes/No Questions and Tag Questions	**Appendix** Unit B: Questions: B-5
Unit 6 Using Relative Pronouns in Adjective Clauses	**Unit 13** Adjective Clauses with Subject Relative Prounouns **Unit 14** Adjective Clauses with Object Relative Pronouns or When and Where	**Chapter 13** Adjective Clauses

NorthStar: Listening and Speaking Level 4, Third Edition	Focus on Grammar Level 4, Third Edition	Azar's Understanding and Using English Grammar, Third Edition
Unit 7 *Make, Have, Let, Help* and *Get*	**Unit 10** *Make, Have, Let, Help* and *Get*	**Chapter 15** Gerunds and Infinitives (2): 15-8, 15-9
Unit 8 Phrasal Verbs	**Unit 11** Phrasal Verbs: Review **Unit 12** Phrasal Verbs: Separable and Inseperable	**Appendix** Unit E: Preposition Combinations See also Appendix 1: Phrasal Verbs, in *Fundamentals of English Grammar*, Third Edition
Unit 9 Present and Past— Contrasting Verb Tenses	**Unit 1** Simple Present and Present Progressive **Unit 2** Simple Past and Past Progressive **Unit 3** Simple Past, Present Perfect, and Present Perfect Progressive	**Chapter 2** Present and Past, Simple and Progressive: 2-1, 2-2, 2-5, 2-9, 2-10 **Chapter 3** Perfect and Perfect Progressive Tenses, 3-1, 3-2
Unit 10 Future Perfect and Future Progressive	**Unit 5** Future and Future Progressive **Unit 6** Future Perfect and Future Perfect Progressive	**Chapter 4** Future Time: 4-5, 4-6

AUDIOSCRIPT

UNIT 1: Information Overload

2A. LISTENING ONE: *News Resisters*

Bob Edwards: Since you're listening to this program, odds are you're not taking the advice of Dr. Andrew Weil. He's written a book titled *8 Weeks to Optimum Health* and he recommends reducing your daily intake of news.

Andrew Weil: And then I asked people over the course of eight weeks to extend this to two days a week, three days a week and so forth until the last week you get up to a whole week of no news.

BE: Weil is not the only one trying to get people to take a break from coverage of daily events. NPR's Margot Adler reports on a growing number of people who bring new meaning to the phrase "no news is good news."

LISTEN FOR MAIN IDEAS

BE: Since you're listening to this program, odds are you're not taking the advice of Dr. Andrew Weil. He's written a book titled *8 Weeks to Optimum Health* and he recommends reducing your daily intake of news.

AW: And then I asked people over the course of eight weeks to extend this to two days a week, three days a week and so forth until the last week you get up to a whole week of no news.

BE: Weil is not the only one trying to get people to take a break from coverage of daily events. NPR's Margot Adler reports on a growing number of people who bring new meaning to the phrase "no news is good news."

Margot Adler: When I was a kid, I loved a baseball novel called *The Southpaw*. It was the first volume of a baseball quartet written by Mark Harris. One of the books, *Bang the Drum Slowly,* became a famous movie. What I only learned recently was that Harris wrote a long essay in the *New York Times* back in the early '70s in which he said reading a daily newspaper was a useless addiction. Thirty years later, Harris still believes that.

Mark Harris: Somebody gets up in the morning and the first thing he or she has to do is get that newspaper, and then they have to have it with the coffee and it's kind of two addictions go together.

MA: Harris left his job with the newspaper and turned to writing novels because, he said, you could focus on much more interesting things that are never considered newsworthy. For example, you could focus on the person who loses in sports or comes in second. He also turned to teaching. Academia turns out to be a place filled with news resisters. Take Gabrielle Spiegel, the chair of the history department at Johns Hopkins University. Perhaps it's understandable that a medievalist who says her period of study ends around 1328 would find daily news, in her words, "ephemeral, repetitive and inconsequential."

Gabrielle Spiegel: But I think my underlying reason is that, you know, life is short. There's only a certain amount of time that you have to spend on things, and I have always believed that there are two things you really need to get through life, and I say this to my children in a sort of nauseatingly repetitive way. The first is a really rich fantasy life so you can imagine what the possibilities are, and the other is a sense of humor so you can deal with what is. And actually I'd rather spend my time on my fantasy life and reading novels than reading newspapers. And I really do think that's why I don't read newspapers.

MA: John Sommerville is a professor of history at the University of Florida and the author of works on the history of religion in England. He has written a book called *How the News Makes Us Dumb: The Death of Wisdom in an Information Society,* and he argues that bias is fixable, but the real problem isn't. His main argument against daily news is the daily part. He argues that dailiness, as he puts it, chops everything down to a standard size, making it harder to get perspective, to know the appropriate size and scale of any problem.

John Sommerville: That one feature by itself, regardless of the competence and the professionalism of the journalist, it's lethal. If dumbness is the inability to make connections, logical connections and historical connections, then you can see how taking in everything on a daily basis is going to hurt our ability to make the connections.

MA: Sommerville prefers quarterlies and says somewhere between weekliness and monthliness you move from entertainment to reflection. And while he does occasionally read newsmagazines, he prefers to read them a month after they come out to maintain perspective. As a historian of religion, Sommerville believes there is a natural antagonism between the news' emphasis on the immediate, and religion, which points toward the more eternal. And it does seem that those involved in spiritual practices are often the most resistant to the daily news barrage.

Tupton Shudrun is a Buddhist nun, a teacher and a student of the Dalai Lama. She says that when you study meditation, you become aware of how your mind is influenced by outside events. She says the media presents problems well, but doesn't give time or space to those helping to remedy the situation.

Tupton Shudrun: And it creates a sense of despair that I think is unrealistic, and that sense of despair immobilizes us from actually contributing to the benefit of society and doing something to help others.

MA: The venerable Tupton Shudrun says she reads a newsmagazine occasionally because as a teacher she needs to get the general feeling of the country, but she chooses what she reads. She, like Weil, advises students to decide consciously how much news to take in and not to assume that the media has a lock on what's important and how to measure success. She also says many people keep themselves plugged in because they don't know how to be alone with themselves. Historian Gabrielle Spiegel agrees.

GS: I think we live in a society that offers us very, very little time alone. And the way children are raised, you know, set in front of televisions, they don't have a lot of time to be by themselves. When my children were little, we used to have a thing called Mommy's hour in which, you know, they had to go in their rooms and just think for an hour or two a day so I could think for an hour or two a day.

MA: While studies show that the majority of Americans don't want to disengage from daily news, when we e-mailed the news staff at NPR for suggestions of people to interview for this story, we got an enormous response, and a surprising number wrote things like, "I would if I could," or "Psst, don't tell anyone." Margot Adler, NPR News, New York.

LISTEN FOR DETAILS

(Repeat Listen for Main Ideas)

Listen again to Listen for Main Ideas.

MAKE INFERENCES

Excerpt One

Mark Harris: Somebody gets up in the morning and the first thing he or she has to do is get that newspaper, and then they have to have it with the coffee and it's kind of two addictions go together.

Excerpt Two

Margot Adler: Academia turns out to be a place filled with news resisters. Take Gabrielle Spiegel, the chair of the history department at Johns Hopkins University. Perhaps it's understandable that a medievalist who says her period of study ends around 1328 would find daily news, in her words, "ephemeral, repetitive and inconsequential."

Excerpt Three

Margot Adler: John Sommerville is a professor of history at the University of Florida and the author of works on the history of religion in England. He has written a book called How the News Makes Us Dumb: The Death of Wisdom in an Information Society, and he argues that bias is fixable, but the real problem isn't. His main argument against daily news is the daily part. He argues that dailiness, as he puts it, chops everything down to a standard size, making it harder to get perspective, to know the appropriate size and scale of any problem.

Excerpt Four

Margot Adler: While studies show that the majority of Americans don't want to disengage from daily news, when we e-mailed the news staff at NPR for suggestions of people to interview for this story, we got an enormous response, and a surprising number wrote things like, "I would if I could," or "Psst, don't tell anyone." Margot Adler, NPR News, New York.

2B. LISTENING TWO: *Does the Media Overwhelm Our Lives?*

Announcer: Millions of Americans wake up each morning to their clock radio, drive to work in their surround sound-equipped car, check their multiple email accounts, surf the web, read the papers and then after a long day, catch the news as they head back home to flick on the tube. . . .

A hundred cable stations at the tip of your remote, the endless waves of the Internet, music, news and talking heads everywhere, telling you what to buy, what to do, what to think—the presence of media all around us, all the time has become an everyday part of life in America. Our guest tonight says this media overload comes at a price, and asks if we're ready to pay it. In his new book *Media Unlimited*, Todd Gitlin says the media does more than surround us, he says it's actually become our life. Are we totally immersed in a media-saturated, speed-addicted world of non-stop stimulation? Have Americans learned to experience and understand the world primarily based on what they experience on TV, the web, the radio? Is the media now the way we live?

We're joined tonight from New York by Todd Gitlin, he's professor of culture, journalism and sociology at New York University, and author of the new book, "Media Unlimited: How the Torrent of Images and Sounds Overwhelms Our Lives." Good evening and welcome, Todd Gitlin. . . . Todd Gitlin, are you there?

Todd Gitlin: Hi, there.

Announcer: Hi, thanks for joining us tonight.

Gitlin: My pleasure.

Announcer: You write that in a society that fancies itself the freest ever, spending time with communications machinery is the main use to which we have put our freedom. Is that a problem, Todd Gittlin?

Gitlin: Well, I think it is: I mean, I think it's a problem on two levels. First of all, the very fact that we're doing it and we're rather oblivious of the fact that this is how we're living is a distraction from the truth: I mean, I think we're evading who we are and that troubles me, but I think there are more particular problems: I think that we have for one thing a sort of national attention deficit disorder: we're on to OJ Simpson, then we're on to Chandra Levy, then we're on to Princess Diana, then we're on to Survivor II, or we're on to the drama of the, you know, the disappeared girl or what have you: and this I think, er, ill equips us to govern ourselves . . . I think it distracts us from, uh, from our discipline, our duty, our common bonds with others. It, it er, puts us in separate camps, little containers, that seal us away from people who are not like ourselves, and although we talk a lot about community, we're actually more interested in hanging out with people who are more or less like ourselves. So I think our civic life is weakened by this. I think also, it's not an accident in this non-stop entertainment world that we have growing numbers of kids who literally can't sit still, uh, who are you know, diagnosed as victims of attention deficit disorder: but Attention Deficit Disorder is what's being cultivated by, by what is really the . . . the de facto curriculum of our time, which is this non-stop world: the average kid is in the presence of these media for about $6^{1}/_{2}$ hours a day and I was, I've been told by teachers that, er, often, a kid, whether in an inner city school or a fancy private school comes to school having already been plunked down in front of the TV or video games or other such equipment for a couple of hours, and wanting the teacher, expecting the teacher to wiggle and flash the way the media do!

3C. PRONUNCIATION: *Reducing and Contracting Auxiliary Verbs*

Exercise 1

1. The United States has become a nation of people addicted to the news.

2. Americans are offered news in many forms.

3. Critics have been concerned about the amount of news we watch.

4. Academics are worried about the amount of news we consume.

Exercise 2

People are offered many sources of news, some of which is available 24/7. The country has become a nation of "news junkies," or people who are addicted to the news. Some academics have started to ask serious questions about the role of the news media in society. Some people believe that the media is focusing on negative stories. Therefore, it focuses less on the important issues that we face. We're being entertained by gossip about celebrities and politicians, but we've stopped worrying about serious problems that affect our society.

UNIT 2: The Achilles Heel

2A. LISTENING ONE: *Dreams of Flying and Overcoming Obstacles*

Bob Edwards: This is the time of year when high school seniors rush to the mailbox to find out which colleges have accepted them. One thing they'll be judged on is their application essay, so *Morning Edition* asked students to share those essays. More than 150 students, parents, and teachers from around the country responded. Five were chosen for broadcast. There'll be one each day this week. Richard Van Ornum of Cincinnati is first.

LISTEN FOR MAIN IDEAS

Bob Edwards: This is the time of year when high school seniors rush to the mailbox to find out which colleges have accepted them. One thing they'll be judged on is their application essay, so *Morning Edition* asked students to share those essays. More than 150 students, parents, and teachers from around the country responded. Five were chosen for broadcast. There'll be one each day this week. Richard Van Ornum of Cincinnati is first.

Richard Van Ornum: When I was little, I dreamed I was flying. Each night, I was up in the air, though never over the same landscape. Sometimes in the confusion of early morning, I would wake up thinking it was true and I'd leap off my bed, expecting to soar out of the window. Of course, I always hit the ground, but not before remembering that I'd been dreaming. I would realize that no real person could fly and I'd collapse on the floor, crushed by the weight of my own limitations. Eventually, my dreams of flying stopped. I think I stopped dreaming completely.

After that, my earliest memory is of learning to count to 100. After baths, my mother would perch me on the sink and dry me, as I tried to make it to 100 without a mistake. I had to be lifted onto the sink. An accident with a runaway truck when I was four had mangled my left leg, leaving scars that stood out, puckered white against my skin. Looking at the largest of my scars in the mirror, I imagined that it was an eagle. It wasn't fair, I thought, I had an eagle on my leg, but I couldn't fly. I could hardly walk, and the crutches hurt my arms.

Years later, in Venice, I had the closest thing to a revelation I can imagine. Sitting on the rooftop of the Cathedral of San Marco, I wasn't sure what life had in store for me. I was up on a ledge in between the winged horses that overlook San Marco square. To the left, the Grand Canal snaked off into the sea, where the sun cast long crimson afternoon shadows across the city. Below me, in the square, pigeons swirled away from the children chasing them and swooped down onto a tourist who was scattering dried corn.

Somewhere in the square, a band was playing Frank Sinatra. It was *Fly Me to the Moon,* I think. Up on the roof of the cathedral, it seemed to me the pieces of my life suddenly fell together. I realized that everyone is born with gifts, but we all run into obstacles. If we recognize our talents and make the best of them, we've got a fighting chance to overcome our obstacles and succeed in life. I knew what my gifts were: imagination and perseverance. And I also knew what my first obstacle had been: a runaway truck on a May morning with no compassion for preschoolers on a field trip. But I knew that the obstacles weren't impossible. They could be overcome. I was proof of that, walking.

That night, for the first time in years, I dreamed I was flying. I soared through the fields of Italy, through the narrow winding streets of Venice and on beyond the Grand Canal, chasing the reddening sun across the sea.

BE: The college essay of Richard Van Ornum, who attends the Seven Hills School in Cincinnati.

LISTEN FOR DETAILS

(Repeat Listen for Main Ideas)

MAKE INFERENCES

Excerpt One

Richard Van Ornum: When I was little, I dreamed I was flying. Each night, I was up in the air, though never over the same landscape. Sometimes in the confusion of early morning, I would wake up thinking it was true and I'd leap off my bed, expecting to soar out of the window.

Excerpt Two

Richard Van Ornum: Of course, I always hit the ground, but not before remembering that I'd been dreaming. I would realize that no real person could fly and I'd collapse on the floor, crushed by the weight of my own limitations. Eventually, my dreams of flying stopped. I think I stopped dreaming completely.

Excerpt Three

Richard Van Ornum: Years later, in Venice, I had the closest thing to a revelation I can imagine. Sitting on the rooftop of the Cathedral of San Marco, I wasn't sure what life had in store for me. I was up on a ledge in between the winged horses that overlook San Marco square. To the left, the Grand Canal snaked off into the sea, where the sun cast long crimson afternoon shadows across the city. Below me, in the square, pigeons swirled away from the children chasing them and swooped down onto a tourist who was scattering dried corn.

Excerpt Four

Richard Van Ornum: That night, for the first time in years, I dreamed I was flying. I soared through the fields of Italy, through the narrow winding streets of Venice and on beyond the Grand Canal, chasing the reddening sun across the sea.

2B. LISTENING 2: *The Achilles Track Club Climbs Mt. Kilimanjaro*

Narrator: They climbed one of the world's tallest mountains- a group of disabled climbers from the New York area. It's a story of reaching new heights, and overcoming great odds. Monica Pellegrini introduces us to those inspirational athletes.

Climber 1: I thought a few times going up that I wouldn't make it. . . . um . . . I almost turned back around twice.

Monica Pellegrini: Mount Kilimanjaro, in the northern part of the African nation of Tanzania. Scaling it is no small task for your average climber, but for a group of seven from New York's Achilles Track Club, it was a much greater challenge. They are all disabled in some way. Five are blind. One is deaf and asthmatic. The other, a cancer survivor and amputee.

Climber 2: It was a lot more difficult than I had expected. Er . . . a difficult climb, and the altitude really did affect a lot of us. But we persevered, and the majority of the athletes were able to make it.

MP: The accomplishment makes the group the largest of disabled athletes to ever climb Mount Kilimanjaro—an expedition they call a testament to the human spirit, and a chance to empower themselves and others.

Climber 3: I just wanted to reach deep down, and grab all the energy I had, and keep on going. Because behind accomplishing this physical challenge for myself, I knew there was a greater message we were all carrying.

MP: The group kept a diary of their travels online, and even when the going got tough, they buckled down, turning to each other for inspiration as they continued on the trail to the peak.

Climber 4: I heard it was going to be hard. I just didn't imagine it was going to be so tough.

MP: Tough, yes, but an experience that will not be forgotten any time soon.

C1: When you're experiencing this wide open space, wind, the sunshine, the strength of the sun like you've never felt before . . .

MP: The adventure began on August 28th and ended this past Sunday, when the group, along with their 18 volunteer guides from the Achilles Track Club, reached the summit.

C1: Getting to the top was definitely the high point.

MP: Monica Pellegrini, UPN 9 news.

3C.   PRONUNCIATION: *Thought Groups*

Exercise 1

1. When Richard was little, he dreamed he was flying.

2. He looked at his scar and imagined it was an eagle.

3. When he visited Venice, he realized that he had great gifts.

4. He suddenly realized that he could overcome his obstacles.

5. The essay he wrote about his experience was chosen for broadcast.

UNIT 3: Early To Bed, Early To Rise . . .

CD 2, Track 28:

Linda Wertheimer: From NPR News, this is All Things Considered. I'm Linda Wertheimer.

Noah Adams: And I'm Noah Adams. The new school year began in many parts of the country today. Youngsters who got used to a summer schedule of sleeping late each morning found themselves rudely awakened by alarm clocks or by eager parents, but not in Minneapolis, Minnesota. For some time now, high schools there have opened their doors an hour and a half later than schools elsewhere. The decision to move the start time was based on growing scientific evidence about the sleep needs of adolescents. Michelle Trudeau spoke with students in Minneapolis and reports on how the schedule change is working.

Michelle Trudeau: This is South High School in a quiet neighborhood 10 minutes from downtown Minneapolis. Here, in a large assembly hall, many of the school's 2,000 students gather each morning. It's the hub and heart of the school, alive with movement, with young voices chatting, joking, greeting, connecting. At the far end of the hall, above the cafeteria entrance, a banner reading 'Cappuccino and hot chocolate,' students dashing in for a last quick shot at breakfast and caffeine. It's 8:40 in the morning. First period is about to begin.

Unidentified Student #1: Hey.

MT: For the fourth year now, all Minneapolis high schools and all 12,000 students will start school at 8:40 AM. That's nearly an hour and a half later than the way it used to be when first bell rang at 7:15.

Unidentified Student #2: I did have to get up a lot earlier. I think I got up at like 5:50 or 6, which is pretty rough.

Unidentified Student #3: At about 6:00, my sister would come in my room and attempt to wake me up after my alarm had been going off for about 20 minutes.

Unidentified Student #4: Getting up early, I just remember, was really difficult, yeah.

Unidentified Student #5: When you're that tired, your showers go from eight to 10 minutes from 18 to 20 minutes.

Unidentified Student #6: It's kind of a psychological thing when you wake up in the morning and go to school in the dark. It really sucked.

MT: Minneapolis is the largest school district in the country to change their high schools to a later start time. The impetus came in the spring of 1994 when every school district in the state received a powerful letter from the Minnesota Medical Association. The physicians urged that all high schools eliminate early start times, citing scientific evidence that teen-agers aren't getting nearly enough sleep and that this has significant impact on their learning and safety.

Unidentified Student #7: Go to first hour, biology with Mr. Kanum, and I'd find myself sitting in there and hearing him speak but not knowing a thing he said. I thought I was like in a foreign language class or something.

MT: Starting high schools later cost the Minneapolis district nothing. They did it by rearranging their busing schedule. And they hired this woman to measure the actual impact on students.

Ms. Kyla Wahlstrom (University of Minnesota): Let's see, now if I can get the right . . .

KW: We're getting closer, getting closer. Ah, here we are.

MT: Kyla Wahlstrom, education researcher at the University of Minnesota. Her office on campus is housed ironically in a former high school building. Over the past three years, Wahlstrom's collected a massive amount of information; so much so that she's had to appropriate the old school lockers to hold all the data on student grades, attendance, sleep habits, moods, sports participation, after-school jobs. It's the largest and longest evaluation of high school start times ever undertaken.

KW: So we have survey information from over 7,000 students.

MT: Students like these seniors at South High, the last class to have experienced the earlier start time as freshmen.

Unidentified Student #8: I could definitely tell I would waste my mornings away till about third hour when I woke up.

Unidentified Student #9: I don't know if I ever slept through it, but I might as well have been because I certainly wasn't paying attention.

Unidentified Student #8: Through at least second hour, I had no clue what was going on.

MT: But sleep researchers do have some clues as to what's going on in the brains and bodies of teen-agers.

Unidentified Man #1: OK. Room one's all set.

MT: In Providence, Rhode Island, there's a very unusual summer camp for teen-agers.

Ms. Mary Carskadon (Brown University): We call it our sleep camp, but it's not like a real camp with horseback riding and swimming.

MT: It's a research lab housed underground and run by pioneering sleep researcher Mary Carskadon of Brown University. In this windowless environment, all outside time cues are eliminated, so no sunlight, no clocks, no MTV, no contact with the outside world; just uniformly dim light day and night as the teens play, read, eat and, of course, sleep for three full weeks.

MC: And what we do is sort of take them out of time as if we blasted off from Earth and we're in our own little time capsule.

MT: Out of the real time of the external world, allowing the teen-agers to sleep and wake to the rhythm, the circadian rhythm, of their own internal, biological clocks. They're hooked up to equipment that records their brain waves, muscle activity, heart rates, their waking and their sleeping. And what Carskadon has discovered flies in the face of some long-held assumptions about teen-agers. First assumption, teens don't need as much sleep as when they were younger. Not true at all, says Carskadon.

MC: They continue to need nine hours plus sleep every night. They weren't needing less sleep.

2A. LISTENING ONE: *Teen Sleep Needs*

Track 29:

Michelle Trudeau: Teenagers, when allowed to, sleep nearly nine and a half hours every night—as much as young children. But unlike young children, even when teens do get their full sleep, they're still out of sync with everybody else. They have waves of sleepiness in the daytime, and then surges of energy in the evening, making them wide awake late at night. But not, Carskadon has discovered, for the reasons most of us assume.

LISTEN FOR MAIN IDEAS

Track 30:

Mary Carskadon: We kind of always thought that adolescents stayed up late because they liked to—which they do—and because there's plenty of things to do—which there are. . . .

MT: But there's also a big push from biology that makes teenagers such night owls. It comes from that mighty sleep hormone, melatonin.

MC: Melatonin is a wonderfully simple signal 'cause it turns on in the evening,

MT: You're getting sleepy. . . .

MC: And it turns off in the morning.

MT: And you awaken. During adolescence, melatonin isn't secreted until around 11:00 P.M., several hours later than it is in childhood. So the typical teenager doesn't even get sleepy till that melatonin surge signals the brain that it's night, no matter how early the teen goes to bed. And the melatonin doesn't shut off till nine hours later, around 8:00 A.M. But of course most high schools start around 7:30. The result is all too evident. A teenager's body may be in the classroom, but his brain is still asleep on the pillow.

Student: I'll wake up and I'll just feel miserable, just kind of like ugh, what's wrong with me, you know?

William Dement: An adolescent, and particularly the adolescent in high school, is almost bound to get severely sleep deprived.

MT: That's William Dement of Stanford University. Bill Dement *is* Dr. Sleep, captivated by the mysteries of sleep for decades, creating the specialty of sleep medicine. As a scientist, Dement has contributed more to our understanding of what happens to each of us at night during those hours of unconsciousness than perhaps any other researcher. These days, Dement makes frequent forays out of his lab—an ambassador at large from the field of sleep research. Teenagers, parents, and school authorities need to know more about the science of sleep, he says, and how important it is to young people's health.

WD: I've been accepting every invitation that I get to speak to high school students. So I go to a high school and it'll be 10:30 in the morning, or 2:00 in the afternoon, whenever it is, several hundred students in an auditorium, and I'll just watch them, as I'm talking.

MT: Doing a little spontaneous field research.

WD: And after ten minutes of sitting, particularly if the lights are dim, I would say, almost without exception, they are all struggling to stay awake. Ten minutes!!

MT: This shows up in lab studies too. The typical teenager when monitored in a quiet environment during morning hours will fall asleep in less than three and a half minutes.

WD: It's just like magic. It's like somebody turned on some kind of gas . . . in the auditorium. And they all look gassed.

MT: Not gassed, just severely sleep deprived. Short about two hours of sleep every school night, accumulating into what Dement calls "sleep debt." And most teenagers are up to their drooping eyelids in sleep debt: An estimated 85 percent of high school students are chronically sleep deprived, unable to stay fully awake throughout the school day. And it's not just falling asleep in class; it's also riding a bike, playing sports, using tools, driving. . . .

Calene: Uum, he hit a tree one night when he was driving.

MT: Calene, a South High student, talking about his friend.

C: And he told me he fell asleep for a couple of seconds, and next thing he knew, he hit a tree.

Ronald Dahl: You can have a second where your eyelid blinks and you are not taking information or making judgment.

MT: Researcher Ronald Dahl from the University of Pittsburg.

RD: But if that occurs when you're at the wheel, you travel 60 feet in that second.

C: The report was that if he would have hit, like, three inches to the left, he would have probably been dead. You know, three inches could have changed everything.

MT: Reaction time, alertness, concentration, all slowed down by insufficient sleep. The Federal Department of Transportation estimates teenage drivers cause more than half of all fall-asleep crashes.

RD: But in addition to those straightforward effects on attention and the ability to stay awake and alert, there are more subtle effects on emotion.

MT: Dahl is studying how adolescents balance their cognitive thoughts and their emotions. When tired, he says, teens are more easily frustrated, more irritable, more prone to sadness. And their performance on intellectual tasks drops.

LISTEN FOR DETAILS

(Repeat Listen for Main Ideas, track 30)

CD 2, Track 31:

MT: Mark, accepted to MIT this year, remembers the daily struggle.

Mark (Student): I had math first hour, which is rough to have first hour, because it's a lot of thinking.

RD: The ability to use the thinking part of the brain, the planning, strategic part of the brain to control feelings is what is affected by being sleep deprived.

Mark: If I don't get enough sleep, obviously I don't function real well, and I'm cranky, I guess, and I'm not real fun to be around.

MT: For researcher Kyla Wahlstrom, the evaluation of the ambitious experiment begun three years ago in the Minneapolis high schools is nearly complete. Final results won't be known for another couple of months, but Wahlstrom says early indications are that starting school later underscores what sleep researchers have discovered about adolescent sleep needs.

KW: The students whose schools are starting later are not staying up later. Teen-agers tend to fall asleep somewhere between 11 and 11:30, and 11:21 is the mean.

MT: Right on schedule, sleep researchers would say, given the shift in teen-agers' biological clocks. So the late start time, Wahlstrom concludes, really does give teens over an hour of extra sleep each school morning. But what parents and school districts across the country also want to know is does starting high school later in the morning improve academic performance?

KW: We're seeing an indication that something is happening in the Minneapolis schools. We're seeing a clear trend line that shows that there is an increase in grades earned by the students in the Minneapolis schools.

MT: Another trend line suggests better school attendance and less tardiness by Minneapolis students. Now these trends lines, while encouraging, are not conclusive proof that a later start time improves academic performance. The third year of data analysis is required to determine if these trends can reach statistical significance, the gold standard of research results. These early findings are strengthened, though, by surveys, adds Wahlstrom. Parents say their teens are easier to live with. Teachers, too, report that their students are now more alert, more awake actually, in class. And students say their school performance is improved since starting high school later each morning.

Unidentified Student #11: Just that extra hour and a half gives you time to get everything together before coming to school.

Unidentified Student #12: And so it does help I a lot. I can feel it, definitely, in the morning.

Unidentified Student #13: I need probably, like, nine or 10 hours of sleep to be, like, at optimum performance.

Unidentified Student #14: In my eyes, sleep is sacred.

Unidentified Student #15: Sleep is really important. I need that sleep.

MT: Michelle Trudeau, NPR News, Minneapolis.

LW: India's extremely hot discovery, next on All Things Considered.

MAKE INFERENCES

Excerpt One

Mary Carskadon: Melatonin is a wonderfully simple signal that turns on in the evening,

Michelle Trudeau: You're getting sleepy . . .

MC: And it turns off in the morning.

MT: And you awaken.

Excerpt Two

William Dement: An adolescent, and particularly the adolescent in high school, is almost bound to get severely sleep deprived.

Michelle Trudeau: That's William Dement of Stanford University. Bill Dement is Dr. Sleep.

Excerpt Three

Student: I'll wake up and I'll just feel miserable, just kind of like ugh, what's wrong with me, you know?

Excerpt Four

William Dement: And after ten minutes of sitting, particularly if the lights are dim, I would say, almost without exception, they are all struggling to stay awake. Ten minutes!!

2B. LISTENING 2: *Get Back in Bed*

Lian: This is Lian, and, like many of our listeners out there, I'm tired. I'm tired in the morning, I'm tired in the afternoon, and I'm really tired at night. And frankly, I'm tired of being tired. My excuse is that I have two small children who sleep a little, and wake up a lot. Dr. Walsleben, why are we all so tired?

Dr. Joyce Walsleben: We're probably tired because we don't make sleep a priority. And I think as a young mother and a career woman, your days are pretty well filled, and I would suspect that you probably think you can do without sleep or at least cut your sleep short, and one of the things that happens is we forget that sleep loss accumulates, so even one bad night, teamed with another will make an effect on our performance the following day. The other aspect, which you did touch

on, is that even though we may sleep long periods of time, the sleep may not be really of good quality.

L: How serious a problem is sleep deprivation?

JW: Well, it can be very serious, because lack of sleep can affect our performance. It's not . . . We can get cranky and all of that, but if our performance is poor, and we are in a very critical job, we can have a major incident. And there have been many across society in which sleep and fatigue were issues.

The *Exxon Valdez* was one in which the captain got a lot of attention, but the mate who was driving the ship had been on duty for 36 hours. . . . But you can read your local papers; every weekend, you'll see a car crash with probably a single driver, around 2 or 3 A.M., no reason why they would happen to drive off the road, and we all believe that that's probably a short sleep event that occurred when they weren't looking for it.

L: Dr. Walsleben, I know how this sleep deprivation affects me. By the end of the day, with my children, I'm tired and cranky, I'm not making good parenting decisions, I don't have a lot to give my husband when he comes home, and then I just feel too tired to exercise. So I think, "Oh, I'll eat or I'll have a big cup of coffee, and that will give me the energy that I don't have naturally." Are these pretty common effects of sleep deprivation amongst your patients?

JW: They're very common, and so many people accept them . . .

L: I would even say by Friday afternoon, I'm afraid to get behind the wheel of a car, because I just feel like I am not a safe driver on the road. That's how tired I am by Fridays.

JW: I think it's great of you to have recognized that . . . and that's a real, major concern for most of America's workers. By Friday, everyone seems to be missing, probably, five hours of sleep.

3C. PRONUNCIATION: *Contrastive Stress*

Exercise 1

1. I <u>need</u> to go to <u>bed</u>, but I'm <u>feeling</u> <u>energetic</u>.
2. <u>Adolescents</u> wake up <u>late</u>, but <u>children</u> wake up <u>early</u>.
3. <u>Lian</u> is fast <u>asleep</u>, but her <u>children</u> are <u>awake</u>.
4. My <u>husband</u> has <u>insomnia</u>, but <u>I</u> need to <u>sleep</u>.
5. I'm <u>sleepy</u> in the <u>morning</u>, but I'm wide <u>awake</u> at <u>night</u>.

UNIT 4: Animal Intelligence

2A. LISTENING ONE: *The Infinite Mind: Animal Intelligence*

Goodwin: We've assembled a fascinating group of scientists who make a living working with smart birds, smart chimps and smart dolphins. All three of them are pushing the edge of the envelope in the animal intelligence field, and they're here to share what they've learned.

LISTEN FOR MAIN IDEAS

Goodwin: Welcome, all three of you, to The Infinite Mind.

Dr. Pepperberg: Hi.

Dr. Stan Kuczaj: Hi.

Dr. Sally Boysen: Thank you.

Goodwin: Glad to have you. Now let me start with a quick question for each of you. Off the top of your head, what's the smartest thing you've ever seen one of your animals do, thing—you know, something that made you step out and say, "Wow, that's amazing." Dr. Boysen, what about you?

Dr. Boysen: Oh, you would start with me. I—I guess probably the most remarkable thing I've seen lately is an older chimpanzee that we have in the colony who's now 40. We had a—an arrival of an ex-pet chimp who'd been living in a home for 20 years, and she really has difficulty kind of getting around the lab. She has some retinal damage from diabetes. And, quite literally, I—I think that Sara, the older chimp, recognizes that this other chimpanzee, Abigail, kind of just doesn't get it. And we've seen her literally move through the facility, put her arms around Abigail and lead her down to the right door, for example, in the evening when she's supposed to come in for dinner. This is very remarkable behavior for—for a chimp that was born—raised in captivity, who has not socialized with chimps, and yet she really seemed to understand that Abigail needed her assistance. So I think it's—it's—was a pretty remarkable thing to observe.

Goodwin: Dr. Pepperberg, what about you?

Dr. Pepperberg: Ours is very different. I believe one of the things that we found that is—that's really very exciting is Alex's ability to use information that he's learned in one context and transfer that to a completely different context. So, for example, he was trained to respond color, shape, matter or none when objects were shown to him and he was asked, "What's same?" or "What's different?" And then we trained him on a task on relative size. So we'd ask him, "What color bigger?" or, "What color smaller?" And the very first time we showed him two objects of the same size and asked him, "What color bigger?" he looks at us and he says, "What same?"

Goodwin: OK.

Dr. Pepperberg: And—yeah. And then we asked him, "OK. Now you tell us, you know, what color bigger." And he said, "None." And he had never been trained on this.

Goodwin: That is amazing. Dr. Kuczaj, what about you?

Dr. Kuczaj: Well, I have two examples that I'd like to mention. Both of these are spontaneous behaviors involving killer whales. In one example, a young whale was playing with a large disk, which ended up on the bottom of a pool, and it couldn't figure out how to get the disk off the bottom of the pool. And, spontaneously, it blew air bubbles out of its blow hole, which raised the disk off the floor so it could grab it. Another thing that we've observed is—with a number of killer whales is they'll use fish to bait seagulls. As the—the seagulls will get close enough so that then they can try and catch and often succeed in catching the gulls.

Goodwin: OK.

Goodwin: Now, Dr. Pepperberg, it's—parrots are particularly intriguing, of course, because they actually vocalize to some extent a kind of communication. Can you really talk to them like you talk to a human? I mean, what's—what's it like?

Dr. Pepperberg: Well, you can talk to the birds the way you talk to a very young human. They don't speak to us in complete sentences. They don't have the same type of language as we do. We don't even call it language. We just call it two-way communication. But you can come into the lab, you can ask Alex what he'd like to eat, where he wants to go. And he answers numerous questions about colors, shapes, materials, categories, similarity, difference, numbers. So it's—it's like working with a small child.

Goodwin: And you gave us one example. What else has—has Alex learned to do?

Dr. Pepperberg: Well, one—one thing he can do is to answer multiple questions about the same objects, and that's important because it shows that he understands the questions themselves. He's not simply responding in a rote manner to the particular objects.

Alex: Some water.

Goodwin: I think Alex is trying to butt in here. Dr. Pepperberg . . .

Dr. Kuczaj: Good.

Goodwin: . . . do you wanna give Alex the floor here?

Dr. Pepperberg: Alex, do you wanna do some work huh? Here. Listen. What's here?

Alex: Beeper.

Dr. Pepperberg: Very good. It's a little toy telephone beeper. Good birdie. OK. Let's go back to this other thing. What's here? How many?

Alex: Two.

Dr. Pepperberg: Good. Can you tell me what's different? What's different?

Alex: Color.

Dr. Pepperberg: Color, very good. And what color bigger? What color bigger?

Alex: Green.

Dr. Pepperberg: That's right. Saw two keys. One was blue and one was green, and they were the same shape and different color and different size. Very good. He's been asking for water, grapes, go shoulder, all sorts of things while we've been doing this.

Alex: Some water.

Goodwin: At any rate, we really appreciate all of you appearing on The Infinite Mind, and we'll—we're gonna be coming back to this issue. So thank you all very much.

Dr. Pepperberg: You're w—very welcome.

Dr. Kuczaj: Thank you.

Dr. Boysen: Thank you.

Goodwin: Alex, thank you, too.

LISTEN FOR DETAILS

(Repeat Listen for Main Ideas)

MAKE INFERENCES

Excerpt One

Goodwin: . . . Dr. Boysen, what about you?

Dr. Boysen: Oh, you would start with me.

Excerpt Two

Dr. Boysen: And, quite literally, I—I think that Sara, the older chimp, recognizes that this other chimpanzee, Abigail, kind of just doesn't get it. And we've seen her literally move through the facility, put her arms around Abigail and lead her down to the right door, for example, in the evening when she's supposed to come in for dinner. This is very remarkable behavior for—for a chimp that was born—raised in captivity, who has not socialized with chimps, and yet she really seemed to understand that Abigail needed her assistance.

Excerpt Three

Dr. Pepperberg: So we'd ask him, "What color bigger?" or, "What color smaller?" And the very first time we showed him two objects of the same size and asked him, "What color bigger?" he looks at us and he says, "What same?"

Goodwin: That is amazing.

Excerpt Four

Dr. Pepperberg: Alex, do you wanna do some work? Huh? Listen. What's here?

Alex: Beeper.

Dr. Pepperberg: Very good. It's a little toy telephone beeper. Good birdie. OK. Let's go back to this other thing. What's here? How many?

Alex: Two.

2B. LISTENING TWO: *What Motivates Animals?*

Liz: A lot of the work is done in chimps and other apes because they're our closest relatives, and the idea is to put the chimps into a situation that they react to. And it turns out that competition for food is what motivates them to perform. So there's been a series of experiments, one of the more recent ones has to do with putting a chimp head to head with a human, and the chimp wants to reach for food and the human has the ability to pull the food away. And what the chimp readily figures out, is that if it kind of sneaks around a barrier that the human can't see, it can get the food. What that experiment is showing is that the chimp understands that the human is watching them and understands how to manipulate the situation to get what it wants.

Commentator: So I guess there's also been some interesting things done with birds as well, though, which aren't quite as close to us on the evolutionary relationship. We've had at least one study just this year that suggests that birds can remember, plan, or even perhaps, anticipate the future. Is that correct?

Liz: Right. What happened is about ten years ago a couple of researchers realized that some of the skills that you see in chimps and social animals, including us, might also exist in social birds. And so they started a series of experiments, most of them take advantage of what they call caching behavior in which a scrub jay for example or a crow will take a tidbit of food, a piece of nut, whatever, and bury it. And all the experiments are based on the idea that, "OK, if some other bird is watching you bury the food, what do you do? And what they've discovered is that the bird is aware if somebody else is watching, the bird takes evasive action—it will go behind a barrier so that the onlooker can't see what it's doing. It will bury the food in one place and then come back and move it to another place.

Commentator: And I guess part of it sort of plays into this whole question of what cognition really is. I mean, isn't that sort of an extra layer of controversy or disagreement on this whole question?

Liz: Oh right. I mean the definition of cognition and intelligence, even, if humans have to be the most intelligent beings, then we have to define intelligence in terms of what we can and cannot do. So what, one of the prevailing standards is something called 'theory of mind' and that is when you can assess what somebody else is thinking, can judge what somebody else might be doing, can take that information and use it at a later time. And at one point no animal was supposed to have any of that, and of course the experiments with chimps and even with the birds are showing that . . . well, they know about deception, they know when someone can see something they're doing, and they know how to manipulate that—what that person can see.

Commentator: Well Liz, it looks like there's a lot going on on this front. Thanks for coming in today and chatting with us about some of it.

Liz: Well, thank you.

3C. PRONUNCIATION: *Questions with or*

Exercise 1

1. Do you have a cat or a dog?

2. Do you like to visit zoos or parks?

3. Do chimps communicate with sounds or gestures?

4. Can your dog shake hands or roll over?

5. Can that parrot ask or answer questions?

6. Did the speaker talk about the intelligence of cows or horses?

7. Have you read about seagulls or crows?

8. Do you have a fur coat or a leather jacket?

Exercise 2

1. Do you have a cat or a dog?

2. Do you like to visit zoos or parks?

3. Do chimps communicate with sounds or gestures?

4. Can your dog shake hands or roll over?

5. Can that parrot ask or answer questions?

6. Did the speaker talk about the intelligence of cows or horses?

7. Have you read about seagulls or crows?

8. Do you have a fur coat or a leather jacket?

UNIT 5: Longevity: Refusing to Be Invisible

2A. LISTENING ONE: *The Red Hat Society*

Korva Coleman, host: They're popping up around the country: women in red hats. In fact, they've organized their own sorority with more than 3,000 chapters. They celebrate being women and being over 50 years old. Trish Anderton of New Hampshire Public Radio found one chapter of the Red Hat Society at an Independence Day parade this week and filed this story.

LISTEN FOR MAIN IDEAS

Korva Coleman, host: They're popping up around the country: women in red hats. In fact, they've organized their own sorority with more than 3,000 chapters. They celebrate being women and being over 50 years old. Trish Anderton of New Hampshire Public Radio found one chapter of the Red Hat Society at an Independence Day parade this week and filed this story.

Trish Anderton, reporting: It's a classic small-town parade, complete with fire engines, veterans organizations and a float by the high school swim team. But this year, there's something new.

(parade activity)

Unidentified Man: The Red Hats are coming. Yeah, the Red Hats!

Anderton: The Red Hat Society consists of women 50 and older. They've got a black truck with a big hat on it and a red hay wagon some of the members are riding. Others walk alongside and toss candy to the kids in the crowd. Red Hatters dress all in purple, with, of course, red hats. Their goal is to have a good time.

Ms. Maryann Ryan: Well, today's ensemble—I have on a purple ankle-length shift with stars on it.

Anderton: Maryann Ryan is the leader or queen mother of this chapter.

Ms. Ryan: My hat is a wide-brimmed picture hat, with a purple feather boa topped off with a tiara because, after all, I am the queen.

Anderton: The society takes its name from a 1961 poem by Englishwoman Jenny Joseph called "Warning." It begins, "When I am an old woman I shall wear purple with a red hat which doesn't go and doesn't suit me." The narrator goes on to talk about learning to spit and spending her pension on satin sandals and generally enjoying herself. The society's founder, Californian Sue Ellen Cooper, says it's a message women 50 and older instantly understand.

Ms. Sue Ellen Cooper: My particular generation and those older pretty much did put their family ahead of everything, and there's no bitterness about it. It's just we all kind of look at each other and we know that we have given and nurtured and supported and upheld and etcetera, and it's kind of fun to say, "Now, like, let's see, what was it I wanted to do?"

Anderton: Cooper saw the poem years ago and was struck by it. She gave a bunch of her friends red hats. Then they started going out to tea, wearing the colors. Two years ago, a local magazine wrote an article about them. Then phone calls and e-mails started pouring in, and other women began organizing. Now Cooper is the Exalted Queen Mother of a society with over 3,500 chapters. Red Hatters are not overtly political. They don't go in for volunteer work or self-improvement. But they do enjoy solidarity.

(parade activity)

Anderton: Back at the Wolfeboro parade, Judy Harrington marches with a dozen other members of the society. Harrington is wearing a big red straw hat with an American flag. She says at first, it wasn't easy being so flamboyant.

Ms. Judy Harrington: I don't like to come out of my home with my neighbors seeing me in purple and a huge red hat. But when I get with the girls and put the hat on, it's a whole different story.

Anderton: The clothes are important, but not as a status symbol. Red Hatters brag about yard-sale dresses and bargain-basement shoes. Former clothing industry executive Carol Wallace especially enjoys dressing down. She says it signals a sort of detente, an agreement that as older women, they can stop competing with each other.

Ms. Carol Wallace: It's the first time in my life I have been with a group of women and alls we do is love and support each other and laugh our sides off. There's not one of us that are jealous of each other or envious or—it's amazing.

Anderton: Sitting on the sidelines, 35-year-old Kristin Hammond of Connecticut says she's going to wear purple someday.

Ms. Kristin Hammond: I like the fact that they're out here so bold. Most of the time, women over the age of 50 like to pretend they're not.

And I'd like to see that women of all age are happy to be out there, wearing gorgeous hats, being as bold as they can be.

Anderton: That's the point, says Sue Ellen Cooper. The Exalted Queen Mother says the message behind the apparent silliness is that older women refuse to be invisible, even if they have to wear a red sequined baseball cap and purple pants to grab the spotlight. For NPR News, I'm Trish Anderton in Wolfeboro, New Hampshire.

LISTEN FOR DETAILS

(Repeat Listen for Main Ideas)

MAKE INFERENCES

Excerpt One

Ms. Maryann Ryan: Well, today's ensemble—I have on a purple ankle-length shift with stars on it.

Excerpt Two

Trish Anderton: The society takes its name from a 1961 poem by Englishwoman Jenny Joseph called "Warning." It begins, "When I am an old woman I shall wear purple with a red hat which doesn't go and doesn't suit me." The narrator goes on to talk about learning to spit and spending her pension on satin sandals and generally enjoying herself. The society's founder, Californian Sue Ellen Cooper, says it's a message women 50 and older instantly understand.

Excerpt Three

Ms. Sue Ellen Cooper: My particular generation and those older pretty much did put their family ahead of everything, . . . and it's kind of fun to say, "Now, like, let's see, what was it I wanted to do?"

Excerpt Four

Ms. Judy Harrington: I don't like to come out of my home with my neighbors seeing me in purple and a huge red hat. But when I get with the girls and put the hat on, it's a whole different story.

2B.   LISTENING TWO: *On Vinegar and Living to the Ripe Old Age of 115*

Madeleine Brand, host: This Day to Day, from NPR News. I'm Madeleine Brand.

Alex Chadwick, host: I'm Alex Chadwick. We're a little late with this next item, an obituary for a woman who died over the weekend. Susie Potts Gibson is someone to know about anyway, because she had achieved a couple of distinctions. First, she lived to the age of 115, one of the oldest people in the world, and second, she apparently lived not just a long life, but a remarkably happy one as well. Her granddaughter, Nancy Paetz, is on the phone from her office in Huntsville, Alabama. Ms. Paetz, welcome to Day to Day.

Ms. Nancy Paetz: Thank you.

Chadwick: Your grandmother, Susie Potts Gibson, she was born in Mississippi. She lived in Sheffield, Alabama in the same house for 80 years, I read, in an obituary in the L.A. Times. What did she think about being 115 years old?

Ms. Paetz: You know, she was very proud of it. She often referred to herself as one of the oldest people in the world, and she would constantly say, okay, so am I still one of the oldest people in the world?

Ms. Paetz: So that was kind of exciting for her, I think.

Chadwick: She had a secret of longevity?

Ms. Paetz: If you asked her what her secret was, she would tell you that it was probably three things. One, she lived for her pickles. She ate lots and lots of pickles.

Chadwick: Okay, pickles is one.

Ms. Paetz: And vinegar.

Chadwick: Vinegar.

Ms. Paetz: We kept, every time we visited, we had to go and buy big jars of vinegar, and big jars of pickles.

Chadwick: How did she take her vinegar?

Ms. Paetz: Well, she put it on everything. I don't think she ever just drank it, but she certainly drank the pickle juice.

Chadwick: She did?

Ms. Paetz: Oh, yes. Yes, she soaked her feet in it. She put it on any parts of her body that hurt, that was her end all, be all.

Chadwick: All right, pickles, vinegar, and number three . . .

Ms. Paetz: And number three was she didn't take medicines unless she absolutely had to, until the last few years when she really was getting old in her mind, they made her take some of the medicines that she needed in the nursing home, but she was the kind that would never take an aspirin for a headache. She figured it'd go away, and it couldn't be good for you.

Chadwick: She lived alone to the age of 106, and then moved into some sort of assisted living facility there, I read. Weren't you all a little anxious about having your grandmother living on her own, independently, at an age over 100?

Ms. Paetz: Yes, especially since she was so far away, but she's always been a very strong woman and a very stubborn woman, and she would not even allow the conversation to be held, and in fact, when it came time for her to move, she called us on the phone, and she says, okay, the time has come. I've sold my house. I've got me a room. Come move me.

Chadwick: She took care of all the arrangements herself?

Ms. Paetz: Oh, yes. Oh, yes. There was never anything wrong with her mind or her physical abilities.

Chadwick: Nancy Paetz, mourning, but mainly remembering her grandmother, Susie Potts Gibson who died over this last weekend in Alabama at the age of 115. Nancy Paetz, thank you and our sympathies to you.

Ms. Paetz: Thank you very much.

3B. GRAMMAR: *Tag Questions*

Exercise 1

You heard that story about the Red Hat Society, didn't you?

Yes, that sounds like an amazing group, doesn't it?

Exercise 2, Step 2

A: You've heard about the Red Hat Society, haven't you?

B: Yes, I have. It's an amazing story, isn't it?

A: They don't have organizations like that in other countries, do they?

B: Of course they do. You've heard about the International Federation of Women, haven't you?

A: No, what is it?

B: They promote lifelong education for women. They also try to create positive change and peace in the world. It's an international network of women graduates from all cultures. That's a great idea, isn't it?

A: Yeah, it sounds very inspiring. They don't have any chapters in Latin America, do they?

B: Yeah, I think they have a lot of groups throughout Latin America, as well as in Asia and Europe. Why do you ask?

A: Well, because my family's from Latin America. You knew that, didn't you?

3C. PRONUNCIATION: *Recognizing Word Blends with* **You**

Exercise 2

1. Why did you go there?
2. What did you see at the parade?
3. You can come, can't you?
4. They won't let you in without an ID card.
5. How do you get there?
6. Where do you live?
7. You can't come, can you?
8. Where did you go after class?
9. What do you think about that?

UNIT 6: Giving to Others: Why Do We Do It?

2A. LISTENING ONE: *Why We Give*

Goodwin: Probably most gestures of everyday kindness and generosity are never recorded. But when it comes to organized charities, fund-raisers make it their business to know who is giving and why.

LISTEN FOR MAIN IDEAS

Goodwin: Probably most gestures of everyday kindness and generosity are never recorded. But when it comes to organized charities, fund-raisers make it their business to know who is giving and why. With us today is Stacy Palmer, editor of the fund-raiser's weekly bible, The Chronicle of Philanthropy.

Goodwin: Welcome, Ms. Palmer.

Ms. Palmer: Glad to be here.

Goodwin: What studies have been done on volunteering and charitable giving?

Ms. Palmer: Actually, we don't know all of that much about what really motivates people to give. We know how often they give. And about half of Americans volunteer their time and 75 percent of people give money. There have been some polls that give some indication of what—what are some of the kinds of things that make people want to give. And usually, it's the passion for the cause. That's what they really care about. Whatever it is that they're involved with, they care about it a great deal. And that motivates them more than anything else; more than the tax benefits, more than the desire to repay somebody for something. They really care very, very much about whatever it is that they're getting involved in. And that's the biggest motivator.

Goodwin: Do positive appeals work better than negative appeals?

Ms. Palmer: It's hard to tell. It depends on what the issue is. One of the things that politically minded causes often find is that when they have an enemy, they do very well. If they can say that this is the big threat to something, "You better do something now or else something bad will happen," people give in a big way.

Goodwin: Well, what about the difference between volunteering time and volunteering money?

Ms. Palmer: A lot of people have differing attitudes on that, and both are very valuable. But I think people feel better after they volunteer. Writing the check feels good, but I think most people really f—when—when they go to volunteer, they see the direct effects of what they're doing. And that's much more rewarding to them.

Goodwin: Now what's the magnitude of this in terms of percentage of the population? I mean, is there a figure at what-you know, at what percentage of the population give either their time and-or their money?

Ms. Palmer: About 50 percent of people say that they volunteer at least at some point, maybe, just, you know, a short-term volunteering project or something like that. It's a smaller percentage that actually volunteers once a week or—or something like that.

Goodwin: Mm-hmm. Mm-hmm.

Ms. Palmer: But at least half of Americans say they volunteered at some time in the past year. Seventy-five percent of people said they made some kind of a cash donation, and that's often to some kind of a religious institution, which is what commands the biggest share of contributions, but also to multiple other causes. So most people in America do give something.

Goodwin: What about social class? Is that as predictable as it should be?

Ms. Palmer: The very wealthy do give more often, and they give a little bit differently. They tend to like to go to these black tie benefits and do that sort of thing. And they also like to give with their name attached to it. People who are not in that wealthy class tend to give anonymously more often, and say that that's something that they prefer to do.

Goodwin: Would you say that the less-wealthy give a larger percentage of their income?

Ms. Palmer: The evidence is debatable on that, and that's something that economists really disagree on. And I think the biggest group of economists think that the poor do give proportionally more, but there's a strong argument to be made on the other side that the wealthy are giving proportionally more. So that's something that is continuing to be studied, and we hope at some point we'll get a more definitive answer with better data. Part of it is, how do you count what's giving? Is it giving when somebody helps their neighbor and gives, you know, a bunch of their winter clothing to somebody next door? Should you count that as part of charitable giving? It's not part of formal giving . . .

Goodwin: No.

Ms. Palmer: . . . but it's certainly something that one would consider generous. The other problem is getting people to accurately say what it is that they've given in response to what they're being asked. Do you remember what you gave over the past year, honestly? Might you exaggerate it when somebody asks you, "Were you a giving person last year?"

Goodwin: Sure.

Ms. Palmer: All of those things are what researchers are trying to factor out so that they get honest answers.

Goodwin: Other than the—the thing we talked about a minute ago about ca—you know, caring about the cause, are there other reasons that people give? Are there other sort of universals that differentiate a giver from a non-giver?

Ms. Palmer: Usually, it's some kind of moral or religious feeling that also motivates a great deal of people to give. And it seems to come out of a feeling that it's important to, in some ways, give back to society.

Goodwin: Mm-hmm.

Ms. Palmer: And that's often part of a family tradition or something that people have been taught all along the way, that that's something that's vital. And one of the things we're seeing a lot of is efforts to teach very young children how to give because it's clear that it is something that can be taught and something that the more people learn about as part of a tradition stays with them for all of their lives. So you even see kindergarten classes doing United Way fund-raising events. And I think we'll be seeing much more emphasis on teaching children because we can see that that really pays off.

And you see in a lot of schools, too, they—this mandatory service requirement, where they actually have to do commer-community service to graduate. That's part of a way to show people, you know, "Here. I worked on a housing project or I helped clean up a river or I helped do something. Here's the difference that I made."

Goodwin: Mm-hmm.

Ms. Palmer: And that seems to make a huge difference in helping people give all throughout their lives.

Goodwin: Thank you very much, Ms. Palmer, for appearing on The Infinite Mind.

Ms. Palmer: Thank you.

LISTEN FOR DETAILS
(Repeat Listen for Main Ideas)

MAKE INFERENCES

Excerpt One

Goodwin: What about social class? Is that as predictable as it should be?

Excerpt Two

Ms. Palmer: Part of it is, how do you count what's giving? Is it giving when somebody helps their neighbor and gives, you know, a bunch of their winter clothing to somebody next door? Should you count that as part of charitable giving? It's not part of formal giving . . .

Excerpt Three

Ms. Palmer: The other problem is getting people to accurately say what it is that they've given in response to what they're being asked. Do you remember what you gave over the past year, honestly? Might you exaggerate it when somebody asks you, "Were you a giving person last year?"

Excerpt Four

Ms. Palmer: And that's often part of a family tradition or something that people have been taught all along the way, that that's something that's vital. And one of the things we're seeing a lot of is efforts to teach very young children how to give because it's clear that it is something that can be taught and something that the more people learn about as part of a tradition stays with them for all of their lives. So you even see kindergarten classes doing United Way fund-raising events. And I think we'll be seeing much more emphasis on teaching children because we can see that that really pays off.

2B.   LISTENING TWO: *The Mystery Donor*

Kai Ryssdal: Something about winter and all those family gatherings must be inspiring us: Half of all charitable donations are made between Thanksgiving and New Year's. Or, maybe we just realize that the tax year is about to end. Some people, though, have the giving spirit year-round. Amy Radil introduces us to an anonymous Seattle resident who's become something of a guerilla philanthropist.

Amy Radil: I had just done a story about a welfare mother who was having trouble feeding her children, when I got a phone message. The woman in the message, let's call her the Mystery Donor, said she would like to do something, anonymously, to help the woman in my story. She ended up paying off a $1,200 light bill to keep the woman's power from being shut off. Her career as a benefactor really began after she lost her husband.

Donor: My husband died about three years ago and I had access to more money than I needed for expenses. So it was an opportunity to start giving money away.

AR: At age 58, the Mystery Donor lives in a pretty but not extravagant Seattle home. When her husband was alive they gave money but tended to focus on established charities. Now she acts on her own. Altogether she donates a quarter of her income each year, and she says that amount will increase over time. She says she often gives secretly because she's learned that money can change relationships. Her first secret donation was to a massage therapist she knew.

Donor: She was a single mother and so this was really important work. And she broke her leg. And anybody who's been a single mother as I have knows what a catastrophe looks like on its way. And that looked awful to me. So what I did was to give her some money anonymously through having a cashier's check from the bank sent to her from another town.

AR: These small, personal gifts often go to helping single mothers. Their experience echoes her own years ago.

Donor: I know what that feels like to feel desperate and need to care for a child. I was poor as a single mother for a period, looking for a job and had a 1-year-old. I do recall one night where I had to decide whether to buy tuna fish or diapers. And it was down to that before I got my next paycheck. Of course we got the diapers.

AR: She describes the past three years as a learning curve in the art of philanthropy. She contributes hundreds of thousands of dollars each year to her cause of choice: sustainable farming. She belongs to a group, the Women Donors Network, that put her in touch with a University of Montana professor named Neva Hassanein. Hassanein had created a program to help local farmers supply the school's cafeteria food. The Mystery Donor wanted to help expand the program to other institutions. Hassanein says she then proposed having Americorps volunteers work with other colleges to replicate it.

Neva Hassanein: And so we approached this donor with this idea and she loved it, was very excited. And it was in fact her prodding that got us to think outside the box.

AR: Hassanein says working with these freelance philanthropists has its advantages. They're more flexible and responsive than big foundations, she says, who can sometimes push their own agenda. The Mystery Donor says she may create a foundation one day, but right now she enjoys the freedom that comes from giving on her own.

Donor: I really love flying under the radar and writing checks, you know, without having a structure. I certainly consult with a lot of people around what I do to make sure my judgment is as accurate as it can be, but right now this other way is good.

AR: Even when helping someone she knows, the Mystery Donor says she doesn't feel the need to ask whether they've received her gift. She says these gifts are more like being a secret Santa, where secrecy itself is part of the charm. In Seattle, I'm Amy Radil for Marketplace Money.

3C.   PRONUNCIATION: *Intonation in Lists*

Exercise 1

1. The World Wildlife Fund works with governments, local communities, non-profits.

2. How can you help? You can help by giving your time, your money, and your ideas.

3. Communities where adults vote regularly, parents are active in schools, children play on sports teams, usually have lower levels of crime.

4. I need a vacation—I'm tired of waking up early, spending hours on the road, working at night.

5. If you volunteer at the senior center, you'll feel good about yourself, meet new people, and learn more English.

6. Americans give a lot between Thanksgiving and Christmas: There are food drives, coat drives, toy drives.

Exercise 3

A: Are you having a big Thanksgiving dinner at your house?

B: Actually, every year we spend Thanksgiving at a homeless shelter. We decorate the shelter, help with the cooking, serve the guests, and talk to them. Would you like to come?

A: Yes, I really would. For a long time, I've been thinking about volunteering—at a school, the library, a retirement home. But, you know, I never end up doing anything.

B: Great. We can pick you up here Thursday morning, around 10.

A: Should I bring anything?

B: Just your hands, your energy, and a smile. The shelter supplies everything else.

3C. PRODUCTION: *A Public Service Announcement*

Step One

Close your eyes in Chicago and you can hear the sound of zebra braying in Africa. Look hard out your window in DC and you can see the snow-covered peaks of the Andes. Stand on a corner in LA and feel the hot wind of the Sahara brush across your face. The world is that small. We are that connected. Please visit Earthshare.org and learn how the world's leading environmental groups are working together, making it so simple for you to make a difference, because we are many and we are one. Please visit us at earthshare.org to learn more. Earthshare. One environment: one simple way to care for it all.

UNIT 7: What's The Use of Homework?

2A. LISTENING ONE: *Effects of Homework on Family Life*

CD 3, Track 30:

Bob Edwards: Homework can be stressful for the whole family. Too many nights ending in tears and frustration can leave parents with agonizing questions, like how much is too much? NPR's Margot Adler begins a four-part series with a report on what can happen when homework gets out of control.

Margot Adler: Thousands of families have had the experience of homework assignments that become family events: that wooden replica of the Mayflower that Dad and Mom finished after eight-year-old Johnny got bored, the science fair project that went over the top, the Internet search that took the whole weekend. These days, kids and families are doing lots of homework, and many of those parents are finding that the amount of hands-on help required is totally alien to their own experience growing up, where homework was pretty minimal until high school, and parents stayed way out of the picture.

LISTEN FOR MAIN IDEAS

Track 31

Margot Adler: Steven Oloya, a professor of special education, lives outside of Los Angeles. He has five children who have been in public schools and Catholic schools. One of his daughters, Kaitlyn, attends Chaparral High School, and wants to be a teacher.

Kaitlyn: I usually get home around 5:00, and I'm usually doing homework until about 11 or 12 at night.

Professor Steven Oloya: We've had many nights, 1 and 2 in the morning.

Kaitlyn: I'll find myself just getting really, really tired doing my homework. I have to get up and move around to stay awake.

Prof. Oloya: That's a nightly ritual, because around 11:30 she starts to conk out in the chair, and I go, "Kate, Kate, you've got to wake up." We go outside, sprint down the street, sprint back up the street, just to get her to wake up so she can do one more hour of solid, intense reading and studying.

Adler: Oloya isn't the only parent who talks about sleep and homework. Cecilia Bluer thinks back to her daughter's previous year in the New York City public schools.

Ms. Cecilia Bluer: Last year, when she was in the third grade, she got four hours of homework a night. She was up until 11 at night in tears. There were days that I did not take her to school the next day because she was so distraught over not doing homework, and we have gotten

up at 5 to complete her assignment. I just had to give her mental health days. I wasn't the only mother in that class keeping their children out of school so they could just get a full night's sleep.

Adler: The amount of homework that students get has fluctuated throughout American history, and today it varies from school to school. At the beginning of the 20th century, homework was outlawed in the state of California until a child was 15. It was considered child labor. And in the 1920s and '30s there was another movement against homework led by physicians who said that children needed five hours of fresh air and sunshine every day. After Sputnik in 1957, and the report in the 1980s, A Nation at Risk, which warned that the nation's schools were in danger, homework increased, and now many schools give way over the 10 minutes a day per year that is recommended by some educators. Advocates believe homework teaches responsibility, keeps kids off the streets, helps refine study skills and gets parents involved in their kids' schooling. Joyce Epstein, a sociologist at Johns Hopkins University's Center on Schools, Families and Communities, says her research over 20 years gives support for homework.

Ms. Joyce Epstein: It is helpful for showing that youngsters at any grade level who do their work and complete it do do better in school than kids just like them, similar youngsters, who don't complete their work.

Adler: Gary Natriello has also studied homework. He is a professor of sociology and education at Teachers College in New York. In the 1980s, he was involved in researching the effects of homework in high school.

Professor Gary Natriello: And at that time, we produced a paper that showed that in fact if you assigned more homework, the kids who received the homework actually had better standardized achievement tests.

Adler: Years later, Natriello became a parent.

Prof. Natriello: Then I realized that it wasn't just the students, the children who were getting homework. It was also the parents who were getting homework, and particularly as assignments got more creative, which might have been something that I might have recommended in the '80s, and more demanding, which certainly would have been something that I recommended in the '80s, all those additional demands came back to fall on my wife and myself.

Adler: It is the impact of homework on family life that has many parents hopping mad, particularly in a culture where two parents often work and home life hours are already truncated by many social forces. Steven Russo, an administrator at a medical school, has two children in the New York City public schools, a daughter in sixth grade and a son in ninth grade.

Mr. Steven Russo: When you add it all up, you know, your child's in school for 30 hours a week, they're going to have another 10 hours of homework, then they're expected to read between a half an hour to an hour a night, and then there are projects and there's art, you're talking about a 45 to a 50-hour work week for a 10-year-old.

Adler: Sociologist Gary Natriello says at the time he did his research in the '80s, he believed more homework would simply make teachers and students more accountable.

Prof. Natriello: What we weren't counting on was that at the end of the day all of that comes home, and so someone has to then support the students and monitor the students in getting this work done. Or if nothing else, at least has to allow them to stay up late enough to finish the work, and that really changes home life in some pretty substantial ways. I don't think we fully appreciated what that would mean.

Adler: Natriello still believes if you want kids to reach higher standards, homework is necessary, especially in high school. But he says as a parent he now understands homework's hidden costs. Margot Adler, NPR News, New York.

LISTEN FOR DETAILS

(Repeat Listen for Main Ideas, track 31)

CD 3, Track 32:

Adler: Russo and several other parents in New York City's District 3 decided to purposely choose middle schools with less homework. Cecilia Bluer said when she chose a kindergarten, she chose one with homework because she was nervous and wanted a school with rigor, but now she finds she is constantly fighting over homework, a battle she no longer believes in.

Ms. Bluer: I mean, I have a 12-year-old son who has never loaded a dishwasher, never unloaded a dishwasher. He's never taken the garbage out. He doesn't do anything, because it's all about homework.

Adler: Perhaps one of the most fervent anti-homework activists is Etta Kralovec, the co-author, along with John Buell, of "The End of Homework." Kralovec believes parents have the right to set educational agendas for their families.

Ms. Etta Kravolec (Co-author, "The End of Homework"): If some parents want their kids to learn three languages and want their kids to be in AP math, they ought to be free to structure their family time so the kids can achieve that. But that doesn't mean that all parents want that for their kids. A lot of parents want their kids to participate in community activities, in religious activities.

Adler: The other problem with homework, she says, is that you're never sure who's doing it. Steven Oloya adds class and education differences create an inherent unfairness.

Prof. Oloya: Homework reflects the quality of the home, not the child. My children have access to a university, because I'm a professor. I've had my son bring into his class science fairs liquid nitrogen to demonstrate on show and tell day on science in the fourth grade. As a parent who's conscientious and concerned, I'm going to make sure they turn in the very best homework there is, and it's unfair because some parents do not have access to those resources.

Adler: Oloya will go on and on about the bad content of assignments, but his main gripe is again the effect on family life.

Prof. Oloya: None of my children are involved in scouting. They're not involved in anything with our church, anything with the community, and they cannot be because homework pre-empts everything. They already have my children with compulsory attendance laws, and that's their right. The state does not belong in my home at nighttime.

Adler: Sociologist Gary Natriello says at the time he did his research in the '80s, he believed more homework would simply make teachers and students more accountable.

Prof. Natriello: What we weren't counting on was that at the end of the day all of that comes home, and so someone has to then support the students and monitor the students in getting this work done. Or if nothing else, at least has to allow them to stay up late enough to finish the work, and that really changes home life in some pretty substantial ways. I don't think we fully appreciated what that would mean.

Adler: Natriello still believes if you want kids to reach higher standards, homework is necessary, especially in high school. But he says as a parent he now understands homework's hidden costs. Margot Adler, NPR News, New York.

Edwards: Tomorrow an inner-city school in Baltimore where homework is a vital communications link between teachers and parents. A PTA guide that encourages good homework habits is at npr.org. The time is 29 minutes past the hour.

MAKE INFERENCES

Excerpt One

Kaitlyn: I usually get home around 5:00, and I'm usually doing homework until about 11 or 12 at night.

Professor Steven Oloya: We've had many nights, 1 and 2 in the morning.

Kaitlyn: I'll find myself just getting really, really tired doing my homework. I have to get up and move around to stay awake.

Prof. Oloya: That's a nightly ritual, because around 11:30 she starts to conk out in the chair, and I go, "Kate, Kate, you've got to wake up." We go outside, sprint down the street, sprint back up the street, just to get her to wake up so she can do one more hour of solid, intense reading and studying.

Excerpt Two

Ms. Cecilia Bluer: Last year, when she was in the third grade, she got four hours of homework a night. She was up until 11 at night in tears. There were days that I did not take her to school the next day because she was so distraught over not doing homework, and we have gotten up at 5 to complete her assignment. I just had to give her mental health days. I wasn't the only mother in that class keeping their children out of school so they could just get a full night's sleep.

Excerpt Three

Professor Gary Natriello: And at that time, we produced a paper that showed that in fact if you assigned more homework, the kids who received the homework actually had better standardized achievement tests.

Adler: Years later, Natriello became a parent.

Prof. Natriello: Then I realized that it wasn't just the children who were getting homework. It was also the parents who were getting homework, and particularly as assignments got more creative, which might have been something that I might have recommended in the '80s, and more demanding, which certainly would have been something that I recommended in the '80s, all those additional demands came back to fall on my wife and myself.

Excerpt Four

Adler: Steven Russo, an administrator at a medical school, has two children in the New York City public schools, a daughter in sixth grade and a son in ninth grade.

Mr. Steven Russo: When you add it all up, you know, your child's in school for 30 hours a week, they're going to have another 10 hours of homework, then they're expected to read between a half an hour to an hour a night, and then there are projects and there's art, you're talking about a 45 to a 50-hour work week for a 10-year-old.

2B. LISTENING TWO: *A Duty to Family, Heritage, and Country: Another Perspective on Homework*

Ying Ying Yu: I am a good child, obedient. I grew up in China, a country where education is the center of every child's life and a grade less than 85 percent is considered a failure. Grades mean more to us than a mother's smile, more than the murmur of a wish lingering on birthday candles. I had homework during lunch, math and language classes two times a day. There were punishments for not paying attention. I was beaten with a ruler, and I learned to do anything to get a good grade.

I believe in duty, but that belief comes with sacrifice. The achievements I make come with a cost.

I remember first grade, the red scarf flapping tantalizingly in the wind, and wanting more than anything to be the first one to wear it, that, the symbol of responsibility, excellence and loyalty. The first thing that flashed to mind when I put it on was how glad my family would be, how proud the motherland would be of the child it had borne and how my accomplishments would look on a college application.

All my pride, love, self-esteem—they merge into duty. There have been times I wanted to throw away everything, but duty and obligation were always there to haunt me and to keep me strong. I would think: My parents and grandparents brought me up, my country gave me shelter, my teachers spent so much time building my foundations just to have me throw it all away? No, I can't do that! I must repay all that they have done. "I must," "I should," "I have to," all those little phrases govern my life and the lives of many of my classmates. We struggle on because duty reminds us that the awaiting success is not just for us. It's for our families, our heritage and our country.

I used to want to be a gardener. I liked working outdoors and the gritty feel of dirt was much more tangible than a bunch of flimsy words strung together. But I can never grow up to be a gardener. Everything I have done so far points to the direction of becoming a lawyer. That's a job my family wholeheartedly supports.

There is no other choice for someone who's been brought up by such a strict system, someone who has ambition. Here in America, there is almost a pressure to follow your dreams. I don't want any more dreams—dreams are illusions. And it's too late for me to work toward another future, to let the foundations I have built go to ruins.

I believe in the power of duty to impel. Only duty will offer me something true, something worthy of my effort and the support of my family and country. Duty can bring me to an achievement that is greater than I am.

3C. PRONUNCIATION: *Stressed and Unstressed Vowels*

EXERCISE 3

1. Do you agree that kids today sacrifice their childhood to homework?
2. Did your parents monitor your homework?
3. Did you have demanding homework assignments in school?
4. Do you think homework should be abolished in elementary school?

UNIT 8: Good-Bye to the Sit-Down Meal

2A. LISTENING ONE: *French Sandwiches*

Bob Edwards, Host: France, home of the two-hour, sit-down mid-day meal, is witnessing a boom in take-out sandwiches. At noon, customers line up outside Paris bakeries, waiting to buy long, thin versions of a shrimp salad and avocado sandwich, or other iconoclastic delicacies. The variation in eating habits is reflecting a deeper change in French society. NPR's Sarah Chayes reports.

LISTEN FOR MAIN IDEAS

Bob Edwards, Host: France, home of the two-hour, sit-down mid-day meal, is witnessing a boom in take-out sandwiches. At noon, customers line up outside Paris bakeries, waiting to buy long, thin versions of a shrimp salad and avocado sandwich, or other iconoclastic delicacies. The variation in eating habits is reflecting a deeper change in French society. NPR's Sarah Chayes reports.

Sarah Chayes: As with any major shift in something as intimate as eating, the story is complicated. Sociologist Claude Fishlere makes a living studying food habits here.

Claude Fishlere: It starts with a change in the workforce. So it's a feminization, white-collarization, if I can say so . . . services rather than industry. . . .

SC: The result has been a revolution in one of France's core industries—the bakery. Formerly, bakeries here offered a limited range of albeit excellent products—about four kinds of bread, breakfast and dessert pastries. Now, that's just the start.

SC: Au Pain Gourmet, a bakery on the corner of a market street, in the ordinary working-class tenth arrondissement of Paris. It's eight in the morning, and Nicole already has the slicer going, cutting bread for lunch sandwiches. She's making tuna vegetables on whole wheat bread.

Nicole: (speaks French)

SC: "I hate making sandwiches," she says. Tough. It puts bread on her table, too. Au Pain Gourmet, with its glass cases stacked full, does so much sandwich business, it had to hire Nicole especially to make them. Owner Audile Gazier says she's just responding to the demand . . . and letting her imagination run wild. She even tried making a four-course sandwich meal—with the appetizer, then the main dish, then cheese, and chocolate spread alternating down one baguette. It was a bit much for people to swallow.

Audile Gazier: (speaks French)

SC: She says, nowadays people want to eat faster at noon, and leave early at the end of the day. Life is changing, she says; we have to keep up. The changes include women making up almost half the labor force now, and making their tastes known, and men, more likely to be working behind a computer than behind a jackhammer, not needing to eat so much. Sociologist Fishlere:

CF: They also have to pick up the children as early as possible, from the *crèche*.

SC: . . . daycare center.

CF: Daycare center. So basically, they look for something that's very close to what is called fast food. And, eh, the interesting point is that the um, supply that has developed goes well beyond your, uh, basic McDonald's hamburgers.

Unidentified Woman #1: (speaks French)

SC: For example, Au Pain Gourmet's plethora of multishaped, multicontent sandwiches. They're obviously a hit with the lunchtime customers who line up all the way onto the sidewalk. They agree this recent phenomenon is growing.

Unidentified Woman #2: Yes, more and more. It's exploding, this kind of eating.

Unidentified Man: Every baker offers sandwiches.

Unidentified Woman #3: Because before, it was only with ham and butter and now we have salad and tomatoes and Roquefort. Because we eat sandwich, but it's French products in it.

SC: French products in it. That may be the key. Instead of being overrun by McDonald's, as some feared, the French have adapted the idea of fast food and made it their own. Around the corner from Au Pain Gourmet, a quick burger franchise just closed. Sarah Chayes, NPR News. Paris.

LISTEN FOR DETAILS

(Repeat Listen for Main Ideas)

MAKE INFERENCES

Excerpt One

Reporter: It's eight in the morning, and Nicole already has the slicer going, cutting bread for lunch sandwiches. . . . "I hate making sandwiches," she says. Tough.

Excerpt Two

Reporter: It puts bread on her table, too.

Excerpt Three

Reporter: Owner Audile Gazier says she's just responding to the demand . . . and letting her imagination run wild. She even tried making a four-course sandwich meal—with the appetizer, then the main dish, then cheese, and chocolate spread alternating down one baguette. It was a bit much for people to swallow.

Excerpt Four

Reporter: For example, Au Pain Gourmet's plethora of multishaped, multicontent sandwiches. They're obviously a hit with the lunchtime customers who line up all the way onto the sidewalk.

Excerpt Five

Reporter: Yes, more and more. It's exploding, this kind of eating.

2B.   LISTENING TWO: *Food in a Bowl*

Lian Dolan: A couple of years ago, I started noticing a food trend. And it started at Teriyaki Hut. And I noticed a big sign in the window that said: Teriyaki Bowl. And I thought: Ah, Teriyaki Bowl, OK.

And then I saw at El Pollo Loco, which is kind of a fast food Mexican chain—more bowls, more food in bowls—beef bowls, chicken bowls, rice bowls, and I thought: Well rice, that makes sense, that's a cultural thing. You've got to eat rice in a bowl, that makes sense.

But the other day, I was wandering through the frozen food aisle, and I looked up, and now, there's a whole "Food in Bowl" section. And this has nothing to do with cultural food. I just . . . I don't think lasagna needs to be in a bowl. I don't know. Are we just eating too much food, too fast, that we can't eat on a plate anymore . . . that we need a bowl because we can get that closer to our mouth for more shoveling in?

What is the next trend, hands-free eating, like hands-free cell phones? Just forget it. Forget the utensils, just get yourself a nice trough, and put the lasagna in there.

I'm Lian Dolan in Pasadena, and I feel it's my duty as a mother to educate my children to eat on a plate with a knife and a fork.

Julie Dolan: I'm Julie Dolan in Bangkok. And we've got rice bowls, monk bowls. It's pretty much bowl city, here.

Liz: I'm Liz Dolan in New York. And of all the challenging methods of presenting food, I've actually been having the most trouble lately wrestling with things on skewers. Last week I actually beaned someone with a lamb kebab!

UNIT 9: Finding A Niche: The Challenge for Young Immigrants

2A.   LISTENING ONE: *A World Within a School*

Mary Ambrose: Students in cities like New York are used to hearing wide variations of English. In a town where immigrant communities flourish, many dialects and languages mix with standard English. In fact, there's an international high school that encourages immigrant students to use and develop their native tongues while learning English. It's a new approach, and as Richard Schiffman reports, it seems to work.

LISTEN FOR MAIN IDEAS

Mary Ambrose: Students in cities like New York are used to hearing wide variations of English. In a town where immigrant communities flourish, many dialects and languages mix with standard English. In fact, there's an international high school that encourages immigrant students to use and develop their native tongues while learning English. It's a new approach, and as Richard Schiffman reports, it seems to work.

Richard Schiffman: The philosophy of this school is that you learn by doing, and not by hearing the teacher lecture. In this math class, for example, six teams of young people are gathered around lab tables, building their own miniature temple out of cardboard. But to find out what really sets this school apart, you need to get up close.

The four teenage boys at this table are planning their temple in Polish. At the other tables, they're speaking Spanish, English, and Mandarin Chinese. This is not just a bilingual classroom; it's a multilingual one, and the pupils here are all recent immigrants to the United States. Their teacher, Jennifer Shenke, walks around the room, quietly helping out.

Jennifer Shenke: They love building things. This has been really successful, and they've learned a lot of math that they didn't have before, umm, just doing scale and proportion. And, and I feel pretty good about that because they, they didn't know that they were learning it until they had learned it.

RS: Shenke is happy that her pupils are learning math and enjoying themselves in the process, and she's especially pleased that they're teaching one another. She knows that many in her classroom wouldn't be able to follow her if she lectured. So she depends on the pupils who know more English and more math to help teach those who know less. That's what's happening now at the lab tables. They're helping each other out in their own languages. . . .

Priscilla Billarrel: . . . I think what we share the most is a feeling of not fitting in.

RS: Priscilla Billarrel left Chile when she was 14 years old. She says that although they come from all over the world, the students at the International High School understand each other very well.

PB: Since we all are immigrants in here, we all know what['s] to be different feels like, so we support one another. Whenever we have problems with pronunciation[s], or we're missing words or something, whatever we're saying, we correct one another kindly. We don't make fun of each other. That's what I really like about this school. . . .

RS: . . . New York City can be an intimidating place, even for those who have spent their whole lives here. But for young people who have just been uprooted from tight-knit, extended families and traditional communities abroad, the city can seem positively unfriendly. Teacher Aaron Listhaus says that young immigrants don't just need a place to learn English and other subjects. They need, above all else, a place that feels completely safe and welcoming.

Aaron Listhaus: It's particularly important for these students to have a comfort level in a place called school and for that school to feel like home . . . to feel like their needs are going to get met, um, they're going to be listened to, they're going to be valued for who they are and the diverse backgrounds that they come from, and that those things are viewed as what makes them special rather than what makes them a problem.

RS: The fact that immigrant youngsters speak a language other than English, Listhaus says, is seen by most educators as a problem that needs to be corrected. The usual approach is to teach students exclusively in English, and to suppress the use of their native language. Evelyna Namovich, who came to the U.S. three years ago from Poland, remembers what it was like to find herself in a typical New York City school.

Evelyna Namovich: Sometimes it was so difficult because I didn't know what was the subject all about, what was she speaking about, and I would need somebody to translate, even a little bit for me, you know. And we couldn't, because we would have to write something like . . . an essay, er, you know, like punishment, if we spoke Polish.

RS: Evelyna says she was relieved when she transferred to the International High School, where she not only wasn't punished for speaking Polish, she was encouraged to bone up on her native language at the same time as she was learning English. Instructor Aaron Listhaus says that it's important that young immigrants don't lose their languages, as his own immigrant parents from Eastern Europe did.

AL: My parents have a hard time speaking in their native languages at this point. And to me there's something sad about that. Language is more than just the way that you communicate with the world; it's the way that you interpret the world in your own head. So to me, there's something more than just communication that's lost when you lose your native language.

RS: And teacher Kathy Rucker adds that speaking another language also has a practical economic value.

Kathy Rucker: People in the future are going to have to communicate in more than one language, it seems to me, because there's so much rapid travel, there's so much international business.

RS: . . . Today, as also in the past, immigrants to the U.S. often feel the need to assimilate as quickly as possible into mainstream American culture. But there is one place, at least, where new immigrants are being encouraged to keep what is unique to them. From the International High School in New York, I'm Richard Schiffman, for *The World.*

LISTEN FOR DETAILS

(Repeat Listen for Main Ideas)

MAKE INFERENCES

Excerpt One

Richard Schiffman: The philosophy of this school is that you learn by doing, and not by hearing the teacher lecture. In this math class, for example, six teams of young people are gathered around lab tables, building their own miniature temple out of cardboard. But to find out what really sets this school apart, you need to get up close.

Excerpt Two

Priscilla Billarrel: . . . Since we all are immigrants in here, we all know what['s] to be different feels like, so we support one another. Whenever we have problems with pronunciation[s], or we're missing words or something, whatever we're saying, we correct one another kindly. We don't make fun of each other. That's what I really like about this school. . . .

Excerpt Three

Evelyna Namovich: Sometimes it was so difficult because I didn't know what was the subject all about, what was she speaking about, and I would need somebody to translate, even a little bit for me, you know. And we couldn't, because we would have to write something like . . . an essay, er, you know, like punishment, if we spoke Polish.

Excerpt Four

Aaron Listhaus: My parents have a hard time speaking in their native languages at this point. And to me there's something sad about that. Language is more than just the way that you communicate with the world; it's the way that you interpret the world in your own head. So to me, there's something more than just communication that's lost when you lose your native language.

Excerpt Five

Kathy Rucker: People in the future are going to have to communicate in more than one language, it seems to me, because there's so much rapid travel, there's so much international business.

2B. LISTENING TWO: *The Words Escape Me*

I was standing on a train platform in a foreign land.
I was 21 years old,
Excited to be involved, and to do my part, to understand everything I was told.
But they moved too quickly, talked too fast, moved too quickly.
I couldn't even catch my breath.
Frozen in a fast frame, action is blurred.
Loud, too loud, I can't understand your words.
What was I thinking? I can't do this, learn this.
Think I'll just go home,
But I can't go home.
I worked out some bugs, and know where I live.
I can also use your words to order only fish.
I try to eat their food; I miss the meals from home.
I eat too little; I eat too much.
I'm studying hard, but I don't get the jokes.
They think I'm stupid; I can't tell them I'm not.

Writing in this book makes me feel at home.
The words I can't escape they're hiding my best, you know.
What was I thinking? I can't do this, learn this.
Think I'll just go home.
But I can't go home.
Hey, yeah, words escape me, [repeat]
And I can't use my tongue. [repeat] I can't use it like you. [repeat]
Learn the language, talk the language, learn the language, boy. [repeat]

Writing in this book makes me feel at home.
The words I can't escape are hiding my best, you know.
What was I thinking? I can't do this, learn this.
Think I'll just go home.
But I can't go home.
Hey, yeah, words escape me, [repeat]
And I can't use my tongue. [repeat]
I can't use it like you. [repeat]

UNIT 10: No Technology? No Way!

2A. LISTENING ONE: *Noise in the City*

Neal Rauch: It's late. You're tired. Finally, after an exhausting day, you're ready to surrender to the world of dreams. Your head sinks into your pillow. Then . . .

LISTEN FOR MAIN IDEAS.

Steve Curwood: Modern life is full of nasty noises, especially in the cities. Sirens can shatter serenity at any moment and jackhammers, loud music, and useless mufflers can all send us over the edge. For many people in New York City, there's one form of sonic pollution at the top of the list. They're calling for its banning, even though some nervous New Yorkers savor the sound for security reasons. And as Neal Rauch reports, even as the controversy prompts loud debate, some aren't waiting for laws to be passed.

Neal Rauch: It's late. You're tired. Finally, after an exhausting day, you're ready to surrender to the world of dreams. Your head sinks into your pillow. Then . . .

Judy Evans: After being awakened at night many times so that awful feeling, you know, you've just gotten to sleep and then the alarm goes off.

NR: Each night hundreds of people like Judy Evans, a scenic designer and artist who lives in Brooklyn, are jolted out of their sleep by the nagging wail of a car alarm.

JE: You just wait it out but you don't know if that's going to happen again. You don't know when you're going to be reawakened for a second or a third time even.

NR: Often she is, and sometimes a defective alarm will go on for hours.

JE: If one person were standing on the corner with a horn making that kind of noise, they would be arrested. They would be disturbing the peace.

Man: It slowly gets under your skin and eventually drives you nuts.

NR: A music producer and composer, this resident of Manhattan's Upper West Side got fed up with car alarms disturbing his sleep and his work. He got together with some similarly frazzled neighbors and formed a posse of sorts.

Man: We start off with a note saying, "Fix your car alarm, it's disturbed hundreds of people last night." If that doesn't help we quite often use some minor retaliatory step like breaking an egg on their windshield or on the front hood, which doesn't hurt anything but it's a little bit of a mess to clean up.

NR: The "egg man," who prefers to remain anonymous, says some vigilantes take even more drastic action. Like smearing axle grease on door handles.

Man: Another classic is to smear vaseline all over the windshield, which is incredibly hard to get off. So . . . I think in other neighborhoods there might be even broken windshields and things like that.

NR: Lucille DiMaggio was a target of vigilante retribution. It happened one night when, unbeknownst to her, the car alarm malfunctioned.

Lucille DiMaggio: I noticed something on the passenger front door. There were a lot of dent marks. It appeared to me that it looked like the heel of someone's shoe, as if someone had kicked my innocent car, because the alarm hadn't even been going off all night.

NR: The repairs cost her a couple of hundred dollars. To test the theory, Lucille DiMaggio set off her alarm for me in a restaurant parking lot. Not a single person bothered to see if a car was being broken into. Which begs the question: Are car alarms really effective? Judy Evans says absolutely not, not even when she's called the police.

JE: One night, there was a real incredible racket, and a little MG was being mutilated to death. The alarm was going off. So I called 911. Well, about 40 minutes later, the police drove up.

NR: Little remained of the car by then. Ms. Evans, who's taken to sleeping with earplugs and the windows closed, says car alarms should be banned in densely populated and already noisy neighborhoods.

Catherine Abate: The streets are much noisier than they were 20 years ago . . . even 10 years ago.

NR: New York State Senator Catherine Abate represents Manhattan.

CA: The noise affects not only their ability to sleep at night, but for the most part their ability to work during the day. And even parents have come to me and said, "What is the impact on children?" And there are more and more studies that show that young people in particular, that are exposed to a sustained amount of loud noise, have hearing loss. So it's a health issue, it's a quality of life issue.

NR: Enforcement of existing laws, along with new regulations, may be cutting down noise in some neighborhoods. It's now illegal for alarms to run for more than three minutes. After that police can break into a car to disable the alarm or even tow away a wailing vehicle. It's hoped these actions will motivate car owners to adjust their alarms, making them less sensitive so vibrations from passing trucks and the like don't set them off. Even the egg man admits the car alarm situation has improved, at least in his neighborhood. By the way, the egg man has a sidekick: his wife.

Man: When something happens outside she'll say, "Do you think that's eggworthy?" And I'll say, "That sounds like an egg candidate to me."

NR: For Living on Earth, I'm Neal Rauch in New York.

LISTEN FOR DETAILS
(Repeat Listen for Main Ideas)

MAKE INFERENCES

Excerpt One

Judy Evans: You just wait it out but you don't know if that's going to happen again. You don't know when you're going to be reawakened for a second or a third time even. . . . If one person were standing on the corner with a horn making that kind of noise, they would be arrested. They would be disturbing the peace.

Excerpt Two

Lucille DiMaggio: I noticed something on the passenger front door. There were a lot of dent marks. It appeared to me that it looked like the heel of someone's shoe, as if someone had kicked my innocent car, because the alarm hadn't even been going off all night.

Excerpt Three

Catherine Abate: The noise affects not only their ability to sleep at night, but for the most part their ability to work during the day. And even parents have come to me and said, "What is the impact on children?" And there are more and more studies that show that young people in particular, that are exposed to a sustained amount of loud noise, have hearing loss. So it's a health issue, it's a quality of life issue.

Excerpt Four

Man: When something happens outside she'll say, "Do you think that's eggworthy?" And I'll say, "That sounds like an egg candidate to me."

2B. LISTENING TWO: *The Ten Commandments of Cell Phone Etiquette*

John Gordon: The Ten Commandments of Cell Phone Etiquette. This is Future Tense from American Public Media. I'm John Gordon. Dan Briody wrote a column raging against rude cell phone behavior for Infoworld Magazine back in 2000. He suggested a list of do's and don'ts, his Ten Commandments of Cell Phone Etiquette. The article keeps getting passed around the blogosphere and it still looks pretty fresh. The issues Briody raised six years ago, obnoxious ring tones, for example, are as relevant as ever, but Briody says cell phone talkers are a little better behaved than they used to be.

DB: I think people have started to understand you know that there is an acceptable way to use these things, and that there is a sort of understood etiquette around them.

JG: Maybe this one's getting worse, not better, I don't know, as ring tones sort of, sort of become more popular, but your second commandment is "Thou shalt not set thy ringer to play 'La Cucaracha' every time thy phone rings," or Beethoven's Fifth or the Beegees or anything else.

DB: Ring tones have gotten certainly more interesting. Uh, if you need to hear the ring tone, uh, try to make it something that's uh, not going to offend anybody, and uh, you know, you can always set the phone to vibrate, uh, uh, which a lot of people don't seem to know how to do . . . yet.

JG: Your third commandment . . . I'm wondering how this has changed you know, for better or worse over the past few years, you know, since you wrote it, and that is, "Thou shall turn thy cell phone off for public performances."

DB: Yeah. I think this has gotten a lot better, and, and part of that has to do with the fact that prior to many public performances, you will, there will be an announcement saying, "Please turn off your cell phone or turn them to silent mode, umm, so that we don't have any interruptions." So it's just that little reminder, uh, that people give now that has really uh, helped that along.

JG: In one of your commandments, you take objection with people trying to impress others with their cell phones. Uh, is that era over? I mean everyone has 'em now, right?

DB: No, it's not over, unfortunately. Umm, you know, you . . .certainly a cell phone is a fashion statement. You know, what kind of phone you whip out when it rings, uh, means something to people. If you've got a hot pink Razr phone, or if you've got your Treo or something like that, there is a certain amount of a fashion statement involved when, when you're using them.

JG: OK, let's talk about your number one commandment, um, which is not subjecting others to your cell phone conversations. Uh, I'm wondering if we have just sort of become inured to that, and whether that piece of etiquette is eventually just going to sort of . . . go away as, as we get used to it.

DB: Well, I think some people have become inured to it . . . um, I think it depends on the situation. You know, I . . . I ride the commuter train into New York, um, every day. And in the morning, um, I, I don't want to hear people barking on their cell phones on the way in. There are people sleeping, there are people reading the paper . . . it's a quiet time. And, and, and . . . that, and if you're speaking too loudly, you know, you can go into the vestibule of the, of the, of the train and get out of people's earshot. Um, other times, you know, walking down the street, or things like that, I have no problem with it at all. Uh, but uh, but there are, you know, certain situations where it's, it's just rude. It's, it's rude to be, uh, you know, speaking loudly into these things and uh, and having people listen to one side of a conversation.

JG: Dan Briody, Editor of CIO Insight Magazine. His original column appeared in Info World. This is Future Tense. I'm John Gordon.

THE PHONETIC ALPHABET

Consonant Symbols

/b/	be		/t/	to
/d/	do		/v/	van
/f/	father		/w/	will
/g/	get		/y/	yes
/h/	he		/z/	zoo, busy
/k/	keep, can		/θ/	thanks
/l/	let		/ð/	then
/m/	may		/ʃ/	she
/n/	no		/ʒ/	vision, Asia
/p/	pen		/tʃ/	child
/r/	rain		/dʒ/	join
/s/	so, circle		/ŋ/	long

Vowel Symbols

/ɑ/	far, hot		/iy/	we, mean, feet
/ɛ/	met, said		/ey/	day, late, rain
/ɔ/	tall, bought		/ow/	go, low, coat
/ə/	son, under		/uw/	too, blue
/æ/	cat		/ay/	time, buy
/ɪ/	ship		/aw/	house, now
/ʊ/	good, could, put		/oy/	boy, coin

CREDITS

Photo Credits: Page 1 Copley News Service/Scott Stantis; **Page 3** David Sacks/Getty Images; **Page 21** Claudio Peri/epa/Corbis; **Page 24** Adam Woolfitt/Corbis; **Page 26** Corbis/Jupiterimages; **Page 38** Zero-Gravity Corporation/handout/epa/Corbis; **Page 39** (top) Chien-min Chung/Getty Images, (bottom) Yoshikazu Tsuno/AFP/ Getty Images; **Page 41** The New Yorker Collection 1992 Michael Crawford from cartoonbank.com. All rights reserved; **Page 47** Frank Wartenberg/Picture Press; **Page 49** Frank Herholdt/Getty Images; **Page 51** MetroNaps.com; **Page 63** (top row) Shutterstock, Shutterstock, Shutterstock, Robert Blanchard/iStockphoto.com, (bottom row) Shutterstock, Shutterstock, Shutterstock; **Page 64** Shutterstock; **Page 71** Shutterstock; **Page 79** Shutterstock; **Page 83** Michal Heron/Pearson Education; **Page 86** (left) Kevin Farrington/Redhatsociety.com, (right) Mapsofworld.com; **Page 90** Pickles © 2007 Brian Crane. All rights reserved. Used with the permission of Brian Crane and the Washington Post Writers Group in conjunction with the Cartoonist Group; **Page 103** The New Yorker Collection 2000 Frank Cotham from cartoonbank.com. All rights reserved; **Page 105** (top left) Karen Pittleman, (top right) AP Images, (bottom left) Getty Images, (bottom right) Themba Hadebe/AP Images; **Page 127** The New Yorker Collection 2001 Michael Maslin from cartoonbank.com. All rights reserved; **Page 137** Bloomimage/Corbis; **Page 149** The New Yorker Collection 1996 Victoria Roberts from cartoonbank.com. All rights reserved; **Page 152** Paul Seheult/Eye Ubiquitous/Corbis; **Page 172** Arthur Tilley/Getty Images; **Page 178** Orban Thierry/Corbis Sygma; **Page 179** Owen Franken/Corbis; **Page 193** The New Yorker Collection 1998 David Sipress from cartoonbank.com. All rights reserved; **Page 201** Shutterstock; **Page 202** Shutterstock; **Page 210** Alan Mothner/AP Images.

Listening Selections and Text Credits: Page 5 © NPR ® 2000. The text and audio of the news report by NPR's Margot Adler was originally broadcast on National Public Radio's *Morning Edition*® on June 6, 2000, and is used with the permission of National Public Radio, Inc. Any unauthorized duplication is strictly prohibited; **Page 8** excerpt from On Point interview with Todd Gitlin reproduced with permission of WBUR radio; **Page 24** © NPR ® 2000. The text and audio of the news report by NPR's Bob Edwards was originally broadcast on National Public Radio's *Morning Edition*® on March 26, 2000, and is used with the permission of National Public Radio, Inc. Any unauthorized duplication is strictly prohibited; **Page 27** Courtesy of WWOR News, WWOR-TV, Inc. All rights reserved; **Page 29** "The Achilles Track Club Climbs Mount Kilimanjaro." Reprinted by permission of MySpace, Inc.; **Page 44** © NPR ® 2000. The text and audio of the news report by NPR's Michelle Trudeau was originally broadcast on National Public Radio's *All Things Considered*® on September 9, 2000, and is used with the permission of National Public Radio, Inc. Any unauthorized duplication is strictly prohibited; **Page 47** "Get Back in Bed" on Satellite Sisters. Reprinted by permission of ABC News Radio; **Page 66** excerpt from *The Infinite Mind* program "Animal Intelligence" reproduced with permission of Lichtenstein Creative Media; **Page 68** From *Science* Podcast "Cloaking Devices, Animal Cognition, Ancient Beads and More" *Science* 23 June, 2006 [http://www.sciencemag.org/feature/misc/podcast/

SciencePodcast_060623.mp3]. Used with permission from AAAS; **Page 87** © NPR ® 2002. The text and audio of the news report by NPR's Trish Anderton was originally broadcast on National Public Radio's *All Things Considered*® on July 6, 2002, and is used with the permission of National Public Radio, Inc. Any unauthorized duplication is strictly prohibited; **Page 91** © NPR ® 2006. The text and audio of the news report by NPR's Alex Chadwick was originally broadcast on National Public Radio's *Remembrances*® on February 21, 2006, and is used with the permission of National Public Radio, Inc. Any unauthorized duplication is strictly prohibited; **Page 107** excerpt from *The Infinite Mind* program "Altruism" reproduced with permission of Lichtenstein Creative Media; **Page 110** © American Public Media; **Page 124** "Small World" PSA reproduced with permission of Earth Share National; **Page 130** © NPR ® 2003. The text and audio of the news report by NPR's Margot Adler was originally broadcast on National Public Radio's *Morning Edition*® on March 3, 2003, and is used with the permission of National Public Radio, Inc. Any unauthorized duplication is strictly prohibited; **Page 134** "A Duty to Family, Heritage, and Country," ©2006 Ying Ying Yu. Reprinted by arrangement with This I Believe, Inc. (www.thisibelieve.org); **Page 152** © NPR ® 2001. The text and audio of the news report by NPR's Sarah Chayes was originally broadcast on National Public Radio's *Morning Edition*® on May 7, 2001, and is used with the permission of National Public Radio, Inc. Any unauthorized duplication is strictly prohibited; **Page 155** "Food in a Bowl" on Satellite Sisters. Reprinted by permission of ABC News Radio; **Page 172** as heard on PRI's The World, a co-production of the BBC World Service, Public Radio International, and WGBH Boston; **Page 174** "The Words Escape Me" by Steve Coleman. Reprinted by permission of Steve Coleman; **Page 196** "Noise in the City" from Living on Earth, 9/27/96. Copyright © 1996 by Living on Earth. Edited text used with permission of Living on Earth and World Media Foundation. www.loe.org Living on Earth is the weekly environmental news and information program distributed by Public Radio International; **Page 199** © 2006, American Public Media.

Illustration Credits: Dusan Petricic, **Page 142**; Derek Mueller, **Pages 14, 205**; Paul Hampson, **Pages 86, 145, 150, 204**; Aphik Diseño, **Pages 34, 66, 128, 143, 155, 163, 166, 201**; Mapping Specialists, **Pages 26, 86, 169**.

Notes

Notes